C000146074

KIERKEGAARD, EVE AND METAPHORS OF BIRTH

KIERKEGAARD, EVE AND METAPHORS OF BIRTH

Alison Assiter

ROWMAN & LITTLEFIELD

INTERNATIONAL

London • New York

Published by Rowman & Littlefield International, Ltd.
Unit A, Whitacre Mews, 26-34 Stannary Street, London SE11 4AB
www.rowmaninternational.com

Rowman & Littlefield International, Ltd. is an affiliate of Rowman & Littlefield
4501 Forbes Boulevard, Suite 200, Lanham, Maryland 20706, USA
With additional offices in Boulder, New York, Toronto (Canada), and London
(UK)
www.rowman.com

Copyright © 2015 by Alison Assiter

All rights reserved. No part of this book may be reproduced in any form or by
any electronic or mechanical means, including information storage and retrieval
systems, without written permission from the publisher, except by a reviewer
who may quote passages in a review.

British Library Cataloguing in Publication Information Available
A catalogue record for this book is available from the British Library

ISBN: HB 978-1-78348-324-2
ISBN: PB 978-1-78348-325-9
ISBN: EB 978-1-78348-326-6

Library of Congress Cataloging-in-Publication Data

Assiter, Alison.
Kierkegaard, Eve, and metaphors of birth / Alison Assiter.
pages cm
Includes bibliographical references and index.
ISBN 978-1-78348-324-2 (cloth : alk. paper) -- ISBN 978-1-78348-325-9 (pbk. : alk. paper) -- ISBN
978-1-78348-326-6 (electronic)
1. Kierkegaard, S?ren, 1813-1855. 2. Ontology. 3. Kant, Immanuel, 1724-1804. 4. Schelling, Friedrich Wilhelm Joseph von, 1775-1854. I. Title.
B4378.O5A87 2015
198'.9--dc23
2014048169

∞™ The paper used in this publication meets the minimum requirements of
American National Standard for Information Sciences Permanence of Paper for
Printed Library Materials, ANSI/NISO Z39.48-1992.

Printed in the United States of America

CONTENTS

ACKNOWLEDGEMENTS

In the acknowledgements section of one of my previous books I mentioned that I'd never received a grant for this kind of work. This remains true and I have only, in my entire career, had one sabbatical. But there is something I would like to mention.

I was trained as an analytical philosopher, many years ago, and I am lucky enough to have studied at Oxford and gained a BPhil in philosophy. This, I appreciate, gave me skills and openings I would never otherwise have had. However, it also gave me a fear of making bold hypotheses, since, I felt, any such hypothesis was bound to be wrong. Indeed, I would probably have gone so far as to claim that it would ultimately have been meaningless.

Spending the last few years in the company of a group of wonderful continental philosophers at UWE Bristol, however, has radically changed both my outlook and my confidence in the possibility of exercising my imagination and thinking in bigger and bolder ways. While some will doubt my sanity, a few others might at least understand what I mean. So I owe a particularly strong debt to all my various colleagues as well as those who have passed through—usually occupying temporary jobs—our little philosophy group. I would like to mention you all—Mike Lewis, Darian Meacham, Sean Watson, Havi Carel, Tina Chanter, Leone Gazziero, Phil Meadows (who would probably not describe himself as a continental philosopher), John Sellars, Katrina Mitcheson and Dagmar Wilhelm. But my biggest debt is to Iain Hamilton Grant, whose charisma and enthusiasm for philosophy are second to none. It was he, above all others, who both taught me the little I know of Schelling and enabled me to recognize the importance of thinking in bold speculative terms. We also had such fun teaching Schelling and Kierkegaard together. Of course I cannot blame him for all the errors in my thinking. Ironically, none of the above have read this book, but you have all shaped my thinking in different ways.

I would also like to acknowledge generations of students who have influenced my thinking. I owe a particular debt to each final-year group who studied Kierkegaard with me. I am also indebted to those of you who studied Kant with me, both the undergraduates in their second year of study who studied the first and second Critiques with me and the MA students on the module where we read Kant's third Critique. Many of you inspired me but particular mention (because of their love of Kierkegaard) goes to Rose Ziai and Barney Riggs (the latter read this entire manuscript and removed some of the typos as well as giving me feedback on the text). I have also received inspiration and feedback from Will Stronge and Andy Jones. I would like to mention Heather Nunney-Boodan and Rosie Massey, who, after I made a brief mention in a seminar on Schelling of the notion of birth in Schelling, took this a step further and began working on it. The latter has a piece that anyone can read, if interested, in *Agora*, the philosophy magazine produced by UWE students. The former wrote her MA dissertation on the subject.

I would like to acknowledge all the feminist philosophers I have ever known, who, while you have not commented on this, have inspired my thinking over many years. I'd particularly like to mention Christine Battersby, whose work led me to Kierkegaard.

Otherwise, I'd like to acknowledge all the Kierkegaardians I have met and/or whose work I have read and been inspired by. I would like particularly to thank Michael Burns for giving me the confidence to think that it is possible to read Kierkegaard differently.

Finally, I would like to thank Hamid, Ben and also Liane, as well as all my close friends for just being around. I'd also (weirdly again) like to thank all the lifeguards at Hampstead Women's Pond for enabling the cold-water winter swimming that keeps me (partially!) sane and alive!

Some of the arguments in chapters 1 and 2 are based on a piece I wrote, 'Speculative and Critical Realism', *Journal of Critical Realism* 12, no. 3 (2013), 283–300. Some brief sections of chapters 3, 4 and 5 are developments from a piece I wrote, 'Kant and Kierkegaard on Freedom and Evil', *Royal Institute of Philosophy Supplement* 72 (July 2013), 2275–2296.

Alison Assiter
February 2015

ABBREVIATIONS

Works by Kierkegaard, with their standard abbreviations:

CA: Kierkegaard, Søren. *The Concept of Anxiety*. Edited and translated by Reidar Thomte, in collaboration with Albert B. Anderson. Princeton: Princeton University Press, 1980.

CI: Kierkegaard, Søren. *The Concept of Irony*. Translated by Howard V. Hong and Edna H. Hong. Princeton: Princeton University Press, 1989.

CUP: Kierkegaard, Søren. *Concluding Unscientific Postscript to Philosophical Fragments*, vol. 1. Edited and translated by Howard V. Hong and Edna H. Hong. Princeton, Princeton University Press, 1992.

EO: Kierkegaard, Søren. *Either-Or*. Parts I and II. Edited and translated by Howard V. Hong and Edna H. Hong. Bloomington: Indiana University Press, 1987.

EUD: Kierkegaard, Søren. *Eighteen Upbuilding Discourses*. Edited and translated by Howard V. Hong and Edna H. Hong. Princeton: Princeton University Press, 1990.

FT: Kierkegaard, Søren. *Fear and Trembling*. Translated by Alistair Hannay. London: Penguin, 2003.

JP: Kierkegaard, Søren. *Journals and Papers*, 7 volumes. Translated by Howard V. Hong and Edna H. Hong. Bloomington: Indiana University Press, 1967–1978.

PF: Kierkegaard, Søren. *Philosophical Fragments: Johannes Climacus*. Translated by Howard V. Hong and Edna H. Hong. Princeton: Princeton University Press, 1985.

PJ: Kierkegaard, Søren. *Papers and Journals, A Selection*. Harmondsworth: Penguin, 1996.

R: Kierkegaard, Søren. *Repetition and Philosophical Crumbs*. Translated by M. G. Piety, with an introduction and notes by Edward Mooney and M. G. Piety. Oxford: Oxford University Press, 2009.

SLW: Kierkegaard, Søren. *Stages on Life's Way*. Edited and translated by Howard V. Hong and Edna H. Hong. Princeton: Princeton University Press, 1980.

SUD: Kierkegaard, Søren. *The Sickness unto Death*. Translated by Howard V. Hong and Edna H. Hong. Princeton: Princeton University Press, 1980.

TA: Kierkegaard, Søren. *Two Ages: The Age of Revolution and the Present Age, a Literary Review*. Edited and translated by Howard V. Hong and Edna H. Hong. Princeton: Princeton University Press, 1978.

WL: Kierkegaard, Søren. *Works of Love*. Translated by Howard V. Hong and Edna H. Hong. Princeton: Princeton University Press, 1995.

INTRODUCTION

Recently, there has been a revival of interest in reading Søren Kierke-gaard as an ontologist. This means viewing him as dealing with questions about the kinds of entity or process that constitute ultimate reality. Does reality ultimately comprise just one thing or many? Is it made up of 'things' at all, and can we know the answers to these questions? We might even ask the further question: Why is there something, or some process, rather than nothing at all, or no process? What is the meaning of Being per se? This question is quite general and may be different from the answer to questions like: What does it mean to be a human being, a toad, an angel, or a shell on the beach? Recent readers of Kierkegaard have seen him as being interested in such questions and as having some kind of answers to them.

Slavoj Žižek, to take one example of a recent reader of Kierkegaard, considers Kierkegaard's God to be 'strictly correlative to the ontological openness of reality, to our relating to reality as unfinished', reality 'in becoming'. '"God" is the name for the Absolute Other against which we can measure the thorough contingency of reality—as such it cannot be conceived as any kind of Substance, as the supreme thing'.[1] David Kan-gas, to take another recent commentator on Kierkegaard, notes that Kierkegaard is concerned with the nature of time and that he is respond-ing to a view of time according to which a subject is 'a self-mediating drive toward the realization of its being; and its ontological predicates are nothing other than the various stages of the movement of realization. In aiming to realize its telos, the subject unfolds what lies in it—its original

principle—and this unfolding takes place across a temporality; it constitutes a temporality'.[2] Michael Burns, another recent advocate of the ontological reading of Kierkegaard, emphasizes the 'unground' of anxiety, for
Kierkegaard, as contributing to an account of 'how self-consciousness
comes to posit itself in the first place'.[3] A further significant contributor
to these debates is Steven Shakespeare.[4] These recent readings of Kierkegaard stand in contrast to those interpretations, of which there are many,
which claim Kierkegaard's thought to stand in opposition to the German
Idealist tradition in general, to Hegel's thought in particular and, indeed,
to any form of metaphysics or ontology. According to these latter readings, Kierkegaard opposes the abstractions of German Idealist thought in
favour of the 'actuality' of lived experience. The latter readings may,
moreover, be adopting a view of what the 'abstractions' of the German
Idealist tradition amount to, which I will contest in this book.

The new way of viewing Kierkegaard's texts stands alongside a revival of interest in ontology and metaphysics more generally. I will claim in
this book that these recent readers of Kierkegaard are right to suggest that
he is focusing in part on ontological questions and on issues pertaining to
the nature of being as a whole. I will also suggest that the view I will
attribute to Kierkegaard not only has some plausibility as an interpretation of his deep and quirky writings, but is also a view that has much to
recommend in its own right.[5] I will make the bold claim that Being, for
Kierkegaard, following Friedrich Wilhelm Joseph Schelling, can be read
in terms of conceptions of birthing—the capacity to give birth as well as a
notion of a birthing body. I will claim, further, that the story offered by
Kierkegaard, in *The Concept of Anxiety*, about the origin of freedom
connects with a birthing body. I will also suggest that the ontological
view I will attribute to him has some plausibility in its own right.

It is important, of course, to note that Kierkegaard, especially when
writing under the pseudonym Climacus, is concerned above all with subjective passion and with 'faith as the highest passion of subjectivity'[6] and
is highly critical of 'objective' thought and of doctrines that might pass as
'speculative'. However, it is possible to construe this as, at least in part, a
critique not of all forms of philosophizing but of particular philosophical
positions. It may be that there are other options than those listed, for
example, by Edward Mooney. Subjectivity may neither be 'a Cartesian
state of consciousness [n]or a special place from which one can know'.[7]
Mooney's own suggestion of subjectivity as a moral stance that realizes

personality may itself constitute an ontological position. Indeed, the view, often held since Descartes, of the subject as self-positing invokes an ontological claim that Kierkegaard contests.

Recent commentators, as well as challenging the view that Kierkegaard is not concerned with ontological questions at all, have also stood in opposition to Martin Heidegger's reading of Kierkegaard. For Heidegger, 'Kierkegaard remains everywhere philosophically entangled, on the one hand in a dogmatic Aristotelianism that is completely on par with medieval scholasticism, and on the other in the subjectivity of German Idealism'.[8] These recent commentators offer a different view. They attribute the view to Kierkegaard, among others, that reality is, at its core, contingent, or, more strongly, that it is chaotic. While I would like, in this book, to add to the range of thinkers who read Kierkegaard as being concerned with the nature of Being, I will contest this particular view of its nature. I will offer a different understanding of Kierkegaard's work on this subject.

It is important, in offering a theory about the nature of ultimate reality, to recognize one preliminary point. This is that theories about the nature of this ultimate reality are speculative hypotheses. Since Kant's demonstration of the impossibility of proving that God exists, it has not been possible to make claims about how reality must be. Some recent thinkers, however,[9] have claimed that proofs like Kant's of the paradoxical nature of reasoning about ultimate reality suggest that reality must be, at its core, paradoxical. Alain Badiou has argued, for example, that we can derive from contemporary mathematics a claim to the effect that reality itself must be contingent. However, Kant would reply to this that we cannot know that contemporary mathematics gets things right. We cannot make claims about existence from mathematical axioms alone. This is not at all, it is important to reiterate, to suggest that we cannot make speculative hypotheses. But that must be what they are—nothing more than speculative. Kierkegaard, I will suggest, offers a speculative hypothesis, in terms of metaphors of birthing, about the nature of Being. This speculative hypothesis can, however, be given a strong justification.

Kierkegaard was deeply concerned about major ontological questions, but his interest in these questions was not only metaphysical. It was also ethical. Some recent writing on ontology has, in a true post-Kantian vein, lost the concern with the ethical alongside the belief that it is no longer possible to prove, in the manner of many pre-Kantians, the existence of

God, although there are others—Badiou and Giorgio Agamben, to name but two—who link their concerns with ontology to political and ethical interests. Kierkegaard is a post-Kantian who is deeply immersed in Kant's thought. But, unlike many in the German Idealist tradition, his interventions in ontology stand alongside those of the ancient Greeks, for whom major ontological questions were closely related to ethical issues. Plato, to take an exemplary case, was interested in Being partly because he wanted to understand, like his mentor Socrates, in what the good really consists. In his dissertation, *The Concept of Irony with Constant Reference to Socrates*, Kierkegaard argues that Socrates used irony in order to bring about the birth of subjectivity. Indeed, his indebtedness to Socrates is surpassed only by the deep influence on him of the Pauline texts of the Bible and of Luther. He writes: 'Of all old men, Socrates is the greatest'.[10]

Much of the evidence for Kierkegaard's ontological thinking emerges in *The Concept of Anxiety*. This is a text, it is important to note, that he originally wrote in his own name, only later inserting his pseudonym— Haufniensis. In this text, Kierkegaard is concerned with the nature of Being but also with the question of freedom and the origin of the latter. Freedom is inseparably bound up with anxiety. In this text, Kierkegaard's concerns are closely connected with those of Immanuel Kant in his late work *Religion within the Limits of Reason Alone* and also with the preoccupations of Schelling in his *Freiheitsschrift*.[11] Kierkegaard, or Haufniensis, takes up the question that preoccupied both Kant and Schelling, of the possibility of freely acting well but also of freely doing wrong. Kant had criticized the ontological argument for the existence of God, and he had further linked the freedom to do well with the ability to act rationally in following the moral law. The human will, for Kant, insofar as it is free, lies 'in' a realm that is unknowable. His transcendental self, indeed, is located in a shadowy realm somewhere between the phenomenal and the noumenal. In its turn, the noumenal is not devoid of sense, but we humans are able to say little about it. The two most important areas of thought, for Kant, are, famously, the starry heavens without and the moral law within:

> Two things fill the mind with ever new and increasing admiration and
> awe, the more often and steadily reflection is occupied with them: the
> starry heaven above me and the moral law within me. Neither of them
> need I seek and merely suspect as if shrouded in obscurity or rapture

beyond my own horizon; I see them before me and connect them immediately with my existence. [12]

The reason for the existence of the noumenal is primarily ethical, in the broadest sense. Kant, the devout Newtonian, was also a strong believer in the need for and the power of ethical thought and action. Kant was unable to link the moral law straightforwardly with the existence of God, although he does so connect it in the *Critique of Judgment*. He set out to use human rationality—the power that led to Newton's brilliance—to ground the moral law as well. However, humans are not perfectly rational, and this left him with a serious lacuna: If freedom and the moral law are linked, how is it possible freely to do wrong? Morality is 'grounded' in the noumenal and yet we are unable really to say what the noumenal is. We know only that thinking of the universe or nature or the phenomenal world, as a whole, leads to paradox. This then is one root of the view, held by some recent thinkers and derived from Kant and the post-Kantian German Idealists, that reality is, at its core, paradoxical. [13]

Kant was left with the above problem and he was never able fully to resolve it. To restate it: If one is free when one follows the moral law, as Kant claims in the *Critique of Practical Reason*, then how is it possible freely to do wrong? If God ultimately grounds human rationality and the human ability to act well, then what grounds the human ability to do wrong? It is this primarily ethical concern that preoccupies Schopenhauer, with his pessimistic picture of nature as being governed by chaotic forces, and that also interests Schelling, in his *Freiheitsschrift*. It is, moreover, ethical issues that preoccupy Nietzsche.

Kierkegaard's interest in the nature of Being stems primarily from his concern with the ground of both good and evil. His work was partially shaped by Kant's thought on this matter, and yet he did not want to be left with the same difficulty as Kant, of being unable to ground the possibility of wrongdoing. Kierkegaard, I will suggest in this book, offers an account, in *The Concept of Anxiety*, of this ground.

The respective interests of Kant and Kierkegaard in the above ethical question are linked, indeed, with their metaphysical outlooks. Kant split 'Being' into the phenomenal and the noumenal worlds. Kierkegaard's account of Being, by contrast, I will argue in this book, stems from a metaphor. The metaphor can be split into two. It is that of a birthing body and also that of the process of birthing. These metaphors are not new to him—indeed, a version of one of them appears in the work of Kant himself, in his *Critique of Judgment*. It appears also in Schelling's *Freiheitsschrift*. Kant considers, in the *Critique of Judgment*, the following hypothesis: 'he can make mother earth (like a large animal as it were) emerge from her state of chaos, and make her lap promptly give birth initially to creatures of a less purposive form'. [14] Schelling also, in the *Freiheitsschrift*, deploys the metaphor of 'the yearning the eternal feels to give birth to itself' [15] to describe his *ungrund* or his 'unprethinkable'. Kierkegaard, I will argue, develops these metaphors in his own way.

Two commentators on Kierkegaard have considered something close to my reading. One is Christine Battersby, in her work *The Phenomenal Woman*. [16] The other is Edward Mooney. He writes: 'The blindness of philosophers and theologians to Kierkegaard's maternal figures should be read against masculine privileging of death over birth, letting the end of life trump its beginning'. [17]

In Kierkegaard's *Stages on Life's Way*, Johannes speaks of the gods creating woman. In *The Concept of Anxiety*, this metaphor is transformed into a natural process. The natural, however, is not to be read in a reductive, mechanical sense. Rather, woman and man, as free beings, free to do right or wrong, evolved out of a purposive nature. Specifically, the awareness of freedom evolved out of a sexual capacity: the sexuality of a woman, of a being that has a body that can give birth. In its turn, I will argue, the ground of the possibility of right and wrong is Being itself conceived as a body that can birth. Importantly, however, this body is not only a body. Specifically, Being is itself grounded in a notion that cannot easily be described in terms of any kind of substance. Rather, it is grounded in a capacity or a power. Schelling describes this power in terms of a yearning or a longing—the yearning of 'the eternal one' to give birth to itself. Kierkegaard, I will suggest, draws on this metaphor.

Viewing the ground of morality solely in terms of a God who is all good and all powerful is to deny the possibility of grounding evil or wrongdoing. The metaphor of the body that can birth can ground both. It is also a metaphor of nature that contains 'mindedness' and therefore the capacity to give rise to this quality in humans, within itself. In other words, it is a speculative naturalist theory that differs both from pure non-naturalism, which holds that minds are radically different from nature, and from mechanistic forms of naturalism, which hold that nature is inert and dead. Furthermore, it differs, also, from a theory that is becoming popular at the moment, and that, as noted above, is being attributed to Kierkegaard, that reality is chaotic and purposeless.

To attribute to Kierkegaard, however, a view that reality should be read in terms of metaphors of birth might seem not only radically speculative but also clearly wrong, on at least three significant and decisive counts. First, it might seem absurdly wrong in relation to the believer—Kierkegaard—in an eternal, infinite, transcendent God who became incarnated as a temporal, finite, human being (Jesus). Secondly, it might seem wrong in relation to Kierkegaard's reputed misogyny. To quote William McDonald, Kierkegaard's 'earliest published essay, for example, was a polemic against women's liberation. It is a reactionary apologetic for the prevailing patriarchal values'.[18] Finally, and most devastatingly of all, it might seem a purely speculative theory for which there is no support. These three objections might seem insuperable for the thesis I am attributing to him. I shall only hint, in this introduction, at my response.

First, why should one not add another layer of paradox to the already paradoxical claim, present in Kierkegaard's works, that an infinite God became embodied in a finite figure? According to the New Testament, Jesus was born and he was born from a virgin. He was born from a woman. Is it not therefore more plausible to suggest that he was born from something or someone that had the capacity to give birth than to suggest otherwise? Is the metaphor of God as a figure with a white beard more or less plausible than the image of God as a capacity or a power to give birth? Why should the image of an eternal, infinite, and transcendent God not be conceived metaphorically in terms of a power or a capacity? God is, indeed, in the Christian and other religious traditions, conceived in terms of the power of love. The above picture is entirely consistent with this. It is an ontological claim, however, as well as a theological one.

In an extension of this first criticism of the approach I propose to develop, I would like to refer more specifically to some commentators who challenge any connection between Kierkegaard and the German Idealist tradition. Many significant commentators will see at least some of Kierkegaard's work, notably the writings of the pseudonymous Anti-Climacus on 'sin', as being concerned, in the words of Sylvia Walsh, with 'a paradox that can only be believed and repented' and 'that cannot strictly be "thought" at all'.[19] Kierkegaard's dialectic, she writes, is 'never simply a dialectic of concepts'[20] but rather involves an interpenetration of 'thought and existence'.[21] Any attempt, in other words, to try to put into concepts a body of work that is designed to challenge that mode of writing will be doing a disservice to Kierkegaard.

Again, I can only hint at my response to this. It seems to me that some who have claimed, as Walsh does, in her important book, that Kierkegaard is not concerned with conceptual thought at all may have had in view a model of conceptual thought that is challenged by the interpretation I would like to offer. The approach to metaphysics I will defend in this book challenges both 'dead' naturalist determinist forms of pantheism, akin perhaps to some readings of Spinoza's work, and theories deriving from Cartesian dualism that separate out 'thought' from 'extension' or matter.

On the second point above, I will argue that although Kierkegaard has been read as a misogynist, it is possible to read his remarks about women differently. I will suggest that his comments on women are not intended to denigrate women; in fact, they should be read in the opposite way. He actually, I will suggest, valourizes many of the qualities he attributes to women.

Moreover, and this relates both to the second and the third critical points above, many feminist philosophers have pointed out how much of the Western philosophical tradition has operated as though humans were not embodied beings; much of the tradition has denigrated or denied the body. Kant, of course, is notable in this respect. The human, as an ethical being, is conceived—metaphorically of course—as a rational mind. This metaphor is in fact deeply implausible when it comes to the reality of human contingent interactions and yet it has a deep hold over many who are trained in the Western tradition. Why then should we not take seriously the opposing hypothesis, that humans are embodied creatures, and that the speculative ground of the possibility of right and wrong might also be embodied—or that it might rather be a power or a capacity that could issue in an embodied being? This is not, to reiterate, to say that we can know that it must be this way, but why should it not serve as a plausible hypothesis about Being?

Such a hypothesis is consonant with Luce Irigaray's claim that the denigration of matter, the description of it as inert substance, runs alongside a forgetting of the female subject position, and more specifically of the role for birth in the generation of that kind of Being—the human being—that uniquely has the capacity to reflect on its place in nature.

Offering the aforementioned metaphorical role for the body that can birth has the further advantage of ascribing to the very foundation of being a nature, a nature that may, indeed, precede the knowledge any human has of it. It would therefore allow for nature to ground the emergence of the human being.

Irigaray has traced the blind spot—the forgetting of the role of procreation in ontology—back to Plato. She argues that the myth of the Cave, in Plato's *Republic*, inscribes women as 'without voice, without presence'.[22] 'Woman', in the philosophical tradition, has been associated with the body, the material. Moreover, a less frequently acknowledged association, again deriving from Plato, particularly from his view in the *Timaeus*,[23] is that woman is seen as dead matter, merely as a receptacle that receives the generative and the living.

The dark walls of the cave, in Plato's myth, according to Socrates, stand for the visible world—the world of appearance. Outside the cave lies the intelligible world and the real world of Forms, with the Sun standing as the ultimate form, the form of the Good. This form, in Irigaray's reading, is, as Rachel Jones has put it, 'a "father" of "offspring" made in its likeness'.[24] For Irigaray, though, this myth rests upon a blind spot: it turns things upside-down and substitutes an Idea, or a Form, for processes of birth.

I will argue, in this book, that Kierkegaard turns things right-side-up again. I will suggest both that the metaphor outlined above is a plausible hypothesis about Being and that it is a view that we can reasonably attribute to Kierkegaard. I will also, in the course of the book, outline in detail the problem of evil, as it appears in Kant, and I will describe what I will suggest is Kierkegaard's solution to this problem. While I will ascribe the views I will outline, to Kierkegaard in particular, the position I will describe will, I hope, also be of interest in its own right.

There is one final issue I should mention in this introduction. Kierkegaard wrote two sets of works—a set of pseudonymous texts and a second set, published in his own name. I do not feel competent to judge the question of whether or not it is fair to attribute to 'Kierkegaard' works written pseudonymously. Some commentators have done this, while others carefully distinguish the words of, for example, the pseudonymous author of *Fear and Trembling*, Johannes de silentio, or John the Silent, from those of Kierkegaard himself. For the thesis I propose to develop I will use material from a number of works in each of the two categories.

The most detailed engagement is reserved for *The Concept of Anxiety*, for the reasons given above. I will note, and spend a little time on, the fictional names, but the relationship between the pseudonyms and Kierkegaard himself is a huge topic, which deserves more time and space than I have here to give it. I do wish to claim, however, and I am not alone in claiming this, that there is an overall philosophical position that broadly represents that of Kierkegaard himself, across a range of his texts.

In the first couple of chapters I consider the view mentioned above, which has been recently attributed to Kierkegaard, to the effect that reality or Being as a whole is contingent or chaotic. I consider and contest the views of two recent philosophers on this subject, that of Slavoj Žižek and that of Quentin Meillassoux. I discuss Žižek's reading of Kierkegaard offered in his book *The Parallax View*, and Meillassoux's claim, in *After Finitude* and elsewhere, that reality must be contingent and chaotic at its core. While I do not accept that reality need be chaotic, I suggest that there is something important in the work of both thinkers—from Žižek, I take the notion of reality as in process, and from Meillassoux, the view that there is a 'great outdoors', as he calls it, that exists independently of the experience of any finite rational being.

In the third chapter, I outline the problem of freely doing wrong as it appears in Kant's work. I discuss a number of ways, suggested in the literature, of solving the problem but argue that they are, for various reasons, unsuccessful.

Chapter 4 begins Kierkegaard's response to Kant's problem. I begin outlining Kierkegaard's process ontology. Focusing primarily on *The Concept of Anxiety*, I suggest that Kierkegaard is influenced by Schelling. I begin to outline what may be meant by the claim that he is a process ontologist.

Chapters 4 and 5 outline what I believe to be Kierkegaard's response to Kant on freedom and specifically on the freedom to do wrong. I suggest that Haufniensis offers, in CA, a response to Kant that deploys the myth of Eve and Adam and that suggests that freedom 'came into' them at the point at which Eve ate the forbidden fruit. Eve and Adam, then, existed as part of a living and active nature, prior to the act of eating the fruit. I suggest that this account enables Kierkegaard convincingly to respond to Kant's problem. I further begin, in chapter 5, the account of the metaphysic of birthing insofar as I suggest that it is important that freedom first emerges, for Kierkegaard, in Eve, a person who has the capacity to give birth.

Chapter 6 discusses Kierkegaard's view of women and his purported misogyny. I suggest that those commentators who have accused him of misogyny have seen his comments on women in a negative light whereas he intends to valourize the qualities he associates with women. Indeed, I suggest that he sees woman as expressing the view of time and process I attributed to him in an earlier chapter.

In chapter 7 I begin to suggest that Kierkegaard sees the whole of nature in terms of processes of birthing. I continue the argument in chapter 8, looking particularly at *Fear and Trembling*, at what is meant by the claim that Abraham believes by virtue of the absurd, and also examining the weaning metaphors deployed in that text.

Chapter 9 offers some arguments to the effect that the view I have been attributing to Kierkegaard has some plausibility in its own right. I look at some contemporary biologists who outline a theory that has some similarities with this view.

In the tenth and final chapter, I set out to apply the process ontology developed throughout the book, including the metaphors of birth, to the conception of revolution described by Kierkegaard in *Two Ages*.

NOTES

1. Slavoj Žižek, *The Parallax View* (Cambridge: MIT Press, 2009), 79, henceforth PV.

2. David Kangas, *Kierkegaard's Instant: On Beginnings* (Bloomington: Indiana University Press, 2007), 7.

3. Michael Burns, 'A Fractured Dialectic: Kierkegaard and Political Ontology after Zizek', in *Kierkegaard and the Political*, ed. Alison Assiter and Margherita Tonon (Cambridge: Cambridge Scholars Press, 2012), 112.

4. See, for example, Steven Shakespeare, *Kierkegaard, Language and the Reality of God* (Basingstoke: Ashgate, 2001).

5. One interpretation of the metaphysical I will not be attributing to Kierkegaard is a form Anthony Rudd labels 'metaphysics in the bad sense' (see Anthony Rudd, *Kierkegaard and the Limits of the Ethical* [Oxford: Clarendon Press, 1997]). By this he means a form of metaphysics that sets out to view the world scientifically and objectively. This is effectively to disengage from the world.

6. CUP, 132, and elsewhere. Among the important commentators on Kierke-gaard who emphasize this aspect of his thought are C. Stephen Evans, *Kierke-gaard's 'Fragments' and 'Postscript': The Religious Philosophy of Johannes Climacus* (Amherst, MA: Humanity Books, 1999); Edward Mooney, *Selves in Discord and Resolve* (Basingstoke: Routledge, 1996); and Merold Westphal, *Becoming a Self: A Reading of Kierkegaard's Concluding Unscientific Post-script* (West Lafayette: Purdue University Press, 1996).

7. Edward Mooney, 'Postscript Ethics: Putting Personality on Stage', in *Ethics, Love and Faith in Kierkegaard*, ed. Edward Mooney (Bloomington: Indiana University Press, 2008), 39.

8. Martin Heidegger, *What Is Called Thinking*, trans. Glenn Gray (New York: Harper, 1968), 213.

9. I will give some illustrative examples of such thinkers in the following chapter.

10. CI.

11. There are two important thinkers, in the English-speaking world in partic-ular—Michelle Kosch, *Freedom and Reason in Kant, Schelling and Kierkegaard* (Oxford: Oxford University Press, 2006); and Michael Burns, *Kierkegaard and the Matter of Philosophy: A Fractured Dialectic* (London: Rowman & Littlefield International, 2014)—who have made the link with Schelling's *Freiheitsschrift* and Kierkegaard's *The Concept of Anxiety* explicit. Kosch also links CA with the above work of Kant. This connection, as Kosch has pointed out, has been made much more frequently in the German-language literature on Kierkegaard.

12. Kant, CPR.

13. Textual evidence for these claims will be found in chapter 3.

14. See Kant, CJ, 314.

15. Friedrich W. J. Schelling, *Philosophical Investigations into the Essence of Human Freedom*, trans. Jeff Love and Johannes Schmidt (New York: State Uni-versity of New York Press, 2006), 11; Friedrich Wilhelm von Schelling, *Philoso-phische Untersuchungen über der menschlichen Freiheit*, in *Friedrich Wilhelm von Schellings sämtliche Werke*, 14 vols., 2 parts (Stuttgart and Augsberg), 431–433, reproduced by Manfred Schröder (München: Beck, 1927), henceforth SW.

16. Christine Battersby, *The Phenomenal Woman: Feminist Metaphysics and the Patterns of Identity* (London: Routledge, 1998).

17. Edward Mooney and Dana Barnea, *Birth and Love in Fear and Trembling and the Symposium* (website, dated Sunday, 1 December 2013), accessed 21 May 2014.

18. William McDonald, entry on Soren Kierkegaard, *Stanford Encyclopedia of Philosophy*, section 4 (first published 3 December 1996; substantive revision 27 July 2012), available online at Plato.Stanford.edu, accessed 25 January 2015.

19. Sylvia Walsh, *Living Christianity: Kierkegaard's Dialectic of Christian Existence* (University Park: Pennsylvania University Press, 2005), 26.

20. Ibid., 6.

21. Ibid.

22. Luce Irigaray, *Speculum of the Other Woman*, trans. Gillian C. Gill (Ithaca: Cornell University Press, 1985), 265.

23. Plato, *Timaeus*, trans. D. Lee (Harmondsworth: Penguin, 1977).

24. Rachel Jones, in her book *Irigaray* (Cambridge: Polity Press, 2011), offers an important ontological reading of Irigaray. This is a quote from page 45 of her book.

CONTINGENT AND CHAOTIC REALITY

This book sets out, as noted in the introduction, partially to defend the bold claim that there is evidence in Søren Kierkegaard's corpus for the view that the Absolute, or the whole of Being, might be conceptualized in terms, following Friedrich Wilhelm Joseph Schelling, both of a body that can birth and, using the language of Schelling, of a force that 'longs' to give birth to itself. Schelling notes, 'The first beginning for the creation is the yearning of the One to give birth to itself or the will of the ground'.[1] These conceptions of birthing are natural—birth is a natural process. But they are also metaphors of activity, of a process that is not dead and static.

In addition to being metaphors of activity, the claims are metaphysical; they concern the whole of reality. I will suggest that they are also statements about nature. Nature, I will suggest, constitutes the backdrop against which any claim to know anything, expressed by a knowing subject, is made. Both Schelling and Kierkegaard challenge any assumption that some 'I' can gain direct access to a knowable reality either through pure intuition or through some form of direct sensory experience, or indeed through some combination of these two.[2] In *Philosophical Fragments*, Kierkegaard, through Climacus, represents doubt as inherent in thought. There is no foundation to thought in the sense Descartes sought; there will always be something that cannot be captured by a thinking or a reasoning self. This something Schelling conceives of as nature, but nature as active and living and as itself grounded in what he calls an 'unprethinkable' process that cannot be comprehended in the terms that reason normally deploys. This process he depicts in terms of conceptions of birth. I will suggest, in this book, that Kierkegaard adopts something from Schelling's view of nature and that he conceives of the whole of nature in terms of a birthing body and, in turn, the ground of this nature in terms of metaphors of processes of birth. These claims are clearly speculative hypotheses. I will attempt, in the course of the book, to give reasons why it is plausible to adopt them.

I would like, in the first couple of chapters, however, to examine an alternative perspective that has been recently attributed to Kierkegaard by those who have an interest in Kierkegaard's place in the German Idealist tradition, and in the topic of the nature of ultimate Being. These recent thinkers, it is important to note, have revived a concern with metaphysics, following a relative decline in interest in this domain in much philosophy in both the analytical and the continental traditions. I would like to read at least some of Kierkegaard's brilliant and enigmatic works, alongside the interpretations of these recent thinkers, as providing evidence that he engaged in deeply metaphysical questions.

I consider these recent engagements because, like mine, their views represent something of a change in interpretation of Kierkegaard, who has, until recently, been seen as a thinker who is concerned primarily with human existence in relation to a transcendent God. Until the recent focus of interest, Kierkegaard has been read, to reiterate, as focusing on existential 'actuality' and on an ethical and religious reaction against the German Idealist metaphysical tradition.[3] He has been seen by some, then, as the 'father' of the existential tradition[4] and by others as not a philosopher at all.[5] Specifically, as noted in the introduction, his work has been seen to stand against the philosophical idealism of his predecessors. As Reidar Thomte has put it, in the introduction to CA, Kierkegaard 'stands in direct opposition to the philosophical idealism of his day'.[6] The recent interpreters of Kierkegaard, however, stand in opposition to Thomte's reading.

My own intention is not to negate some of the earlier readings, many of which are very important and clearly express something of Kierkegaard's enigmatic and brilliant insights. The new readings, including my own, it is to be hoped, will add to these a dimension of Kierkegaard's thought that may have been neglected in the work of some previous commentators.

In this opening chapter, I will examine a specific component of a view that has been attributed recently to Kierkegaard. This perspective stems in part from a challenge to the ontology that characterizes the perspective of a substantial number of philosophers in the Western tradition, although by no means all, which is that reality is made up of substances with properties. I also would like to challenge this particular metaphysical perspective and to suggest that Kierkegaard, although he does have a metaphysical outlook, does not uphold this one. Perhaps the clearest statement of the position that reality is made up of substances with properties is that of Aristotle,[7] although it is also important to note that in *De Anima*,[8] as well as in Book Theta of the *Metaphysics*,[9] he is concerned with movement—*kinesis*—and life. In Book Theta of the *Metaphysics*, he famously discusses movement, or *kinesis*, and he distinguishes between potentiality, *dynamis*, and 'actuality', *energeia*. However, the perspective for which he is widely known is that 'being qua being' is the study of 'substance'. He writes: 'The question which, both now and of old, has always been raised, and always been the subject of doubt, viz. what being is, is just the question what is substance?'[10] Aristotelian metaphysics, his view of being (*ousia*), followed from his research in the natural sciences (*physica*). Among the categories he outlines in his work on that subject, the primary one is 'substance'. 'Substances', as he writes in his *Metaphysics*, are independent things; the contents of other categories depend upon these.[11] Substance is, for him, both the ultimate substratum of reality and, in the form of both particular and general things, the core component of his ontology. The essence of a thing is its form, and the latter is that which persists through change. The 'essence', then, does not itself come into being. Unlike Plato, however, he does not see this 'form' as separable from matter. He is said to have inaugurated the view that, for many philosophers in the tradition, constitutes metaphysical common sense.

The reading of Kierkegaard proposed by the metaphysicians mentioned in the introduction to this work challenges this Aristotelian commonplace.[12] Like Aristotle, but arriving at very different conclusions, these metaphysicians partially derive their perspective from their contemporary science at the same time that they question an over-reliance on science. A further important component of their views, however, is that they uphold a challenge, first put forward in the post-Kantian German Idealist tradition, to the Kantian phenomenal/noumenal distinction. There is additionally, also within this tradition, as noted in the introduction, a strong regard for Immanuel Kant's proof that it is not possible to prove God's existence, and therefore that the notion of a knowable Absolute grounding meaning in the world is no longer open to us.[13] Rather than deriving the conclusion adopted by some philosophers, however, that we cannot any longer be concerned with metaphysical questions at all, some of them focus, in Slavoj Žižek's words, on 'the primacy of Becoming in human life'. They are concerned with the impossibility, for us limited beings, of 'assuming the point of view of finality'.[14] Interestingly, both those who deny that we can any longer concern ourselves with ultimate reality at all and the recent metaphysicians claim Kierkegaard as their own.[15]

The particular focus, broadly, on the priority of 'Becoming', or of process, over static Being, seems to me to be tremendously important. Indeed, two recent prominent commentators on Kierkegaard's work, both of whom deny that he is a philosopher, emphasize the importance of movement or process in Kierkegaard's writings. As George Pattison has put it, 'Now Kierkegaard too, as we will see, will also seize on temporality as a decisive and characteristic dimension of human existence and provide a strategy whereby to make temporality meaningful'.[16]

However, there are two further aspects of the thought of some of these recent interpreters of Kierkegaard with which I would like to take issue. I will argue that some of the recent commentators have gone too far in the following respects: one is their claim that Being is radically contingent and the other is the further assumption, namely that it is chaotic at its core.[17]

Partial inspiration for the view held by recent philosophers that reality at its heart is contingent can be found in Martin Heidegger. In *Being and Time*[18] and in 'The Origin of a Work of Art'[19] he writes that metaphysicians ask questions about the ground of the world that we experience. This, in turn, presupposes probing the totality of beings, investigating the whole that underlies the world we experience. Metaphysics then appears to assume a God's-eye view of the whole. Humans pretend to become Gods, in order to survey the whole. But this is impossible for perspectival, temporal, and limited beings like us. So the meaning of being becomes an abyss—something lacking. A human perspective on the world is precisely this—a perspective, a finite field of vision bounded by a horizon. Beyond the limits of a person's birth and death is non-being or nothingness, a void.[20]

A related perspective is evident in Jean-Paul Sartre's[21] view that the world and our existence are without reason and therefore in some sense absurd and also, famously, in Friedrich Nietzsche's[22] insistence, in *The Birth of Tragedy*, that there is no meaning to anything.

CONTINGENT REALITY

A significant recent philosopher of contingency, one who has referred in some detail to Kierkegaard for inspiration, is Slavoj Žižek. Referring to Kierkegaard, he suggests that '"God" is the name for the Absolute Other against which we can measure the thorough contingency of reality—as such it cannot be conceived as any kind of Substance, as the supreme thing'.[23] As Michael Burns puts it, '[Žižek's] interpretation allows us to read Kierkegaard's conception of God in a properly ontological light as signifying the primacy of contingency in any attempt to articulate a picture of metaphysical totality'.[24] Žižek claims further, 'What Kierkegaardian "infinite resignation" confronts us with is pure Meaning . . . yet unconditional meaning can occur (and has to appear) only as nonsense. The content of pure Meaning can only be negative: the Void, the absence of Meaning'.[25]

Žižek, then, importantly, it seems to me, suggests that Kierkegaard sees ultimate reality as comprising processes as opposed to things. Moreover, Kierkegaard's conception of movement, he suggests, differs from that of Aristotle.[26] As Žižek puts it, 'This is why German Idealism explodes the co-ordinates of the standard Aristotelian ontology which is structured around the vector from possibility to actuality. In contrast to the idea that every possibility strives fully to actualise itself, we should *conceive of progress as a move of restoring the dimension of potentiality in mere actuality*, of unearthing at the very heart of actuality, a secret striving toward potentiality'.[27] This may indeed be one important component of Kierkegaard's view of process. On the other hand, as Claire Carlisle has pointed out, Kierkegaard began, in 1844, to study Trendelburg, who uses Aristotelian modal categories to criticize G. W. F. Hegel.[28] Whichever view is right, the suggestion that ontology involves processes rather than static beings seems to be important both as a thesis about Kierkegaard and also as a claim in its own right.[29]

In his recent magnum opus, *The Parallax View*, Slavoj Žižek suggests that Kierkegaard continues tropes articulated in the German Idealist tradition but also deepens and radicalizes some of them. By 'parallax' he means the view that there is an 'insurmountable gap between two closely linked perspectives between which no neutral common ground is possible'.[30] One key articulation, for Žižek, of this 'parallax' is Kant's transcendental illusion. Kant's transcendental illusion—the illusion of being able to use apparently common language to discuss phenomena that are mutually untranslatable—is an exemplification of the notion. An illustration of this would be the conception of the 'world as a whole', which is, for Kant, both phenomenal and noumenal. In the gap, for Žižek's Kant, between phenomena and noumena is the 'ultimate parallax', the transcendental self, which itself is neither phenomenal nor noumenal.[31] While it was Kant, writes Žižek, who 'laid the foundations', it was Kierkegaard who noticed that the most 'radical authentic core of being-human is perceived as a *concrete practico-ethical engagement and/ or choice which precedes and grounds every "theory"*, every theoretical account of itself, and is, in this radical sense, contingent'.[32]

Kant, others recognize, argued that theoretical reason presupposes practical reason.[33] But it is Kierkegaard, according to Žižek, who recognizes both the depth of the challenge presented by these Kantian questions and also the existential despair they might lead to, concerning the point and purpose of one's life. It is the very connection between these notions that, for Žižek's Kierkegaard, rather than indicating a break with the German Idealist tradition, in fact suggests Kierkegaard's continuity with that tradition. One reason for this is that Hegel, he argues, radicalizes Kant. Žižek reads Hegel as moving from the Kantian view that there is no access to the Absolute, to the claim that the Absolute itself is 'negativity'. Hegel, according to this reading articulated by Žižek, moves on from Kant by introducing a gap into the very texture of reality.[34] In this reading, then, while Kant posits an unknowable Absolute—the noumenal— which may be complete, Hegel radicalizes Being itself by suggesting a gap in this Absolute. The contradictions Kant articulates in the Antinomies, in CPR, do not merely concern our inability to know the whole; rather, they indicate something about the whole itself.

Žižek, then, argues that there is a fissure in the very heart of Being, and he attributes such a view to Hegel. I do not propose to investigate the accuracy of his view of Hegel, but I would like to engage with his view of Kierkegaard's work, and his claim, which he attributes to Kierkegaard, that reality is ultimately contingent.

ŽIŽEK ON KIERKEGAARD

Žižek notes that Kierkegaard, in *Concluding Unscientific Postscript*, distinguishes 'objective' from 'subjective' thought. The former, which designates a certain type of 'Hegelian' thinking, 'translates everything into results'.[35] 'Subjective thought', by contrast, 'puts everything into process and omits results'.[36] Hegel, Kierkegaard writes in CUP, does not understand history from the point of view of becoming, but rather views it as a 'finality that excludes all becoming'.[37] Žižek claims both that for Kierkegaard, only subjective experience is 'in becoming' and also that Hegel might be construed as engaging in the exact opposite of what Kierkegaard represents him as doing. Žižek suggests that Hegel can be read as noting the contingent process that generated existing necessity. Žižek accepts that such a reading of Hegel may be counterintuitive, but he draws the distinction between viewing history retroactively, from the point of view of finality, and looking at it from the existential position of active engagement with it, where we perceive it as full of possibilities and ourselves as free to engage with it.

He describes this as a contrast between the position of the idealist and that of the materialist. For the former, the situation appears open from the perspective of our own engagement with it and closed from the point of view of finality. For the latter, however, 'openness' goes all the way down; it is 'the All itself which is non-All, inconsistent, marked by an irreducible contingency'.[38] Kierkegaard's theology 'represents the extreme point of idealism: he admits the radical open-ness and contingency of the entire field of reality, which is why the closed Whole can appear only as a radical Beyond, in the guise of a totally transcendent God'.[39] But Kierkegaard is also a materialist, since the above characterization of this position is precisely his view. Kierkegaard's God is not a knowable Absolute. Instead, we have to make a leap of faith, which, to an external observer, can only look like madness.[40] Humans are required, according to Žižek's Kierkegaard, to make the ultimate sacrifice, to dedicate their whole lives to God. There is no guarantee that their sacrifices will be rewarded and they might well be carried out for nothing. Žižek uses Kierkegaard's trope of 'infinite resignation' to characterize this gesture of the ultimate sacrifice that, he suggests, might be a purely empty gesture.

There are, in Žižek's work, many important claims. There are aspects of his corpus that cohere with the reading of Kierkegaard I would like to offer. In a significant claim for my argument, moreover, Žižek gives a key role to women.[41]

However, I would like to take issue with a central aspect of his interpretation of Kierkegaard. I am not wholly convinced by his pessimistic reading of Kierkegaard that the latter offers an interpretation of reality as lacking in meaning and as radically contingent. This latter claim appears to chime with some elements of contemporary science—chaos theory, for example—but also with a view that became prevalent among those philosophers writing at the time of the Holocaust, in their attempts to come to terms with a phenomenon that appeared utterly beyond comprehension. Albert Camus,[42] for example, suggested that life itself, ultimately, is without meaning: it is absurd, and he, in his turn, attributed some elements of his view, once more, to Kierkegaard.[43]

I would like to challenge this aspect of Žižek's work alongside that of another influential recent thinker who argues that reality is ultimately contingent and chaotic, namely Quentin Meillassoux.

MEILLASSOUX

Žižek's is one recent account of the view that reality is, at its heart, contingent and chaotic. Another variation of such a position appears in the work of Quentin Meillassoux, although, as we will see, the latter challenges elements of the Heideggerian perspective. It is also important to note that, unlike Žižek, Meillassoux does not uphold the view that reality is fundamentally made up of processes. Meillassoux, further, does not refer to Kierkegaard, but I'd like to consider his position since he offers a very clear and strong description of the view that reality is contingent or chaotic at its core and a strong argument in support of this perspective. But importantly for me, he also offers a strong argument for the claim, which chimes with a view I believe Kierkegaard holds, that there is a reality conceived partly as nature, external to and prior to the self. The self, therefore, does not itself construct that reality.

Meillassoux[44] has claimed, in a vivid phrase, that much of 'pre- metaphysical' contemporary philosophy—by which he means phenomenology and 'various currents of analytic philosophy'[45]—has lost 'the *great outdoors*, the absolute outside'.[46] This metaphor, for him, conveys the idea of an 'outside' that is not relative to us humans, a domain of reality that

exists in itself whether or not we are thinking of it. Contemporary science, Meillassoux argues, offers evidence for the view that entities,
forces, or capacities in the natural world existed before any human came
into being. The dating of fossils suggests that the universe itself existed
several billion years before human life emerged. Meillassoux labels statements about entities in such a world 'ancestral statements'. In apparent
contrast to this, he contends that 'the central notion of modern philosophy
since Kant is that of *correlation*. By "correlation" we mean the idea
according to which we only ever have access to the correlation between
thinking and being, and never to either term considered apart from the
other'.[47] One cannot, in other words, consider either subjectivity or objectivity independently of the other. The prime example of a 'correlationist'
is Kant but the position also, according to Meillassoux, includes Heidegger.[48] The correlationist, he claims, has difficulty formulating ancestral
statements. The person adopting such a position is only able to understand a statement of the form 'Fossil data suggests the existence of life
forms prior to the emergence of humans' as (something like) 'Fossil data
are given in the present as anterior to givenness' or 'Event Y occurred x
number of years before humans—*for humans*'.[49] A very important point
he makes is that Kant, for whom time is an a priori intuition, is unable to
account for the emergence of the conditions for the taking place of the
transcendental. It is difficult, indeed, for Kant, given his view of time, to
make sense of a time period antecedent to the existence of the human.
Labelling the 'great outdoors' the *arche fossil*, Meillassoux suggests that
we need to do what 'modern philosophy has been telling us for the past
two centuries is impossible: to get out of ourselves, to grasp the in-itself,
to know what is whether we are or not'.[50]

It seems to me that these claims are significant.[51] The position advo-
cated is a form of realism. I would like to defend a claim that is analogous, in some respects, to this, in later chapters. However, there are
further elements of the thought of Meillassoux in particular with which I
would like to take issue. I would like, in the following pages, to consider
some of the claims Meillassoux makes about this 'great outdoors'.

Meillassoux writes that if 'ancestrality' is to be thinkable, then so must
'the absolute', and yet on the other hand, he suggests, Kant has shown,
through his critique of the ontological argument, that we can never infer a
priori the existence of an Absolute. We cannot prove anything at all about
the world as a whole by means of a priori reasoning. As he puts it, 'there

is no "prodigious predicate" capable of conferring a priori existence on its recipient'.[52] Kant's refutation of the ontological argument suggests that we cannot prove, using a priori claims about the properties of God, that God must exist. Kant also claims, more generally, that it is difficult to make any conclusive claim about the Whole or the Absolute. Indeed, attempts to do so, he argues in the Antinomies in the *Critique of Pure Reason*, lead to paradox.

Meillassoux claims that it follows from this that we must reject all real necessity and the principle of sufficient reason. This is the principle that claims broadly that, for any occurrence, there must be a reason why it is thus and not otherwise. Since things could be other than they are, then all we are entitled to conclude about reality is that it is irreducibly contingent. As Peter Hallward puts it, in his piece on Meillassoux in *The Speculative Turn*, for the latter 'nothing is necessary, apart from the necessity that nothing be necessary'.[53]

Meillassoux also draws on David Hume to make his case. He writes that none of the respondents to Hume, and perhaps not even Hume himself, really took on the radical nature of his claim, which is that the laws of nature could change out of all recognition. Hume's claim, according to Meillassoux, that we cannot know that causal laws express necessary truths is effectively a statement about 'the future stability of nature itself'.[54] Rather than merely making an epistemic claim, that we cannot know that the future will be like the past, Hume was really claiming that the same cause may bring about a hundred different effects. According to Meillassoux, it follows that, instead of trying to show why there must be some kind of necessity attaching to the laws of nature, in fact the real problem is to explain why, given the contingency of the laws of nature, there is actually relative stability in the world. Meillassoux argues, then, drawing on his reading of Hume, that contingency is necessary and chaos is omnipotent.[55]

Žižek, as we have seen, draws a similar conclusion, although he argues it differently: that it is impossible for an individual to assume the 'point of view of finality over his own life'[56] and that this leads, for different reasons, to a radically contingent 'core' of being. Both are arguing, in other words, from our finitude, to the kinds of assumption we are entitled to make about ultimate Being.

Meillassoux writes, in *After Finitude*, that 'if the necessity of the causal connection cannot be demonstrated, then this is simply because the causal connection is devoid of necessity'.[57] There is no reason for it to be one way rather than another. As Alain Badiou puts it, in his introduction to *After Finitude*, 'Meillassoux's proof—for it is indeed a proof—demonstrates only one thing that is absolutely necessary: that the laws of nature are contingent'.[58] Contingency, furthermore, is cashed out as 'everything's capacity to be other or the capacity not to be'.[59] In its turn, this means, according to Meillassoux, that 'our absolute, in effect, is nothing other than an extreme form of chaos, a hyper-chaos, for which nothing is or would seem to be impossible, not even the unthinkable'.[60]

Žižek attributes a view similar to this to Kierkegaard and reads Hegel, as we have seen, as suggesting that the 'end' of history suggests its openness; it allows one to grasp that which was in the process of becoming, to see the contingent processes that generated necessity.[61]

Both Meillassoux and Žižek, then, suggest not only that reality, at its core, is contingent but also that it is chaotic. Žižek, as we have seen, argues that Hegel[62] removes the gap separating the Kantian phenomenal from the noumenal and claims that the inconsistencies in our experience of the limits of the phenomenal, rather than depicting merely our experience, in fact demonstrate the nature of reality itself. Reality is contradictory, or chaotic, at its core.

According to some readings, Nietzsche is the philosopher par excellence who has articulated this notion of chaotic being—being as devoid of sense, of any kind of purpose or form. As I wrote in my book *Enlightened Women*,[63] Nietzsche challenges the aforementioned Aristotelian metaphysics of substance with properties. According to Michael Haar, for Nietzsche, the illusion of being an individual self—an individual substance with characteristics—derives from the linguistic structure of 'subject and predicate'.[64] It was grammar that fooled Descartes in his view that there is an 'I' that thinks. A productive use of history, by contrast, would allow us to recognize that each self is distinct; that selves are the effects of forces or powers, and that within the self there is 'chaos'.[65] Ultimately, therefore, there is no reason behind things.

Schelling also appears to presuppose a conception of Being that makes it paradoxical and chaotic. He writes: 'Since nothing is prior to, or outside God, he must have the ground of his existence in himself. All philosophies say this; but they speak of this ground as of a mere concept without making it into something real and actual. This ground of his existence, which God has in himself, is not God considered absolutely that is in so far as he exists; for it is only the ground of his existence'. [66] Schelling goes on to note that God's ground of existence is prior to God's existence and yet, also and apparently paradoxically, God must already exist in order for there to be a ground of his existence. I will return to this in a later chapter.

A more recent and perhaps even more thoroughgoing characterization of a position close to this one is that of Gilles Deleuze and Felix Guattari, in *A Thousand Plateaus*. [67] Deleuze and Guattari refer to Kierkegaard on a number of occasions in this text. One significant claim they make is to offer a counter to the substance-property model of ontology through musical refrain. Within music there is movement that is not easily outlined in terms of a series of spatialized moments. Music links past and present in a nonlinear fashion. A musical piece offers some stability within a chaos of possibilities, a chaos of force fields. A rhythm suggests alternative ways of conceptualizing the world than in terms of discrete entities, discrete substances. Identity, in this world, however, is not lost. Rather there is scope for a more open notion, a more fuzzy conception. In *What Is Philosophy*, they define chaos 'not so much by its disorder as by the infinite speed with which every form taking place in it vanishes. It is a void that is not a nothingness but a *virtual*, containing all possible particles and drawing out all possible forms, which spring up only to disappear immediately, without consistency or reference, without consequence. Chaos is an infinite speed of birth and disappearance'. [68]

In this chapter, I have presented two recent and significant accounts of the nature of ultimate reality and the reasons given for suggesting that this reality is contingent and chaotic at its core. I have summarized something of the views of both Žižek, who draws on Kierkegaard, and Meillassoux. In the chapter that follows, I would like to offer some responses to these arguments.

NOTES

1. Schelling, SW, 7; Friedrich Wilhelm von Schelling, *Of Human Freedom*, trans. James Gutmann (Chicago: Open Court Publishing House, 1936). Love and Schmidt translate *sensucht* as the 'yearning' of the one. Schelling, *Philosophical Investigations into the Essence of Human Freedom*, trans. Jeff Love and Johannes Schmidt (Albany: State University of New York Press, 2006), 59, VII; SW, 395. Future references to the text will be to the Love and Schmidt edition.

2. 'Foundationalism' is challenged in detail and depth by Richard Rorty in *Philosophy and the Myth of Nature* (Oxford: Blackwell, 1983) and also by John McDowell in *Having the World in View* (Cambridge: Harvard University Press, 2009). The view, however, is also questioned by Kant in the *Critique of Pure Reason* when he argues, throughout the Transcendental Aesthetic and the Transcendental Analytic, both that intuitions require concepts and, further, that this combination presupposes something 'outer' to the self.

3. See, for example, Alister E. McGrath, *The Blackwell Encyclopedia of Modern Christian Thought* (Oxford: Blackwell Publishing, 1993).

4. See, for example, Claire Carlisle, *Kierkegaard: A Guide for the Perplexed* (London: Continuum, 2009).

5. George Pattison, who is a major and significant Kierkegaard commentator, writes, in his book *The Philosophy of Kierkegaard* (Chesham: Acumen, 2003), 'To speak of "the philosophy of Kierkegaard" is, it may be said, problematic. . . . Kierkegaard did not offer a rounded "philosophy", in the sense of a conceptually grounded and logically consistent worldview' (1). For Pattison, Kierkegaard's authorship is 'essentially non-philosophical' (1), although it is important to note that, like Kierkegaard's own work, Pattison's commentary on Kierkegaard is also deeply philosophical. I could make the same point about the work of Claire Carlisle, another commentator who argues that Kierkegaard is not a philosopher at the same time that she offers philosophical commentary on his work. Perhaps the appropriate conclusion to draw is that philosophy itself, as viewed by these two commentators, is seen in a certain way that excludes the 'process' philosophy of Kierkegaard?

6. Reidar Thomte, introduction to CA, xi.

7. Aristotle, *Metaphysics*, trans. W. D. Ross (London: Penguin, 2004).

8. See Hugh Lawson-Tancred, *De Anima* (London: Penguin Classics, 1986).

9. Indeed, Claire Carlisle, in *Kierkegaard's Philosophy of Becoming, Movements and Positions* (New York: State University of New York Press, 2005), offers a picture of Kierkegaard as a process philosopher that specifically derives from his relationship to Aristotle.

10. Aristotle, *Metaphysics*, 1028b3–4.

11. Aristotle, *Metaphysics*.

12. I should note that there are those who attempt to refute a broadly 'Aristotelian' metaphysical position and to establish that the alternative perspective I shall advocate must be the true one. I am doubtful, though, as to whether they will be successful or indeed, as noted in the introduction, whether it is possible to provide such a demonstration in this domain of philosophy. There have been many attempts to deny the existence of universals and the existence of abstract objects. But there are also attempts to show that there can be no concrete objects. One example of such an argument runs something like this: (i) A concrete object

is supposed to be identical over time. (ii) For an object to be identical with itself, it must satisfy Leibniz's law; (iii) but, at different times, any one concrete object will have different properties. Therefore, there can be no proper concrete objects.

However, there will be many alternative ways of defending some version of a substance ontology. One could, for example, argue that it is not necessary, in order to believe in some notion of a concrete entity, to suppose that it is literally the exact same thing over time. I believe, additionally, that it would be very difficult to offer necessary and sufficient conditions for something's being a process. Indeed, I think, as noted earlier, with Kant, that one cannot establish what must be the case about Being as a whole, since this presupposes that we can step outside Being and examine it, which is precisely what we cannot do.

13. There is an important qualification that must be made to this, however, which I will elaborate in a later chapter.

14. Žižek, PV, 84.

15. See the text below for some spelling out of this point.

16. Two prominent commentators, as noted, on Kierkegaard as a process philosopher are Claire Carlisle, *Kierkegaard's Philosophy of Becoming, Movements and Positions* (Albany: State University of New York Press, 2005); and George Pattison, *The Philosophy of Kierkegaard* (Chesham: Acumen, 2005). The quote is from the latter text, page 17. For more discussion of Kierkegaard's process philosophy, see chapter 4.

17. There are several significant contemporary philosophers, including Alain Badiou (see, for example, Alain Badiou, *The Adventure of French Philosophy*, trans. Bruno Bosteels [London: Continuum, 2012]) and Catherine Malabou (see Catherine Malabou, *The Future of Hegel: Plasticity, Temporality and Dialectic*, trans. Lisabeth During [London: Routledge, 2005]), who take a view analogous to this.

18. Martin Heidegger, *Being and Time*, trans. John Maquarrie and Edward Robinson (Oxford: Blackwell, 1993).

19. Martin Heidegger, 'The Origin of a Work of Art', in *Poetry, Language, Thought*, trans. Albert Hofstadter (New York: Harper and Row, 1971).

20. I am indebted to Mike Lewis, particularly his *Heidegger beyond Deconstruction* (London: Continuum, 2007), for this view of Heidegger. Any errors of interpretation are mine.

21. Jean-Paul Sartre, 'Existentialism Is a Humanism', in *Existentialism from Dostoevsky to Sartre*, ed. Walter Kaufmann (Ohio: Meridian Books, 1964), 287–311.

22. Friedrich Nietzsche, *The Birth of Tragedy* (Cambridge: Cambridge University Press, 2010).

23. Ibid., 79. See also Aristotle, *Metaphysics*, 991a–1046a.

24. Michael Burns, 'A Fractured Dialectic: Kierkegaard and Political Ontology after Žižek', in *Kierkegaard and the Political*, ed. Alison Assiter and Margherita Tonon (Cambridge: Cambridge Scholars Press, 2013), 107.

25. Žižek, PV, 85.

26. Kierkegaard did engage deeply with Aristotle and particularly with the latter's notion of movement. In 1841, he read Tenneman's *Gesichte der Philosophie*, and his journal entries reflect his interest in Aristotle (see Carlisle, *Kierkegaard's Philosophy of Becoming, Movements and Positions*, 15–16). I will suggest, in this book, however, that Kierkegaard's notion of process or movement may be different from the interpretations both of Hegel and of Aristotle.

27. Žižek, PV.

28. See Carlisle, *Kierkegaard's Philosophy of Becoming, Movements and Positions*, 122.

29. I will return briefly to this question in chapter 4.

30. Žižek, PV, 4.

31. Ibid., 22.

32. Ibid., 75.

33. See Onora O'Neill, *Constructions of Reason: Explorations of Kant's Practical Philosophy* (Cambridge: Cambridge University Press, 1989).

34. See Žižek, PV, 27.

35. Žižek, PV, 76.

36. Ibid.

37. Slavoj Žižek, quoting Kierkegaard: CUP, 272, quoted in PV, 76.

38. Žižek, PV, 79.

39. Ibid.

40. Ibid., 80.

41. Ibid., 81.

42. Albert Camus, *The Myth of Sisyphus*, trans. Justin O'Brian (London: Penguin, 2005).

43. One recent feminist thinker who has, importantly, focused, against the trend of much 'post modern' feminist theory, on nature, but who sees this nature as unpredictable and indeterminate, is Elisabeth Grosz (*Time Travels* [Durham: Duke University Press, 2005]).

44. In correspondence with Michael Burns, Quentin Meillassoux has said that 'reckoning with the work of Kierkegaard would constitute an "ultimate finality of my system"'. Quoted in Burns, 'A Fractured Dialectic', 11.

45. Quentin Meillassoux, *After Finitude* (London: Verso, 2009), 6.

46. Ibid., 7.

47. Ibid., 5.

48. Meillassoux writes of Heidegger that he 'clearly exhibits the correlationist "two-step"' (Ibid., 8).

49. Ibid., 13.

50. Ibid., 27.

51. There are philosophers who constitute exceptions to this 'correlationist' post-Kantian norm. The critical realists (see the important work of Roy Bhaskar, *A Realist Theory of Science* [London: Verso, 1997]) constitute one such group of people. I will argue later on that Kierkegaard is another theorist who accepts this claim.

52. Meillassoux, *After Finitude*, 32.

53. Peter Hallward, *The Speculative Turn: Continental Materialism and Realism*, ed. Levi Bryant, Nick Srnicek, and Graham Harman (Melbourne: re.press, 2011), 130.

54. Meillassoux, *After Finitude*, 86.

55. Ibid., 64.

56. Žižek, PV, 84.

57. Meillassoux, *After Finitude*, 91.

58. Ibid., vii.

59. Ibid., 62.

60. Ibid., 64.

61. See Žižek, PV, 78.

62. This is, of course, an unusual reading of Hegel. Žižek, in PV, sees a continuity between the work of Hegel and that of Kierkegaard. Another person who reads Hegel in a similar fashion is Catherine Malabou, *The Future of Hegel: Plasticity, Temporality and Dialectic*, trans. Lisabeth During (London: Routledge, 2005).

63. Alison Assiter, *Enlightened Women* (London: Routledge, 1996), 9.

64. Michael Haar, *The Uses and Abuses of History* (London: Bobbs Merrill, 1957).

65. Ibid., 71.

66. Schelling, *Philosophical Investigations into the Essence of Human Freedom*; SW, 356–358. I should like to refer to Will Stronge's MA thesis, *An Inquiry into the Concept of Chaos and Matters Connected Therewith: A Reading of Nietzsche and Schelling* (Kingston University, 2013), for an excellent discussion of Schelling.

67. Gilles Deleuze and Felix Guattari, *A Thousand Plateaus* (London: Verso, 2004); see also Gilles Deleuze and Felix Guattari, *What Is Philosophy?*, trans. Hugh Tomlinson and Graham Burchell (New York: Columbia University Press, 1994). Another philosopher, as noted earlier, this time a feminist, who has emphasized the role of nature in understanding sex discrimination but who also sees this nature as unpredictable, constituted by cuts and ruptures, is Elisabeth Grosz, in *Time Travels*.

68. Deleuze and Guattari, *What Is Philosophy?*, 118.

2

A CHALLENGE TO CHAOS

In the previous chapter, I presented the views of two prominent recent philosophers who have argued that reality is contingent or chaotic at its core and who have, at least in the case of one of them, attributed this view to Søren Kierkegaard. I would like, in this chapter, to assess these views, focusing particularly on that of Quentin Meillassoux. I focus on his version, despite the fact that he does not directly attribute it to Kierkegaard, because it seems to me to be a particularly clear and strong expression of the position.

SOME RESPONSES TO THE VIEWS OF THE PREVIOUS CHAPTER

The claim that reality is ultimately contingent, or indeed, that it is chaotic, has not gone unchallenged. There have been two main kinds of critical response to Meillassoux, in particular, and these will also apply to at least some of the other variations on the position, including that of Slavoj Žižek. Both critical responses are expressed in a recent book about a position that has come to be known as 'speculative realism', *The Speculative Turn*.[1]

One criticism is that Meillassoux confuses metaphysical and natural necessity.[2] Meillassoux infers from the critique of metaphysical necessity that there is no necessity for anything at all. There is no cause or reason for anything to be the way it is rather than some other way. However, as

Hallward puts it, '[Meillassoux's] insistence that anything might happen can only amount to an insistence on the bare possibility of radical change'.[3] But the abstract logical possibility of change has little to do with real alternations in nature. One can argue, moreover, with Adrian Johnston,[4] that a question is arising about Meillassoux's, Žižek's, and others' transposition of an epistemological problem—the problem of whether the future will be like the past and our inability to know this, or the problem of our not knowing how to characterize claims about the universe as a whole—into an ontological claim that our ontology is characterized by absolute chaos or contingency.

Meillassoux deploys Cantorian set theory to argue against Hume's solution to his problem of induction. He avers that Hume's solution, which depends on the observation that like causes have preceded like events in a large number of cases in the past and so it is likely that this will continue in the future, itself rests upon the assumption of a closed probabilistic universe that is undermined by Cantor. He argues that 'it is possible to construct an unlimited succession of infinite sets, each of which is of a quantity superior to that of the set of whose parts it collects together. But [Zermelo-Frankel's proof] is that this set cannot be totalised'.[5] Meillassoux's own translation of this into his ontology is that 'the totality of the thinkable is unthinkable'.[6] Meillassoux does admit that there might be other set-theoretic assumptions that contradict this one, and yet 'the mere fact that we are able to assume the truth of his [Cantor's] axiomatic enables us to disqualify the necessitarian inference, and with it every reason for continuing to believe in the necessity of physical laws'.[7] But it is difficult to see how this claim follows. Meillassoux has both accepted that the set-theoretic assumption might be false and also claimed that if it is true then we must deny the necessity of the laws of nature. Clearly, though, if it is not true then we don't have to deny this necessity. There might, in other words, be set-theoretic axioms that assume the thinkability or even the knowability of an infinite totality or, indeed, of a totality of all possible infinities. Moreover, even if we accept Cantorian mathematical assumptions, it does not follow from the mere possibility that the laws of nature might change an infinite number of times, and, indeed, that there may be different conceptions of infinity, that the actual universe is chaotic. As Hallward argues, it is not clear why Meillassoux's assumptions should apply to 'the time and space of our existing universe'.[8]

In the collection, Meillassoux responds to his critics. He quotes an analytical philosopher—Nelson Goodman—who, he argues, dissolves what is effectively an ontological problem—the question of whether the future is like the past—into an epistemic one. Meillassoux writes: 'Can a conclusive argument be made for the necessity or *the absence of necessity* of observable constants? Alternatively: is there any way to justify either the claim that the future must resemble the past or the claim that the future might not resemble the past?'[9] He argues that Hume's discovery is that an entirely rational world would also be entirely chaotic, because reason cannot prohibit a priori that which goes against the purely logical necessity of noncontradiction.[10]

Further, Meillassoux writes, 'in supposing the ontological legitimacy of the Cantorian conception of the infinite, we distinguish the infinite from the All, since the infinite of the possible cannot be equated with its exhaustion (every infinite set has a determinate cardinality, which another infinite set is capable of exceeding)'.[11] From this decision 'results the possibility of clearly distinguishing between the notions of contingency and chance'.[12] Meillassoux also argues that the thesis of 'anthropism'—the emergence of life forms—is actually, given the above, likely to be extremely rare.

I would like to suggest, though, that there are a number of possible responses to this. First of all, perhaps it is indeed the case that reason cannot explain a perfectly rational world. But it does not follow from the fact that reason cannot explain itself that the presence of reason in the world cannot be explained. Maybe it is true that in the universe of all logical possibilities, the emergence of life is rare, but this surely does not detract from the fact that the explanation of the emergence (if it is indeed 'emergence' at all, rather than always having been there in some form) is an extremely hard task in a universe in which there are life forms; and one may suggest that, in this universe, life forms go all the way down to the smallest particles of matter and the most apparently inorganic 'thing' (see Tom Nagel's[13] recent work for a discussion of this). The emergence of reason, then, in such a world can be given some explanation.

Moreover, it is possible to respond to Meillassoux, also, as follows: Gottfried Leibniz believed he could formulate a picture of the universe that is mathematically derived. Meillassoux is, like his teacher Badiou, reviving this tradition, but using an ontology derived from Cantorian set theory combined with an ontological version of Hume's problem of induction.

I personally am entirely happy with the partial return, in the work of a number of these thinkers, to a quasi-pre-Kantian frame. However, it seems to me to be vital that claims about metaphysics, or 'first philosophy', in Aristotle's words, remain *hypotheses* about Being or beings. A universe that fits with contemporary, as opposed to Leibnizian, mathematical principles is one founded on that set of axioms. There might, however, be other axioms, and the assumption that it is necessary that the laws of nature be contingent is true only for the Cantorian assumptions Meillassoux makes, that themselves might not be the case.

It therefore seems to me to be imperative that hypotheses about Being or beings or Becomings are treated exactly that way, as hypotheses. Any hypothesis I attribute, as I will later in the book, to Kierkegaard must remain that—a hypothesis. It will be a reading of his work and it will be a speculative hypothesis about ontology.[14] Moreover, there might be very good reasons for thinking in a radically different metaphysical frame from this one of mathematical possibilities. There might, instead, be good reasons for formulating, with Levi Bryant (and others), a more naturalized universe of difference and of capacities and powers. One can, after all, at least make the claim that it is more difficult to derive a living nature, or, indeed, a living thought that can impact nature, from mathematical assumptions alone than from a living nature. Kierkegaard himself, writing in *Concluding Unscientific Postscript*, writes that mathematical relations are given and yet they tell us nothing about existence.[15]

I believe that, rather than supposing what must be the case from mathematical possibilities, we ought to be thinking metaphysically about the kind of world that would best allow us to explain the hard problems in our world—for example, the fact of the existence of life forms and consciousness, and the possibility of freedom. What metaphysical frame actually allows us to explain this?

Moreover, is it not an assumption about the universe to claim that 'things can be other than they are'? Does this not assume that the universe comprises static things that might be other than they are? Both thought and nature might, as Žižek suggested, primarily be made up of living processes. It is true, moreover, if one sees the world through a static spatialized frame, that the claim 'God exists' is a simple tautology. But this claim would not be a 'simple' tautology if the claim were cashed out as 'God has come into existence'. This predicate, construed in such a manner, might indeed be 'prodigious'.[16]

It is very important, it seems to me, to reiterate, then, that we do not return to one aspect of pre-Kantian metaphysics, and that is to suggest, in quasi-Leibnizian fashion, that we know the way the universe must be. In Meillassoux's case, the claim about the way we know the world to be is very different from that of Leibniz—Meillassoux's view is that the laws of nature not only are but also must be radically contingent. However, the similarity between Meillassoux and Leibniz is that both claim to know the way the world must be (even though Meillassoux seems to recognize that this claim is speculative). But despite my own and others' reservations about some aspects of Immanuel Kant's philosophy, after Kant we cannot make claims about the way the universe or nature must be.

A RESPONSE TO GIRONI

There is one point, therefore, pertaining to the above, on which I would like to take issue with Fabio Gironi's[17] admirable piece on speculative realism. Gironi argues that one thing speculative realists, including Meillassoux, ironically, have in common with the Kant of the first *Critique* is, in Henry Allison's reading, a rejection of a 'theocentric paradigm of a purely intuitive, God warranted cognition commonly accepted by all pre-Kantians'.[18] Kant's challenge, Gironi argues, was to the idea of a theocentric model of a pure God-given intuition of a 'real world'. Early realists, prior to Kant, claimed to know things in themselves only on the basis of a prior commitment to the perfect knowledge of God. In Gironi's view, the speculative realist shares Kant's doubts about this 'theocentric' guarantee of a reality exceeding our present epistemic grasp. The speculative realist, according to Gironi, however, is not led back to a rationalism of intellectual intuition but rather towards 'a naturalized transcendental realism'.[19] Gironi also claims that the speculative realist is not a monist. Now, while I agree with him that the speculative realist (as opposed to the Kierkegaardian ontologist) is 'conjoined with an ontological commitment to immanence' (although I doubt the truth of the claim that 'no reality transcends the world'[20]), I do not accept the former claim. I do not accept that speculative realists, or Kierkegaardian process philosophers, are necessarily (or even contingently) not theocentric (in the pre-Kantian sense), nor do I accept that they are not monists. Indeed, Meillassoux actually uses the words 'intellectual intuition'[21] to describe our 'intuition' of absolute contingency.[22]

One key intellectual precursor of Friedrich Wilhelm Joseph Schelling, who influenced Kierkegaard, is Benedict de Spinoza, notably his monism. For Spinoza, God and Nature are one. According to Spinoza, consciousness is to be understood as a mode of being. For Spinoza, in contrast to René Descartes, there is only one substance. Body and mind are modal expressions of the attributes of substance. The latter are thought and extension. In his *Ethics*, Spinoza argues that there cannot be two things with every property in common. There cannot, in other words, be two absolutely identical things. He argues that there must also be a substance with all possible attributes—an infinite substance. God must exist because God is a substance and existence is part of the notion of substance.[23] If there are several substances, they will be distinguished from one another either by a difference in attribute or by a difference in their modifications. An attribute is what constitutes the essence of a substance, and a 'modification' is that which exists in something other than itself.[24] But the attribute of being more than one will be a difference among substances. Therefore, there can be only one substance.

This kind of argument is mathematically or logically derived, like those of Meillassoux, although it is obviously derived from pre-Cantorian set-theoretic assumptions. It is an argument for the equivalence of God (as the Absolute) and Nature. Kant's point against the 'rationalists', however, was precisely that we cannot prove the existence of anything in the world—Absolute or not—from mathematical assumptions alone. Famously, he argued that we cannot infer any ontological claim from purely formal, logical, or mathematical truths. Moreover, one can argue that the limitation of this kind of system is precisely that it restricts matter to a dead and determinist domain and thought, again, to an atemporal field. Both thought and matter, by contrast, might instead be construed as living and dynamic. Thought, as noted by Žižek, in this alternative speculative hypothesis, following Schelling and Kierkegaard, will be an active, dynamic process. So the thought 'The body is a body' would become a process of actively combining two thoughts together in one. Matter, as well, might then be construed as it really is, as living and active, and then, finally, reflection will be a process of reflecting on the infinite in the finite.

Now, while I do not accept, Kant notwithstanding, that it is wrong to make claims about the Absolute or about Being, it is, however, precisely for Kant's reasons that we must be 'speculative' about the nature of this reality. We cannot prove (in epistemic terms) anything about the Absolute—that it is radically contingent or necessary or perfect or anything else—precisely because it lies outside the domain of possible evidence. This is a point strongly noted by Kierkegaard throughout his work.

Therefore, contrary to Gironi's claim, there is no way of separating the naturalized or mathematically derived claims of speculative realists from 'theocentric' claims. God and Nature may, with Spinoza or even, for radically different reasons, with Schelling, be the same thing, but this is precisely an assumption, akin to a mathematical a priori. Good reasons can be given for it, but it cannot be proven in the way in which, for example, Hume wanted proof of the laws of nature.

There can be good reasons for believing in a nature of some kind that lies outside thought and that may be capable indeed of grounding thought. However, these reasons cannot constitute knowledge in the strict sense claimed by some speculators. It is a *petitio principii* to claim, for example, that because we require nature to ground thought then there must be such a nature. That is like claiming that because we need water the existence of water must be necessary. Instead, it is perfectly possible that thought is not grounded at all. We can provide good reasons for a particular account of how mind arises from nature, and I will do so later in this book. But providing good reasons for a speculative account is very different from claiming, as Meillassoux does, that reality must be as we describe it.

So I have two reservations about the above metaphysic. First, it seems to me, contrary to the claims of some of the above metaphysicians, that we cannot know the way reality must be—that it is contingent or that it is necessary. Moreover, I have reservations about some of the arguments that have been proffered to prove that reality is, at its deep core, contingent or chaotic.

Bearing this sceptical caveat in mind, it seems to me, on the other hand, that there is something deeply significant about one aspect of the above perspective. One component of the views of both Žižek and Meillassoux that seems to me both to be important in its own right and to be Kierkegaard's outlook is that there is something that precedes the perspective of limited finite beings like us.[25] The claim upon which Meillassoux grounds his work—the view that Kantianism renders it difficult to account for the evidence of contemporary science that nature preexisted the human—is surely very important. A realist view that sees reality as existing outside the 'experience' of beings like us surely makes better sense of contemporary science than does the Kantian view that the subject, through the transcendental schemata of the imagination, constructs the world.

But there is a second reason deriving from contemporary science for accepting at least one aspect of Žižek's view in particular. This is that, in my limited understanding, contemporary physics assumes that appearance is ordered—organized into forms—through the constellation of a range of force fields. Each one of the following—a rock, a cloud, or a tsunami—represents the coming together of various force fields. As hypothesized by contemporary physics, 'things' emerge because dissipative systems are at rest given a certain flow of forces. Stability and identity, on the model, then, emerge from systems of force fields. At some point, on the other hand, such systems may cease to be stable. As energy is removed from the system, destabilization could occur at any moment.

There is one caveat to the above. It is also scientific investigation, in its broadest sense, that leads, and not only in Descartes' or Aristotle's times, to the substance-property metaphysical model. It is the requirement, in any investigation, that we can generalize from particular instances of, for example, a particular drug working in a small number of cases that presupposes 'individual substances' to which conceptual properties can be ascribed. So while the 'process' model may have much to commend it, the substance model cannot be ruled out altogether.

Notwithstanding this latter point, the two aforementioned points represent significant reasons for accepting a crucial aspect of Žižek's version of the above metaphysic—his claim that reality is made up of processes rather than things. But it is not only contemporary science that challenges the 'substance' model of reality. As Luce Irigaray and Christine Battersby,[26] in their very different ways, have both argued, the above view of ontology, derived from the 'substance-property' aspect of Aristotle's thought, has shaped Western thinking about human subjectivity in general and about women in particular in ways that may not have been helpful. While some notion of 'essence' is important in characterizing how it is that something can remain the same through change, it is odd, Battersby has argued, from a phenomenological perspective of one's own embodiment, to view the body as a 'container' for the self—a 'thing' that 'houses' a self. She quotes the cognitive semanticist Mark Johnson, who writes: 'Our encounter with containment and boundedness is one of the most pervasive features of our bodily experience. We are intimately aware of our bodies as three-dimensional containers into which we put certain things (food, water, air) and out of which other things emerge (food and water wastes, air, blood etc.)'.[27] Battersby writes: 'As I read Johnston's and Lakoff's account of embodiment, I register a shock of strangeness: of wondering what it would be like to inhabit a body like that'.[28] Perhaps it is a testament to the change in commonplace metaphysical assumptions since Battersby wrote *The Phenomenal Woman* (it came out in 1998) that many people might now share her view that that view of the body is strange.

One further reason for conceptualizing nature, including conscious nature, in terms of processes as opposed to inert substances ironically comes from Kant and from an epistemic attempt to defeat the sceptic. In his *Paralogisms*,[29] in the first *Critique*, Kant argues, in various formulations, against Descartes' conclusion in his *Meditations*. Kant claims that Descartes was not entitled to conclude from the occurrence of doubting and, therefore, thinking that he existed as a 'thing that thinks'. He was entitled, rather, to conclude only that 'thinking occurs'. Kant himself does not draw from this the conclusion that processes are significant, and yet he demonstrates, here, that Descartes, the arch-sceptical epistemologist, was entitled to conclude only that there is a process of thinking, rather than a substance that thinks.

AN ALTERNATIVE HYPOTHESIS

Bearing in mind that it is not possible to determine the way ultimate reality must be, I would like, in the remainder of this book, to derive from Kierkegaard's works an alternative speculative hypothesis, the hypothesis that reality is made up of processes and that these can be conceived in terms of metaphors of birth. I would like, further, to suggest that the hypothesis has some plausibility in its own right. I would like to set this speculative hypothesis in a specific context: what I consider to be Kierkegaard's, or Haufniensis', response to a problem that occurs in Kant's work. In the chapter that follows, therefore, I will outline this problem in Kant's thought.

NOTES

1. This book, edited by Levi Bryant, Nick Srnicek, and Graham Harman, *The Speculative Turn: Continental Materialism and Realism* (Melbourne: re.press, 2011), is a collection of articles on a position that has been attributed to Quentin Meillassoux, Iain Hamilton Grant and others, described as 'speculative realism'.

2. See Hallward, *The Speculative Turn*, 138.

3. Ibid., 139.

4. Adrian Johnston, 'Hume's Revenge: Adieu Meillassoux', in Hallward, *The Speculative Turn*, 92–114.

5. Ibid., 104.

6. Ibid.

7. Ibid., 105.

8. Hallward, *The Speculative Turn*, 139.

9. Ibid., 225, his own emphasis.

10. Ibid., 226.

11. Ibid., 231.

12. Ibid.

13. Tom Nagel, *Mind and Cosmos* (Oxford: Oxford University Press, 2012).

14. James Ladyman and Don Ross have made a similar point, drawing on C. S. Peirce, in 'The World in the Data', in *Scientific Metaphysics* (Oxford: Oxford University Press, 2013).

15. CUP, 110.

16. Schelling refers in his *Freiheitsschrift* to 'the profound logic of the ancients' (SW, 342). One can only speculate on what he means by this, but it seems to me that, at the very least, he is expressing something like the point made here. Tautology, Schelling writes, means 'a saying of the same' (SW, 342), but in order for it to mean anything, an action has to take place.

17. Fabio Gironi, 'Between Naturalism and Rationalism: A New Realist Landscape', *Journal of Critical Realism* 11, no. 3 (2012), 361–387.

18. Allison 1983/2004, cited in Gironi, 'Between Naturalism and Rationalism', 376.

19. See Gironi, 'Between Naturalism and Rationalism', 376–377.

20. Ibid., 378.

21. Quentin Meillassoux, *After Finitude* (London: Verso, 2009), 82.

22. This notion has been critiqued by Ray Brassier, 'The Enigma of Reason', *Collapse II*, ed. R. McKay (Oxford: Urbanomie, 2007).

23. This argument was famously criticized by Kant, who argued in the *Critique of Pure Reason* that 'existence is not a predicate or a determinate of a thing'. Existence is not an attribute of a thing in the sense in which redness or its smell are properties of the thing. Rather, the thing's existence must be presupposed in order to attribute anything to it.

24. Benedict de Spinoza, *Ethics*, ed. and trans. Edwin Curley, with an introduction by Stuart Hampshire (Harmondsworth: Penguin Classics, 1994), part 1, definitions 4 and 5.

25. Žižek, PV.

26. Christine Battersby, *The Phenomenal Woman: Feminist Metaphysics and the Patterns of Identity* (Cambridge: Polity Press, 1998).

27. Mark Johnson, *The Body in the Mind, the Bodily Basis of Meaning, Imagination and Reason* (Chicago: University of Chicago Press, 1987), 21.

28. Battersby, *The Phenomenal Woman*, 41.

29. Kant, CPR, 2nd division, book 2, chapter 1, 'The Paralogisms of Pure Reason', 328–368.

3

KANT, FREEDOM AND EVIL

As I wrote in the introduction to this book, I would like to place Søren Kierkegaard's work in the context of the German Idealist tradition. In the two previous chapters, I considered the approach of a couple of prominent recent philosophers, one of whom has, as I would like to, located Kierkegaard's work in this tradition. However, I have contested one aspect of the outlook of these recent philosophers. In the present chapter, I would like to revert, historically, to Immanuel Kant, and to outline one of the difficulties in his thought, a problem to which some of his successors set out to respond.

There are a number of respondents to Kant in this tradition who have noted perceived difficulties in Kant's thought, including, among his immediate successors, Jacobi, Maimon, Fichte and Hegel.[1] I should like, as noted previously, however, specifically to outline a different reading of Kierkegaard's view of ultimate reality that draws, as does Slavoj Žižek, on Kierkegaard's relationship to Friedrich Wilhelm Joseph Schelling, but which also offers a response to the specific difficulty in Kant's thought that I will outline in this chapter.

In common with the perceived lack of concordance, in the literature, between Kierkegaard and the German Idealist tradition, in general, it is also true that Kant and Kierkegaard are two philosophers who are not usually bracketed together. Yet for one important commentator, Ronald Green, in his book *Kierkegaard and Kant: The Hidden Debt*,[2] a deep similarity between them is seen in the centrality both accord to the notion of freedom. I agree with his assessment of the centrality of this notion for both philosophers. Kierkegaard, for example, in one of his journal entries, expresses a 'passion' for human freedom.[3] Green writes that for Kant 'to say that we are rationally free to choose immorality does not explain why we should choose to do so, but it is just Kant's point that there can be no explaining this choice'.[4] He suggests that, for Kierkegaard, as for Kant, 'sin is inexplicable'. Kierkegaard, according to Green, 'insists that we cannot "explain" actions based on freedom since they are neither logically nor causally necessary'.[5] This seems to me, however, to be the precise point at which Kierkegaard disagrees with Kant. First, Kierkegaard writes that 'to want to give a logical explanation of the coming of sin into the world is a stupidity that can only occur to people who are comically worried about finding an explanation'.[6] Kierkegaard does indeed agree with Kant that there can be no speculative comprehension—at least in the Kantian sense—of 'this Christian problem'.[7] But this does not mean that sin is inexplicable altogether for Kierkegaard. I will suggest, in this chapter, that there is a link between the difficulty Kant has explaining the origin of freedom and the well-known problem that exists in his thought, of showing how it is possible freely to do wrong, or more specifically, how it is possible for Kant to hold a person responsible for radical evil.[8] I will outline some elements of Kant's ontology, notably his references to causal powers in the *Critique of Judgment*, that may connect with this difficulty.

Evil, or extreme wrongdoing, is a very serious and major problem in our contemporary world. The awareness of its prevalence is undoubtedly greater than it would have been in Kant's time. Its force in the twentieth century, indeed, is highlighted in Hannah Arendt's characterization of it as epitomized in the Nazi concentration camps and in the experimental laboratories set up to 'kill the juridical person in man'.[9] The conditions that gave rise to extreme evil, not only in the contemporary world but also throughout a considerable period of history, are also outlined in Giorgio Agamben's[10] conception of 'bare life' and in his account of the conditions that allowed for the creation of such a concept. In yet more powerful words on the subject, Hans Jonas writes of the way in which 'evil' 'forces its perception on us by its mere presence'.[11]

Haufniensis, the pseudonymous author of *The Concept of Anxiety*, although he uses the word 'sin' and although he is clearly concerned with the biblical and specifically Lutheran notion, I believe is also interested in wrongdoing and evil per se, and I believe he is interested in responding to

Kant on this subject. Green, moreover, notes that the Kierkegaard or Haufniensis of CA was steeped in Kant and particularly in a reading of *Religion within the Limits of Reason Alone*.[12]

FREEDOM AND EVIL

In a significant recent article, much of which I agree with and applaud, Roe Fremstedal[13] argues that Kierkegaard was not only familiar with Kant's concept of radical evil but in fact approved of it.[14] I concur with Fremstedal's point that 'Kant and Kierkegaard share the view that the ethical requirement has an unconditional nature',[15] but it seems to me that it is precisely this unconditional nature of the ethical requirement that makes it very difficult for Kant to hold a second view that Fremstedal attributes to him. This view, shared by Kant and Kierkegaard, is that 'sin results from a choice', and, as Fremstedal writes, 'put in Kantian terms sin is a category of spirit not a category of nature' and 'evil is a concept of freedom'.[16]

This, it seems to me, is precisely the position Kant would like to hold—he does not want to endorse the Leibnizian or the Socratic view that moral evil is not a fully free choice. Kant does not want to uphold the perspective that views evil as a cosmological problem—a matter of ignorance, of not knowing what is the right thing to do. As he puts it in *Religion within the Limits of Reason Alone*, evil 'must proceed from the individual's own choice'.[17] Kant does not want evil or sin to be either a pure weakness or a matter of irrationality. But it is precisely this view—that evil is a category of spirit rather than nature—that, it seems to me, is difficult for Kant to hold, because it conflicts with others of his strongly held arguments about freedom and the moral law.

Kant, of course, recognizes the magnitude of the problem of freedom, alongside the difficulties posed by reasoning about the world as a whole and the nature of the human mind. It is noteworthy that these same questions, despite the radically different world in which we live today, remain key problems in contemporary metaphysics and philosophy more generally.[18]

Famously, in the opening paragraphs of the *Critique of Pure Reason*, Kant refers to the 'peculiar fate' of human reason, which is 'burdened by questions which, as prescribed by the very nature of reason itself, it is not able to ignore, but which, as transcending all its powers, it is also unable to answer'.[19] One illustration of this 'fate' is the problem of freedom. In the thesis of the Third Antinomy in the first *Critique*, Kant identifies a power of spontaneity or freedom that conflicts with the operation of the universal principle of causation in the phenomenal and natural world. This is an 'absolute spontaneity' that 'begins of itself'.[20] He argues that such a spontaneity can be assumed to exist and that beings like us—finite rational beings—have freedom of this nature. Indeed, he claims that such spontaneity is a presupposition of the possibility of there being a phenomenal world at all. He writes, 'We have to remain satisfied with the a priori knowledge that this latter type of causality must be presupposed'.[21] As reasoners of any kind, therefore, we must assume freedom. Moving on from this, in the *Groundwork of the Metaphysics of Morals* he argues that freedom of the will is also a presupposition of the moral law that is unconditionally valid for the rational will. The objectivity and necessity of the moral law depend upon transcendental freedom. Kant writes, 'With the idea of freedom the concept of autonomy is now inseparably combined, and with the concept of autonomy the universal principle of morality'.[22] As we are potentially rational beings, so are we potentially free: 'as belonging to the intelligible world [we are] under laws which, being independent of nature, are not empirical but grounded merely in reason'.[23] By contrast, insofar as we are sensible beings, we are governed by laws of nature. Indeed, in the third *Critique*, Kant explicitly describes 'man' as a moral agent; 'man considered as a noumenon'.[24] Man, in this case, acts from a 'causality that is teleological'.[25]

I would like, at the outset of this chapter, briefly to outline Kant's view of the relation between freedom and the moral law. His view of this relation appears in the *Critique of Pure Reason*, in the *Groundwork of the Metaphysics of Morals*, and in the *Critique of Practical Reason*.[26]

There is an argument that can be found in the first *Critique* and also in the *Groundwork*, which Henry Allison has labelled the Reciprocity Thesis.[27] According to this, there is a mutual entailment between the following claims:

1. The rational will is free.
2. The moral law is unconditionally valid for the rational will.

In the *Groundwork* much of the argument is about freedom of the will being a presupposition of the practical standpoint of the moral law.[28] A 'free cause' is one that operates in accordance with a special kind of causality—a causality in accordance with a law. If human beings were 'holy wills' then they would necessarily follow the universal and necessary principle of morality. In such a case the moral law would simply describe the operation of its will. Human beings, or finite rational beings, are mostly construed as not being holy wills; nevertheless, as rational beings, they have the capacity to act in accordance with the representation of laws. The moral law then becomes a normative law for them. This is what Kant identifies as practical reason. Rational animals have the capacity to produce (or to receive in some interpretations—see Robert Stern[29]) laws. These laws—normative laws—in their turn become universal and necessary for all rational beings.

Indeed, while Kant appears to develop a different argument for the relation between freedom and the moral law in the *Critique of Practical Reason*, he nonetheless continues to accept the mutual entailment of freedom and the moral law. 'Freedom and unconditional practical law reciprocally imply each other'.[30] 'The moral law', he writes, 'is a law of causality through freedom'.[31] As sensible beings, finite rational beings are described here as heteronymous, while as rational and moral beings they are autonomous.

Brute animals respond mechanically to their desires. Brutes cannot resist their impulses. Kant's argument for the objective validity of the moral law and its applicability to all rational beings depends upon his identification of morality and rationality.

Apart from the issue of dualism, which has been extensively dealt with in the literature,[32] there is clearly a problem here[33]—if freedom is equivalent to the rational self-determination of moral agents when they are following the moral law, then rational beings are not free when they are not following the moral law. At the very least, there is a tension between these arguments and Kant's desire to hold the view that sin results from free choice.

SOME INTERPRETATIONS OF THIS PROBLEM

It is no doubt the case that there are a number of ways of reading Kant's notion of freedom,[34] and it is also true that many contemporary commentators argue that we can read him as a compatibilist with regard to freedom and determinism.[35] But Kant himself, as indicated particularly by the Third Antinomy and as noted above, clearly wanted to defend an incompatibilist and libertarian account of freedom. He believed that genuine freedom required no less than this. The incompatibilist account is his notion, outlined above, of 'transcendental' freedom. It is this that grounds his strong view that behaving well and badly are not matters that come in half measures—his moral rigorism. Kierkegaard follows Kant in this regard. Both believed, in other words, that the source of free norms must be outside the phenomenal world—for Kant the determinist world of Newtonian physics and for Kierkegaard the finite limited world of human interaction. While Kierkegaard adopts this aspect of Kant's view, there is nonetheless an important difference between their respective views. Kierkegaard's transcendent is, in an important sense, both 'outside' the world of experience of limited finite beings and 'inside it' as well. God, for Kierkegaard, grounds freedom, but God is also the ground of nature. These notions will be clarified later on in the text.

I would like, in the following sections of this chapter, to outline some interpretations of the problem of freely doing wrong for Kant, and some attempts, on the part of commentators, to resolve the problem. I would also like to note a link, and a further tension, between Kant's views here and his perspective on purposiveness expressed in the *Critique of Judgment.*

A Strong Reading

One reading I would like to mention of the relation between free will and the moral law makes it out to be very strong indeed. A contemporary of Kant, Carl Schmid, suggests that, at least sometimes, Kant makes the connection between these two so strong that he effectively becomes an 'intelligible fatalist'.[36] The moral law causally determines the free will.[37] There are certainly passages in the Kantian corpus that appear to support such a reading. For example, in the *Groundwork of the Metaphysics of Morals*, Kant writes, 'If reason infallibly determines the will, the actions

of such a being that are cognised as objectively necessary are also subjec-
tively necessary'.[38] Kant's references to the 'holy will', despite his recognition, noted above, that we cannot have such a will, sometimes suggest
this reading. He sometimes intends the notion of the 'holy will' to be a
description of the finite rational will insofar as it operates intelligibly. The
self, therefore, viewed as intelligible agent, must be seen as perfectly
moral. It is clear, in this extreme reading of the notion, that immoral
agents fail to be free. Recognizing that this leaves him with the difficulty
of explaining the freedom to do wrong, in his late work *Religion within
the Limits of Reason Alone* Kant concerns himself with the problem of
freely doing wrong and discusses the origin of evil.[39]

It is important to note that the active purposive element, for Kant, in
relation to this first interpretation of the relation between freedom and the
moral law, is not nature but the moral law. Kant both believed that there
are purposes in nature, at least nature as viewed by finite rational beings,
and was convinced that purposes must be unscientific.[40] It was his strong
conviction that the purposiveness of, for example, a blade of grass—the
capacity of the grass to grow—could not be incorporated into the proper
scientific Newtonian and mechanical notion of causation. Purposes can
neither be specularized—made visible to the eye—nor can they be mechanically configured. Purposes cannot be seen. Yet Kant does not seem
to worry about the idea that the moral law becomes an active causal force.
This seems intuitively odd, since it is difficult to conceptualize a logical
form—the moral law—as having powers or capacities. Even if there is a
relation of entailment between the moral law and the free will, at least
one of these must shape the self that acts. We cannot 'see' causal powers
in nature and this vexes Kant. No more, however, can we 'see' the operation of the will, and this does not seem to concern him.

A Second Interpretation of the Relation

An alternative, developed partly in *Religion within the Limits of Reason
Alone*, to the above 'rational fatalist' reading of all free actions is that
some free actions, those that are wrong or evil, are freely undertaken but
grounded in some other force—outside time and space—than the moral
law. This is the second interpretation of the relation between freedom and
moral law I would like briefly to discuss.

When criticizing the Stoic view that evil consists in the mere lack of knowledge of what is good, Kant writes:

> So it is not surprising that an Apostle represents this *invisible* enemy, who is known only through his operations upon us and who destroys basic principles, as being outside us and indeed an evil *spirit*. . . . As far as its practical value to us is concerned, moreover, it is all one whether we place the seducer merely within ourselves, or without; for guilt touches us not a whit less in the latter case than in the former, in as much as we would not be led astray by him at all were we not already in secret league with him.[41]

In the above passage the 'evil spirit' functions in an analogous fashion to God. One grounds the moral law and the other would ground evil or wrongdoing. In the third *Critique* Kant argues that physical teleology needs to be supplemented with a moral teleology, for physical teleology on its own, 'if it proceeded consistently, instead of borrowing, unnoticed, from moral teleology, could not provide a basis for anything but a *demonology*, which is incapable of providing a determinate concept of the deity'.[42] If the proof of teleological causation in the third *Critique* were only a proof of a physical form of cause, then the ground of this might be some kind of being outside time and space—a demon analogous, perhaps, to Descartes' evil demon.[43] Kant offers a moral proof of the existence of God: when we act freely from the moral law we are acting as though we are pure rational beings. This is, Kant writes, 'the idea of the supersensible within us',[44] and it gives rise to an idea of the supersensible outside us; a supersensible Being that grounds morality in nature—at least insofar as it is supposed to be a teleological whole. The Supreme Being, therefore, is conceived by analogy with our own 'supersensible' capacity—the capacity to act freely in accordance with the moral law. Correspondingly, Kant hypothesizes a 'spirit of an originally more sublime destiny' that tempts human beings into evil.[45] He writes that the absolutely first beginnings of evil, as with the first beginnings of good, are incomprehensible to us finite limited beings. Now, this second interpretation has a distinct advantage: it provides evidence of genuine metaphysical or transcendental freedom to do wrong.

The interpretation has, however, a number of disadvantages. First, it would undermine the crucial argument of the second *Critique* that freedom and the moral law reciprocally imply one another. Some free acts would be grounded in some other unfathomable source while free and moral acts would be grounded in pure reason and the moral law.

A second objection to this notion, proposed by Gordon Michalson, is that, as he puts it, 'devilishness would mark the limit point beyond which no moral regeneration would be possible'.[46] According to his reading of 'devilishness', the notion would remove altogether our moral capacity; 'freely willing to reject the moral law would mean exercising reason for the sake of being irrational'.[47] Perhaps the difficulties pertaining to this interpretation, in the end, stem from the radical separation that parallels other separations, of the grounds for doing good from those for acting wrongly.[48]

Another way of putting the problem is that if a person chose to act in accordance with the devil, then he or she might also lose the capacity to act from the moral law, and one of Kant's arguments against suicide is precisely that it prevents the person from continuing to act as an autonomous and free agent.[49]

This argument of Kant's has him locating the ground of freedom in some being conceived by analogy with ourselves as purely rational beings. This being is a perfectly rational one that 'gives birth to' our moral capacity. So the grounding of nature, rather than being within nature, is displaced onto some perfectly rational being that lies outside nature. Then, in parallel, since it is clearly hard to place the capacity for wrongdoing in this rational nature, there is some perfectly evil being—the counterpoint or the mirror image of the perfectly rational being. This alternative being gives rise to the capacity in us for evil. Both lie outside nature. But is it not perfectly possible for nature itself to operate as the ground? I will return to this point.

A Third Interpretation

A third interpretation I would like to consider is the following: Kant sometimes hypothesizes an inner self—a 'disposition' that 'chooses', on certain occasions, to subordinate the moral law to something else. In *Religion within the Limits of Reason Alone*, he gives a number of possible readings, compatible with this interpretation, of what happens when a person does wrong. For example, he writes: 'The ground of evil cannot lie in any object determining the power of choice through inclination, not in any natural impulses but only in a rule that the power of choice itself produces for the exercise of its freedom i.e. in a maxim'.[50]

A number of contemporary commentators have offered alternative interpretations of Kant's view of what it means freely to do wrong that fit with this notion of a 'disposition' to choose a maxim. Michalson calls this a 'disposition' to subordinate, within a maxim, the moral law to some sensuous inclination.[51] So the account of freely doing wrong, then, involves this 'disposition' to choose a maxim. Sometimes the will may choose a maxim that conflicts with the moral law. This is the view defended by Fremstedal in the article mentioned earlier in the chapter.

Now, rather than being shaped by internal material forces that might sometimes lead to good and sometimes not, we have a further causally efficacious mental element—a disposition to choose a causally active rational self or to choose to subordinate this causally active self to a sensuous capacity.

Allen Wood, for example, suggests that freedom is the capacity to act according to rational norms. He claims that, in acting freely, the agent is acting from a special kind of causality. A will acts not only according to laws but also 'according to their representation'.[52] The law of a free cause must be one 'it represents to itself'. The free self, in this reading, is a 'disposition' to choose some law. I would like to focus at slightly greater length on this third interpretation of the relation between freedom and the moral law since it is the one that is often adopted in the contemporary literature.

What is the 'rule' that the power of choice itself produces? Kant describes some 'natural predispositions' that can lead to good. There are also predispositions to 'merely mechanical self-love'; there are dispositions to self-preservation; there is the desire for propagation and there is a 'social drive'. Sometimes, moreover, Kant writes, the individual may be 'frail' insofar as he or she only indecisively incorporates the moral maxim. On yet other occasions, individuals place self-love above the moral law. In these various readings, then, for Kant, desires would overpower the rational will.

A number of difficulties have been pointed out, however, pertaining to this notion of a 'disposition' or choice of disposition: *Gesinnung*. One is that, as Michalson points out, 'Kant is able to salvage a theory of freedom only by sealing it off from temporality',[53] and the free will is a 'purely intelligible faculty not subject to the form of time, nor consequently to the condition of succession in time'. [54] Where, then, does the 'disposition' sit? Is it outside time as well, or is it partly in time and partly outside it? If it is outside time, how then can Kant make sense of moral change—moral conversion or simply a change of heart that occurs in sequential terms? In these circumstances, as Kant is aware, 'he could become a new man only by a kind of re-birth'. [55] Lewis White Beck has noted that if the soul, the rational self, is not subject to temporal conditions, then it is difficult for us to make sense of the notion of endless progress. [56] There is also the point that the notion may commit Kant to two selves too many. The 'disposition' becomes a kind of third element that is neither phenomenal nor noumenal. There may then be three selves: the psychological phenomenal self, the noumenal 'dispositional' self, and, thirdly, the subject's choice of disposition. Alternatively, this 'third self' may be problematic in a different way. It may be a 'blind spot' that links the noumenal and the phenomenal. [57]

It might be suggested that one can discuss Kant's notion of freedom while setting aside what seems to be an implausible metaphysic. Allen Wood, for example, notes that Kant distinguishes 'metaphysical' from 'practical' freedom. A 'transcendentally free' cause is a first cause, one that can be effective independently of any prior cause. Practical freedom, on the other hand, is the kind of freedom we attribute to ourselves as agents. [58] He suggests a 'reconstruction' of Kant that focuses on 'practical' freedom. [59] It is important to point out that while this account is clearly there in Kant's writings, one cannot easily remove altogether the metaphysical notion without denying a crucial component of Kant's theory of freedom—its libertarian aspect. In a Kantian framework, the only way one can hypothesize a genuinely free form of causation is by supposing that there is some other kind of self from the phenomenal one that operates according to some different and mysterious notion of causation. [60]

Leaving this aside, Wood suggests, as noted, that freedom is the capacity to act according to rational norms. The law that the free self 'represents to itself' is one under which it considers its actions from a practical standpoint. Wood draws the analogy of a chess player: she moves the bishop in accordance with the rules of chess. The explanation of the action will be in terms of the agent's intentions. Freedom, in this view, would not be either causally—in some sense of cause—or descriptively related to the will; rather, freedom would be some notion that may be

inexplicable but that involves the ability to choose either to subordinate
the moral law to something else or to follow the moral law. The rules of
morality, then, operate rather like the rules of chess, but they are rules
that we must presuppose, like the rules of logic, in order to act rationally.
Wood suggests, and Onora O'Neill[61] makes a similar point, that we must
presuppose freedom in representing ourselves as competent to decide
between compatibilism and incompatibilism.

But there seem to me to be parallel difficulties with this revised notion. In Wood's chess player analogy, exercising the freedom to do wrong
could be viewed either as failing properly to move one's bishop or as
failing to play at all. It is difficult, though, to regard either of these actions
as truly free, in the sense in which the chess player who plays the bishop
according to the rules is acting freely. When a chess player fails to move
the bishop properly, the player is trying to move it correctly but failing.
But it would involve some contorted thinking to describe Hitler's actions,
for example, as involving him trying hard to follow the moral law but
failing.[62] In fact, wrongdoing, in the chess player analogy, would be
simply failing to act properly within the rules of the game or failing to fall
within the domain of chess—morality—at all, and so the action would not
be imputable. Moreover, the explanation offered by several commentators seems to leave Kant open to the charge that he is using a sleight of
hand, both suggesting that actions governed by sensuous inclination are
fully determined and arguing that the will can choose to subordinate the
moral law to sensuous inclination. To offer an analogy: if I simply smoke
a cigarette, I am acting from inclination, but if I reflect on this and decide
to subordinate the maxim that considers the consequences of smoking to
my desire, then my action is free. To use Frankfurt's notion of first- and
second-order desires: I might carefully consider the second-order desire,
but still act on my first-order desire.[63] The difficulty, though, is that the
two actions are the same. Kant sometimes speaks against himself, of
freely taking sensuous motives as determinant of one's action.

Moreover, and finally on this, Wood and O'Neill both make the point
that we must presuppose our own freedom in representing ourselves as
rational beings. But the fact that we must presuppose our freedom does
not show that we are free.

I would like to mention, at this point, one more ingenious argument
designed to prove that Kant can offer an account—an a priori and
transcendental account—of the freedom to do wrong, or of an evil pro-

pensity. This is an argument presented by Seiriol Morgan in his excellent paper.[64] Morgan hypothesizes the following thought experiment: imagine the Kantian free will deciding before it enters the world how it is going to make its choices. Such a will would be a free causality so it would have to choose its principle for itself. The self would be a pared-away self: it would have pared away its desires, its emotions, its sociality, its history. Such a self would not therefore be able to choose self-love, since this is an inclination in the phenomenal world and it would be outside the agent's control. But, Morgan argues, this self has the ability to choose to adopt negative freedom as opposed to positive freedom. The former would be, in these circumstances, complete absence of restraint. Such a self, then, would set out to maximize its freedom from restraint, and this would involve its prioritizing its inclinations when they conflict with the choices of others, so curtailing their freedom. The will then would prioritize self-love over morality. Such a will would effectively be an evil will in Kant's sense. This, briefly summarizing a detailed and complex argument, would be an a priori and transcendental argument resting only on the assumption that there are such acts as evil acts among humanity.

My reservation, however, about this argument is threefold. First, it seems to me that the assumption underlying the thought experiment is analogous to the 'original position' of John Rawls.[65] But, in a parallel criticism to that of Michael Sandel and Michael Waltzer of Rawls, such a self wouldn't have the ability to make a choice between positive and negative freedom because being able to draw such a distinction presupposes more than the spontaneous will would have at its disposal. The concept of negative freedom presupposes understanding the notion of constraint, understanding what it would mean to constrain others, and the 'spontaneous will' outside the world could not possibly, in the circumstances outlined, know or understand these matters.

Secondly, it seems to me that the notion of freedom such a will would have would not really be Kantian, since even the strong notion 'absence of all constraints' does not mean the same thing as being 'self' caused. It is the latter Kant wants for his strong notion of freedom. Imagine a billiard ball that is unconstrained by any other billiard ball or any other impediment at all. This would not be the same thing as describing the billiard ball as acting from its own causality.

Even if Morgan were to argue, in response to this, that the self would be choosing to prioritize its inclinations and this would be different from simply going along with one's inclinations, it wouldn't answer the point fully. Inclinations, after all, differ from simply being passively affected by something external. Following an inclination to smoke, for example, is different from being hit in the face by a cricket ball. The agent has some control over the former but none over the latter. So it is difficult to understand the force of the distinction between choosing to follow an inclination and simply following an inclination.

Moreover, and finally, some of the inclinations of such an agent would surely be harmless or even good. Characters who have been depicted as evil have usually had some good and other-directed inclinations. So choosing to follow all one's inclinations would not necessarily even be equivalent to prioritizing self-love over morality. The argument, therefore, seems to me to have its limitations, but it is exactly the form that an argument for the existence of an evil will in Kant would have to take.

Some Related Issues

Although there could be other ways in which Kant might show how the freedom to do wrong is compatible with his view of the freedom to act well in accordance with the moral law, it is difficult for him to do so, given his view of nature and of human nature. Kant's view of nature is limited by his Newtonianism. For the latter, a position that Kant took up in his early writings as well as in the later, the quantity of matter remains always the same and every change has an external cause. For Newton as well as for Kant, nature is a determined system: a system consisting in a collection of substantial things, externally related to one another, through mechanical causation. For Kant, the categories shape the nature of matter as the sum of appearances. Kant's view of natural science has it deal with substantial bodies dependent upon external forces for change. Yet Newton himself found it difficult, within his framework, to account for the force of gravity.[66]

Kant's view of mechanical nature shapes his perspective on the free self as a radically different kind of thing. The self, then, becomes a divided entity. It is divided between a phenomenal, desiring, natural thing determined by Newtonian causal principles and a rational and free being, shaped by the moral law. Even if we view these two elements as aspects of one whole, as Allison does,[67] there remains a divide between the sensory and desiring element of the self and the element that strains to be as rational as possible.[68] In his third *Critique*, Kant does consider some aspects of the natural world in a teleological fashion. Yet he does not believe that nature itself can be purposive: 'We have no a priori basis whatever for the following presumption: how purposes that are not ours, and that we also cannot attribute to nature (since we do not assume nature to be an intelligent being), yet are to constitute or would constitute a special kind of causality, or at least a quite distinct lawfulness of nature'.[69] Purposiveness 'is not a character of things outside me but a mere way of presenting them within me'.[70] In CJ, rational beings are the predominant exemplifications of purposiveness: 'man' becomes the ultimate purpose in the world. 'Man' is a natural purpose, although it is only that we judge reflectively that he is purposive. For Kant in the third *Critique*, the ideal of the beautiful consists in the rational being acting morally.[71]

To judge that something is purposive is to make a 'reflective judgment' or a noncognitive judgement that doesn't constitute any objects.[72] There can, Kant argues, be no conception of matter that has it contain purposiveness within itself.[73] Even a tree, which appears to exhibit a different notion of causation from the mechanical, is only seen this way by analogy with our own causality in terms of purposes.

Ultimately, then, there is something that transcends the natural and that grounds the actions of free beings. Kant is led, partly because of his view of the natural, to see the origin of human evil as 'inscrutable' or irrational. I would now like to go on to discuss this.

In *Religion*, Kant argues that the story, in scripture, of the origin of the first sin involves a mistake. It presents as first in time what ought to be logically first. Evil, in the end, for Kant, is innate. He writes, 'The rational origin of this perversion of our will remains inscrutable to us'.[74] Since, apart from maxims, no determining ground can or ought to be adduced, we are led back endlessly in the series of subjective determining grounds, without ever being able to reach the ultimate ground. Our innermost wills are opaque to us.[75] Knowing myself always to possess the ability to subordinate reason to impulse, this casts a pall over all my future free choices. Kant rejects the following view: 'The most inept is that which describes it as descending in an inheritance from our first parents'.[76]

The Adam story, according to Kant, is 'inept'. Why is this? There are at least three reasons:

1. Because the story is set up to take place in time, whereas the free
   will is not in time.
2. Because it does not explain what it purports to explain. It simply
   presupposes it. If we can resist temptation, then the story of Adam
   is no explanation of why we do wrong.
3. If, on the other hand, evil is exterior to humanity, then seduction is
   impossible to resist. God therefore punishes us for something that
   is beyond our control. This would be a classical determinist reading
   of the origin of evil.

The origin of evil, therefore, cannot be explained. In scripture, the origin
of evil is depicted as having a temporal beginning; this beginning is
presented as a narrative, where its essence appears as becoming first in
time. But, Kant writes, evil does not start from a propensity; rather, it
begins from a transgression of the moral law. Instead of following the
moral law, man—or Adam in the biblical story—looked about for another
incentive. He then made it his maxim to follow the law of duty not as
duty but with regard to other aims. He began to call into question the
severity of the commandment which excludes the influence of all other
incentives. For Kant, therefore, in those of us apart from Adam, sin origi-
nates from an innate wickedness in our nature. This notion of the 'innate',
for him, if it is read in a quasi-logical fashion, simply means a given,
something that cannot be explained.

In his third *Critique*, Kant sets out to unite 'the immense gulf between
nature and freedom'.[77] The work is partly concerned with teleological
judgements or maxims describing how we ought to judge nature. For
Kant, a thing can be viewed as a natural purpose 'if it is both cause and
effect of itself'.[78] In the case of natural purposes, the parts depend upon
the whole. A tree, for example, is self-organizing in three ways: (i) the
tree produces itself in relation to its species—'within its species, it is both
cause and effect'[79]; (ii) the nourishment taken in by the tree enables its
development; and (iii) the various components of the tree depend on and
link with one another.

However, as noted, a judgement that something is purposive is regulative only and does not constitute any object. This contrasts with Kant's
discussion of causation in the Second Analogy, in CPR, where the category of causation is significant in constituting objects in space and time.
In the first *Critique* Kant argues that, in order for representations to

constitute objects, these representations must not be associated in a haphazard or arbitrary fashion. That is, as one commentator puts it, after challenging a number of other interpretations on the subject, 'the representations must themselves be *connected according to rules*'.[80] In Kant's own words, representations 'in so far as they are in these relations (in space and time) connected and determinable according to the rules of the unity of experience are called objects'.[81]

Experience, in this interpretation, can only be represented as an object, for Kant in CPR, if it stands under a rule: the house, in Kant's example, must have a particular spatial location, at a given time; it must also be composed of a particular set of parts, and these various parts must be connected in some determinate fashion.

Matters are different, however, in relation to teleological causation, or judgements of purposiveness, in CJ. Here, rather than offering an account of the conditions under which we can know objects, Kant is concerned with matters of beauty, with biological growth, and with morality. The objects that are 'constituted' by the category of causation in the first *Critique* are not necessarily themselves purposive. It is simply that, in some cases, we judge them as though they are. For Kant, moreover, in CJ, the ultimate exemplification of purposiveness is not a tree or any other plant but 'man' acting as a moral agent.[82] We rational beings have to suppose, for the understanding of morality, 'man' to be the ultimate purpose. 'Man' acting as a moral agent is the purpose against which we judge the purposiveness of everything else. Kant writes that 'man is the only being on earth that has understanding and hence an ability to set himself limited purposes of his own choice, and in this respect he holds himself lord of nature; and if we regard nature as a teleological system then it is man's vocation to be the ultimate purpose of nature, but always subject to a condition; he must have the understanding and the will to give both nature and himself reference to a purpose that can be independent of nature, self-sufficient and a final purpose'.[83]

Kant's Newtonian view of the natural world, then, led him to believe that the objects constituted by the category of causation were not living and active, like a tree, but rather inert and 'dead', as we might intuitively view a billiard ball. On the one hand, Kant offers a detailed and full account of the nature of teleological causation. On the other hand, he believes that, rather than objects like a tree really being purposive, it is simply that we judge them as though they are purposive. So instead of seeing purposiveness as existing in the natural world, he sees the best exemplification of purposiveness as the rational will. We might claim, then, that he reverses real purposiveness in nature and projects it into the rational will of 'man' when 'he' acts well as a moral agent. Instead of seeing the processes of birth and growth as the best exemplifications of purposiveness in nature, he sees the rational will as fulfilling this role. However, coming full circle, this makes it difficult for him to offer an account of how this 'free' self can also do wrong.

One might argue, then, that Kant reverses the process of birth, from a mother or some equally clear-cut exemplification of this into a 'lord' of nature who becomes the ultimate purpose, so long as this 'lord' uses his understanding and his will effectively.

Elsewhere in the third *Critique*, however, Kant offers a completely different picture. There is a section that, although not often noted in the commentaries, is recognized as, in a significant sense, prefiguring Darwin. Kant talks, here, about genera of animals sharing a common schema; about their having been produced according to a common archetype. He suggests that the species of animals is 'produced by a common original mother'.[84] He writes, as noted, 'He can make mother earth (like a large animal as it were) emerge from her state of chaos, and make her lap promptly give birth initially to creatures of a less purposive form, with these then giving birth to others that became better adapted to their place of origin and to their relations to one another, until in the end this womb itself rigidified, ossified, and confined itself to bearing definite species that would no longer degenerate, so that the diversity remained as it had turned out when that fertile formative force ceased to operate'.[85]

What is wrong with this account, according to Kant? I find two reasons in Kant's work for rejecting this account. First, he writes: 'In giving this account, the archaeologist of nature will have to attribute to this universal mother an organisation that purposively aimed at all these creatures, since otherwise it is quite inconceivable [how] the purposive form is possible that we find in the produce of the animal and plant kingdoms. But if he attributes such an organisation to her then he has only put off the basis for his explanation. This is no explanation at all'.[86]

In other words, Kant is arguing, using his metaphysical account that derives in part from his Newtonianism, coupled with his perspective on morality, that the only way this kind of view of the origins of purposiveness can function is if this 'mother' had a super intelligence and could 'see' her capacity to produce her effects. But this would effectively turn her into the supersensible ground considered earlier. The material and biological processes of birth cannot, for Kant, function as the ground, basically because the ordered nature that we know is itself produced by us and produced by us in a fashion that is shaped by a Newtonian view of causation.

Secondly, Kant argues, against the view of a 'mother earth', that those who think in terms of the whole think of it in terms of an 'all encompassing substance'—which is Spinozism, and only therefore a more determinate version of pantheism. So, in this objection to his own account, Kant has removed the process element of the 'mother' and of the evolution of other species and turned it into inert, mechanical matter, which, being inert and mechanical, clearly cannot ground a process system. Putting this differently, then, it is hard for Kant to see the earth as a living system analogous to a 'mother' because the science he so admired and accepted did not allow this. Yet he was, even in proposing this metaphor, and in thinking about the processes by which trees grow, thinking ahead of his time and in process terms.

For Kant, the Newtonian, to reiterate, the categories shape the nature of matter as the sum of appearances. Kant's view of natural science has it deal with substantial bodies dependent upon external forces for change. This, then, is one reason why he cannot accept the metaphor of the earth as a 'mother'.

But another reason has to do, surely, with Kant's view of women and his picture of the nature of inner bodily space. Christine Battersby has pointed out how difficult it is for Kant, in his view of the nature of space and time and of matter, to account even for his own inner bodily space, let alone for that of a body that is capable of giving birth. Knowledge of things in space presupposes 'outer sense' and knowledge of such matters is knowledge of something other than the 'I'. Time is the form of inner sense. So, as Battersby puts it, 'Kant needs a body in order to be a self; but the body he needs is neither self nor not self'.[87] Of course, this 'inner bodily space' includes the 'purposiveness' of the female body in producing another self from within itself. The capacity of a body to 'birth', therefore, is inexplicable because it is literally outside (actually 'inside') his view of space.

Moreover, women, for Kant, are refused the kind of personhood that entails free will and pure rationality. Women are fully animal and human.

However, frequently they are denied the status of 'persons' in the sense of being full moral agents. They are grouped together with 'domestic servants, apprentices, hairdressers and other "passive" citizens'.[88] They therefore cannot have the 'active' thinking capacity that goes along with being a person.

It seems to me that these various views of Kant's are connected. The difficulty he has in explaining the possibility of freely doing wrong is linked with his perspective on nature and with the model of causation he takes, expressed in the Second Analogy, to be the definitive model. Even if one tries, and I have discussed one attempt to do this, to detach Kant's view of practical freedom from his metaphysic, it is hard to escape this difficulty. This, in its turn, I have suggested, gives rise to the difficulty Kant has, of explaining the origin of freedom.

In this chapter, I have discussed a number of interpretations of what it might mean, for Kant, freely to do wrong. I have suggested that each one of these interpretations is problematic. The difficulty Kant has with this issue, I have argued, is connected with his Newtonianism. His Newtonian view of the natural world makes it difficult for him to see 'purposes' as really existing in natural objects. Instead he sees the paradigm exemplification of 'purposiveness' as the rational self, acting well as a moral agent. This account, though, fails to provide a place for the person who does wrong.

I will move, in the next section of the book, to outline how Kierkegaard, while he shares Kant's strong notion of freedom, offers a very different perspective on the human being and on nature. This both allows him to explain the origin of freedom and exempts him from Kant's problem.

NOTES

1. One very useful summary of responses to Kant from his immediate successors and his contemporaries is Frederick Beiser, *The Fate of Reason: German Philosophy from Kant to Fichte* (Cambridge: Harvard University Press, 1987).

2. Ronald Green, *Kierkegaard and Kant: The Hidden Debt* (Albany: State University of New York Press, 1992). A number of scholars have recently begun to notice the links between Kant and Kierkegaard—see below for some examples. A further philosopher who noted this link a while ago was Alasdair MacIntyre, in *After Virtue* (Notre Dame: University of Notre Dame Press, 1981), 42.

Yet another is Paul Ricoeur, in 'Philosophy after Kierkegaard', in *Kierkegaard: A Critical Reader*, ed. Jonathan Ree and Jane Chamberlain (Oxford: Blackwell, 1998).

3. JP vol. 1a, 72; also see Green, *Kierkegaard and Kant*, 147.

4. Green, *Kierkegaard and Kant*, 158.

5. Ibid., 160.

6. CA, quoted in Green, *Kierkegaard and Kant*, 161.

7. Kierkegaard, 1851 journal entry; elsewhere Kierkegaard writes: 'Speculative thought has understood everything, everything everything! The ecclesiastical speaker still exercises some restraint; he admits that he has not yet understood everything; he admits that he is striving—poor fellow that is a confusion of categories!—"If there is anyone who has understood everything" he says, "then I admit that I have not understood it and cannot demonstrate everything"'. CUP, 31.

8. In their notes to volume 2 of Kierkegaard's *Journals and Papers*, Hong and Hong note: 'Kierkegaard criticizes Kant's concept of radical evil. Where Kant thinks thought must stop, at "das Ding an sich", according to Kierkegaard the new actuality begins, which has its ground in a transcendent relationship and which ultimately has the characteristic mark of the absurd' (JP, vol. 2, 611).

9. Hannah Arendt, *The Origins of Totalitarianism*, 3rd ed. (New York: Harcourt Brace, 1951), 447.

10. Giorgio Agamben, *Homo Sacer: Sovereign Power and Bare Life*, trans. Daniel Heller-Roazen (Stanford: Stanford University Press, 1998).

11. Hans Jonas, *The Imperative of Responsibility: In Search of an Ethics for the Technological Age* (Chicago: Chicago University Press, 1984), 27.

12. This link has also been noted by other commentators, for example, Kosch (2009) and Fremstedal (2012). Indeed, Fremstedal points to some references to Kant and rigorism in a number of Kierkegaard texts, including CA and EO.

13. Roe Fremstedal, 'Original Sin and Radical Evil: Kierkegaard and Kant', *Kantian Review* 17, no. 2 (2012), 197–225.

14. Ibid., 198.

15. Ibid., 198.

16. Ibid., 199.

17. Kant, RA, 6, 34–35.

18. For some examples among the many I might refer to, see the work of John McDowell, for instance, *Having the World in View* (Cambridge: Harvard University Press, 2009); and Galen Strawson et al., *Consciousness and Its Place in Nature: Does Physicalism Entail Pan-psychism?*, ed. Anthony Freeman (Exeter: Imprint Academic, 2006).

19. Kant, CPR, Avii.

20. Ibid., A447, B475.

21. Ibid., A448, B476; Kemp Smith edition, 413.

22. Kant, GM, 4:452.

23. Ibid.

24. Kant, CJ §84, 323.

25. Ibid.

26. Kant, GM; and Kant, CPrR.

27. Henry Allison, *Kant's Transcendental Idealism: An Interpretation and Defence* (New Haven, CT: Yale University Press, 1983). Allison's label is quoted approvingly in A. Wood, *Kant's Ethical Thought* (Cambridge: Cambridge University Press, 1999), 171; see also Michelle Kosch, *Freedom and Reason in Kant, Schelling and Kierkegaard* (Oxford: Clarendon Press, 2006). Moreover, there are probably a number of different notions of freedom in Kant's work. Lewis White Beck, for example, counts five different notions of freedom in Kant's work. See Lewis White Beck, 'Five Concepts of Freedom in Kant', in *Philosophical Analysis and Reconstruction*, ed. Stephan Korner and J. T. J. Scredznick (Dortrecht: Nijhoff, 1987), 31–51.

28. See GM, 4:446–447.

29. See Robert Stern, *Understanding Moral Obligation: Kant, Hegel, Kierkegaard* (Cambridge: Cambridge University Press, 2012).

30. Kant, CPrR, 26. Original German edition of Kant's works, *Kant gessamelte Schriften* (Berlin: Walter de Gruyter, 1900), vol. 5, 29.

31. Kant, CPR, 29.

32. See, for example, Peter Strawson, *The Bounds of Sense* (London: Methuen, 1966). For a solution to the problem, according to which the self is not two distinct things—a phenomenal and a noumenal 'thing'—but is, rather, one self, viewed under different aspects, see Allison, *Kant's Transcendental Idealism*.

33. This argument has been very well spelt out by Kosch, *Freedom and Reason in Kant, Schelling and Kierkegaard*.

34. See note 150 in Beck, 'Five Concepts of Freedom in Kant', 31–35.

35. For one such prominent interpretation, see Christine Korsgaard, *The Sources of Normativity* (Cambridge: Cambridge University Press, 1996).

36. C. C. E. Schmid, *Versuch Einer Moralphilosophie* (Jena: Cröcker, 1790), 50.

37. Guyer notes that 'there are numerous passages in the second *Critique* that suggest that, as in the *Groundwork*, Kant still conceives of the moral law as the causal law of the noumenal will. The possibility—in these circumstances—of freely chosen immoral actions remains inconceivable'. Paul Guyer, *Kant* (Oxford: Routledge, 2006), 225–226.

38. GM, 4:412.

39. Kant, RA. This problem may befall all attempts to argue that reasons can be causes. See Kosch, *Freedom and Reason in Kant, Schelling and Kierkegaard*, 52, note 13; see also Wood, *Kant's Ethical Thought*. I would also like to thank Michelle Kosch, whose defence of the view that Kant is an incompatibilist about freedom inspired this chapter.

40. See Kant, CJ. See also Immanuel Kant, *Gesammelte Schriften* 5 (1902).

41. Kant, RA, 52.

42. Kant, CJ, 33, paragraph 86; Kant, *Gesammelte Schriften*, 444 (AK).

43. See Gary Banham, *Kant's Practical Philosophy: From Critique to Doctrine* (Basingstoke: Palgrave Macmillan, 2006), chapter 5, for a discussion of this.

44. Kant, *Gesammelte Schriften*, 474.

45. Appears in RA as 'a spirit of an originally loftier destiny'.

46. Gordon Michalson, *Fallen Freedom: Kant on Radical Evil and Moral Regeneration* (Cambridge: Cambridge University Press, 1990), 73.

47. Ibid., 75.

48. A contemporary and revised account of Kant and the diabolical, which parallels this point, is offered by Alenka Zupancic, *Ethics of the Real* (London: Verso, 2000). She writes that '"diabolical evil" would occur if opposition to the moral law were to be elevated to a maxim' (90). Effectively, Zupancic argues, insofar as the moral law is a command, that says 'do this or that', then opposition to it cannot consist in showing that it is wrong but rather the opposition would itself become a new moral law. This would, of course, not at all be what Kant would have wanted for his moral law.

49. Kant writes in GM, 11, 4:398, that 'to preserve one's life is a duty'.

50. Kant, RA, 6, 21.

51. See Michalson, *Fallen Freedom*, 41. I find something like this interpretation also in Alenka Zupancic (2000), Korsgaard (1996), O'Neill (1989), and Allison (1990). Allison suggests that the *Gesinnung* is the practical counterpart of the transcendental unity of apperception (208). Is there not, however, as Zupancic claims, a difference between the *Gesinnung* and the active choice of disposition (37)? Zupancic argues that the *Gesinnung* is the 'blind spot' that separates the phenomenal from the noumenal (37).

52. Allen Wood, *Kant's Ethical Thought* (Cambridge: Cambridge University Press, 1999), 172.

53. Michalson, *Fallen Freedom*, 84.

54. Ibid.

55. Kant, RA, 42–43.

56. Lewis White Beck, *Commentary on Kant's Critique of Practical Reason* (Chicago: University of Chicago Press, 1960 [1984]), 266–267.

57. Alenca Zupancic, *Ethics of the Real, Kant and Lacan* (London: Verso, 2000), 37.

58. See Wood, *Kant's Ethical Thought*, 172.

59. On this point see also Korsgaard, *The Sources of Normativity*.

60. This is what leads Kant to say, in *Religion*, that the 'disposition must have been adopted by free choice for otherwise it could not be imputed'. Kant, RA, 20.

61. O'Neill argues that the Categorical Imperative is the 'supreme principle of all reason'. Onora O'Neill, *Constructions of Reason: Explorations of Kant's Practical Philosophy* (Cambridge: Cambridge University Press, 1989), chapter 3.

62. The difficulty with doing this stems, it seems to me, from problems with the view of evil that continues to see it as a privation of the good. Evil, in this view, is simply the negation of the good, as the Stoics believed, rather than a counter-force in its own right. Kant, we know, wanted to see evil as a positive force, but this interpretation, it seems to me, may bring him back to the earlier notion of evil.

63. See Harry Frankfurt, 'Freedom of the Will and the Concept of a Person', *Journal of Philosophy* 68 (1971), 5–20.

64. Seiriol Morgan, 'The Missing Formal Proof of Humanity's Radical Evil in Kant's Religion', *Philosophical Review* 114, no. 1 (January 2005).

65. John Rawls, famously, in his work *A Theory of Justice*, (Oxford: Oxford University Press, 1973) argues for a view of justice that incorporates both principles of liberty and principles of equality. He deploys a notion he labels the 'original position' where each person decides principles of justice behind what he calls a 'veil of ignorance'. Essentially the way in which he describes this is that people would make decisions on principles of justice without knowing their position in society, their social status, their intelligence or their views of the good. Each person would be, in these circumstances, he argues, disinterested and rational. Critics objected that the outlook is untenable: feminist critics argued that the model of reasoning adopted is implicitly masculine whilst others argued that it is not possible simply to abstract away from the particularities of our situations in the way that is demanded by the theory (see, for example Michael Sandel, *Liberalism and the Limits of Justice*, Cambridge University Press: Cambridge, 1982, and Michael Walzer, *Spheres of Justice*, Blackwells: Oxford, 1983).

66. See Isaac Newton, *Philosophical Writings*, ed. A. Janiak (Cambridge: Cambridge University Press, 2004).

67. See Allison, *Kant's Transcendental Idealism*.

68. It is important to note that Kant does have a concept of 'feeling' that includes non-sensory gratification. This concept includes the feeling associated

with following the moral law as well as the feeling of disinterested pleasure that is associated with judgements of pure beauty. But this is a different kind of feeling from sensory pleasure.

69. Kant, CJ, §61, 235.

70. Ibid., §62, 242.

71. Ibid., §17, 83.44.

72. Ibid., first introduction, section V, 400.

73. The principle that nature is purposive in itself Kant calls hylozoism. He argues that there can be no such notion of matter. Such a position inappropriately suggests that there is an analogue to intentionality in matter (see CJ, §65, 254). Furthermore, if one were to accept such a notion, then it would imply that judgements of beauty are 'merely' empirical judgements, which, according to his theory of the nature of beauty, they are not.

74. Kant, RA, 38.

75. Ibid., 17–18.

76. Ibid., 35.

77. CJ, 175–176.

78. Ibid., 370.

79. Ibid., 371.

80. Steven M. Bayne, *Kant on Causation: On the Fivefold Routes to the Principle of Causation* (New York: State University of New York Press, 2004), 109, his italics. Bayne sets out, in this book, to challenge and refute a number of interpretations of Kant's argument in the Second Analogy, including those of Lovejoy, Strawson, Bennett, and Guyer.

81. Kant, CPR, A494/522.

82. Kant, CJ, 400.

83. Ibid., 318.

84. Ibid., 304.

85. Ibid., 304.

86. Ibid., 305.

87. Christine Battersby, *The Phenomenal Woman: Feminist Metaphysics and the Patterns of Identity* (London: Routledge, 1998), 70.

88. Immanuel Kant, *The Metaphysics of Morals*, ed. and trans. Mary Gregor (Cambridge: Cambridge University Press, 1996), 92. This quote was drawn to my attention by Battersby, *The Phenomenal Woman*, 64.

4

KIERKEGAARD AND SCHELLING ON PROCESS

Immanuel Kant begins, in Enlightenment vein, with the link between freedom and the moral law. For him, freedom is freedom from domination by our passions; it is freedom to act in a way that controls passion. But this leaves him with two problems: first, it is hard for him to ground evil, and second, it is difficult for him to show how the self is free when it does wrong. Søren Kierkegaard or Haufniensis,[1] by contrast, begins, in CA,[2] by attempting to account for wrongdoing or evil.[3] In this chapter I will outline the influence of Friedrich Wilhelm Joseph Schelling on Kierkegaard and describe the latter's 'process' philosophy. The following chapter will describe Kierkegaard's response to Kant.

Unlike Kant, Kierkegaard has a unified picture of the self as existent and active in the natural world, like other natural objects, although the self is also grounded in a God that in some sense transcends this world.[4] In CUP, referring to Kant, Climacus writes, 'A scepticism that confiscates thinking itself cannot be halted by being thought through, because this must indeed be done by thinking, which is on the side of the mutineer. It must be broken off. To reply to Kant within the fanatical *Schattenspiel* [shadow play] of pure thinking is precisely not to reply to him.— The only *an sich* that cannot be thought is existing, with which thinking has nothing at all to do'.[5] In *The Concept of Anxiety*, Haufniensis writes, possibly with Kant in mind, 'Every fantastic notion of entering into a pact with evil etc. whereby a person becomes entirely evil, must be abandoned'.[6] Further, he notes: 'In the demonic, freedom is posited as unfreedom, because freedom is lost'.[7]

Kierkegaard, unlike Kant, then, I will suggest in this and subsequent chapters, can account for the freedom to do wrong partly because he has a view of the self as an active natural being, in a process of becoming, but also immersed in a natural world that may preexist it. I will suggest that Kierkegaard's or Haufniensis' view of nature is influenced by that of Schelling. Schelling's view of nature is a picture of a living and active nature, one that does not exclude freedom. Ultimately, this living and active nature is construed, for both, I will suggest, in terms of metaphors of birth. Kant, as we saw in chapter 3, gives a detailed and clear account of the operation of purposes in nature.[8] Yet he does not see such purposes as 'really existing'. Rather, for him, we—rational finite beings—judge nature reflectively as though it were purposive. In his *Freiheitsschrift*, by contrast, following from his view of nature as living, Schelling writes that pantheism is not incompatible with the 'the most lively feeling of freedom'.[9]

Kierkegaard's self is embodied and he is concerned with human intersubjective experience. This does not mean that his self is solely natural, but it is important that it is not conceived purely as a mind. The conception of a self that is capable of birthing is also significant for him.

KIERKEGAARD AND SCHELLING

It is important to note that a number of significant commentators on Kierkegaard have downplayed the influence of Schelling upon him. There is a general reason for this; it is the same reason many commentators have claimed that Kierkegaard breaks with the German Idealist tradition. According to these commentators, to reiterate, Kierkegaard is an anti-systematic writer, a 'polemical and sceptical'[10] thinker, who believes in a transcendent God and whose thought runs contrary to systematizers like Schelling and G. W. F. Hegel. I will continue responding to this point throughout the book. My hint at a response here, however, is that Schelling may have been wrongly read, by some of these significant commentators, as a determinist pantheist whose thought is incompatible with the relation between an individual self and a transcendent God.

But there is also one very specific piece of evidence that has been adduced to deny any connection between Schelling and Kierkegaard. Kierkegaard went, in 1841–1842, to Berlin. Alistair Hannay,[11] in his biography of Kierkegaard, writes that 'the ostensible motivation for the trip [to Berlin] had been to hear Schelling's lectures on the Philosophy of Revelation'.[12] Kierkegaard, he notes, had been excited to hear of a philosophical system that might 'sweep' Hegelianism aside. Kierkegaard sat in the lectures alongside Engels, Burkhart and possibly also Bakunin. According to Hannay, however, Kierkegaard was 'quickly disenchanted'[13] both by the lectures and by the man himself, 'a most insignificant man to look at . . . like a tax collector'.[14] Kierkegaard also came to believe, according to the standard story, that 'Schelling talks quite insufferable nonsense' and that Schelling was 'too old' to give lectures.[15]

Others who play down the influence of Schelling on Kierkegaard include Neils Thulstrup, who writes that Kierkegaard was only interested in Schelling for his criticisms of Hegel.[16] Alan White claims that Schelling's strongest influence was negative.[17]

Jon Stewart, despite his strongly critical reading of Thulstrup, argues that Kierkegaard cannot have gone to Berlin to use Schelling to critique Hegel, for he had 'no particular polemic with Hegel'[18] at the time. In Stewart's reading, Schelling, like Hegel, offered an 'abstract' reading of the notion of 'actuality' against the existential and contingent interpretation of the notion held by Kierkegaard himself.

Yet it is this very concept—the concept of 'actuality'—as Daphne Hampson[19] recognizes, in Schelling's work, as the latter struggles with the problem of speaking of evil as a positive force, that caused Kierkegaard's heart to 'leap for joy' as he listened to the (by then elderly) Schelling's lecture.

Moreover, Hannay himself recognizes the importance of the notion of 'becoming' for Kierkegaard, a motif that is deeply Hegelian as well as Schellingian, and he further notes that 'angst' or anxiety was 'part of the vocabulary of the German Idealists, not least of Hegel's but also Schelling's'.[20]

Furthermore, there are commentators[21] who have noted the influence of Schelling on Kierkegaard. One significant commentator who does believe in the influence is Reidar Thomte, who writes, in his introduction to his translation of CA, 'What interested Kierkegaard, in particular, was Schelling's critique of Hegel's rationalistic system, and upon his return [from listening to Schelling's lectures in Berlin] in 1842, he turned to the study of Leibniz, Descartes and Aristotle, as well as the anti-Hegelian work of Trendelburg'.[22]

Also, as Michelle Kosch[23] points out, the standard account relies largely upon Kierkegaard's initial enthusiasm and then disenchantment with Schelling's Berlin lectures. However, several considerations challenge the view that this is the end of the matter. First, Kierkegaard continued to acquire Schelling's works after he had attended the lectures in Berlin. Most importantly of all, for the specific purposes of my argument in this book, there are strong resemblances between the text of Schelling's *Freiheitsschrift* and CA. Both texts, for example, refer to anxiety as the 'dizziness of freedom'.[24] I will note other similarities between the two texts later in the book.

As Kosch has also argued, Schelling's works would have been widely known in the context in which Kierkegaard was working and he would not have had to rely on attendance at the Berlin lectures. One specific example of this, as Habib Malike points out, is H. C. Ørsted, who was a distinguished author in his own right and rector of the university where Kierkegaard studied. Schelling's *Naturphilosophie* was a major influence upon Ørsted.[25]

There are, indeed, a few positive references to Schelling in other works of Kierkegaard. For example, in *The Book on Adler*, a text that is concerned with the concept of a revelation and with what it means to 'have' a revelation, Kierkegaard notes Hegel's *Logic* and, quoting the latter, in a footnote, he writes:

> To speak of thought or objective thought as the heart and soul of the world may seem to be ascribing consciousness to the things of nature. We feel a certain repugnance against making thought the inward function of things, especially as we speak of thought as marking the divergence of man from nature. It would be necessary, therefore, if we use the term thought at all, to speak of nature as the system of unconscious thought, or, to use Schelling's expression a petrified intelligence.[26]

This quotation seems important, for it stresses the very aspect of Schelling's thought which, it seems to me, allows Kierkegaard, or, at the very least, Haufniensis, to offer an alternative account of the freedom to do wrong to that of Kant. Ultimately, Kierkegaard will argue that both perfect goodness and pure evil are impossible for us finite living beings.

Schelling

Schelling, in his *Freiheitsschrift*, makes a very large claim. He writes: 'The whole of Modern European philosophy since its inception (through Descartes) has this common deficiency that nature does not exist for it and that it lacks a living basis'.[27] The *Freiheitsschrift* presents an active process ontology that, significantly, 'precedes our thinking of it'.[28] In other words, there is Being before thought. Each activity can be depicted in terms of ground and consequent and this distinction, in turn, underpins Schelling's system. Every organic being is dependent upon another with respect to its genesis. As Iain Hamilton Grant has put it, 'nature itself must furnish the only possible basis for a philosophy of freedom'.[29] Nature itself is, ultimately, as noted above, 'grounded' in a process that deploys birthing metaphors.

Philosophy can offer a natural history of our mind. In their turn, though, for Schelling, free actions shape nature. Speech, as well, is part of this dynamic nature. As Bernard Freydberg puts it, for Schelling, whoever utters the sentence 'The body is a body' is unifying two thoughts in one. 'The *tauto* in tautology names the gathering of two non-identical thoughts'.[30] The expression of the thought is an act of gathering two thoughts into a unity. Freydberg further argues that when the philosopher thinks about thinking something different again occurs. Through thinking, for example, about the operation of the law of identity, thought, which occurs in time, directs thought to occur atemporally, and therefore to think outside immediacy, imagining the atemporal ground of the whole. A dynamic thought and a dynamic being are aspects of the process of nature's evolution. The subjective and the objective are unified and each, in turn, is itself an evolving, living process. However,

> we have, then, one being (*Ein Wesen*) for all oppositions, an absolute identity of light and darkness, good and evil. . . . There must be being *before* all ground and before all that exists, thus generally before any duality—how can we call it anything other than the original ground or the non-ground [*ungrund*]?'[31]

This notion—an *ungrund*—which precedes all differentiation is simultaneously ground and excess of ground.[32] Some have described the domain outside duality as an 'abyss'. It seems to be both without reason and without meaning or purpose.[33] But, as we shall see in a later chapter, it can also be read in terms of metaphors of birth.

Evil or sin, for Schelling, arises when the self takes itself to be its own ground. As Schelling writes, 'The general possibility of evil consists, as shown, in the fact that man, instead of making his selfhood into the basis, the instrument, can strive to elevate it into the ruling and total will and conversely to make the spiritual within himself into a means'.[34] It is important to note that Kant himself had recognized, although, as I will elaborate later, he understood this in a very different way, that evil results from a form of self-love.[35] I will return later to this notion and to an explanation of what it might mean.

For Schelling, in the *Freiheitsschrift*, things are abstractions from collections of processes. His interpretation of, for example, the sentence 'S is P' differs from that of both Aristotle and Hegel. In Aristotelian logic, the sentence 'S is P' ascribes a property to a subject. 'S' cannot be both 'P' and 'not-P' at the same time. For Hegel, in his *Science of Logic*, by contrast, 'P' is subsumed under some more general concept and, at that more general level, 'P and not-P' are subsumed under some 'R'. So, if the claim is 'The body is blue', both blue and not-blue are subsumed under the concept 'colour'. But for Schelling, the position is different again. For him, the claim would be read as 'The body manifests itself bluely'.[36]

In Schelling's process system, unlike that of Hegel, as he has been read by many,[37] there is an irreducible remainder in nature that 'can never be resolved into reason'.[38] For Schelling, everything participates in a process of becoming. The ground does not reveal itself as a ground until the existent has come into being. The existent is dependent upon its ground for its 'becoming' but not in its being.

Schelling uses the metaphor of birth: 'Man is formed in the maternal body; and only from the obscurity of that which is without understanding (from feeling, yearning, the sovereign [*herrlich*] mother of knowledge) grow luminous thoughts'.[39]

Kierkegaard also adopts a process ontology, and not only in CA. Before returning to continue with Kierkegaard's response to Kant on freedom and evil, I would like to spend the remainder of the chapter considering Kierkegaard's conception of the self and his process ontology. I will briefly outline some respects in which his thinking on ontology is different from the view of Kant on the subject.

Kierkegaard's Self

Kierkegaard writes, 'Ethics begins with the actual'.[40] Human beings, for Kierkegaard, are, in contrast to Kant's view, 'a synthesis of the psyche and the body but also a synthesis of the temporal and the eternal'; the self is the 'synthesis of the infinite and the finite'.[41] This, indeed, is very close to a claim of Schelling's to the effect that 'spirit is therefore neither finite nor infinite . . . but rather in it is the original unification of the finite in the infinite'.[42] Thought must be located in living reality; those philosophers who attempt to ground reality within thought will remain caught up within thought. Human beings, for Kierkegaard, are natural living beings, but with the capacity both to reflect on their natures and to take up and to be guided by some moral ideal. They become certain kinds of self after the emergence of freedom. This process, which I will outline in a moment, constitutes the self as a synthesis of soul and body. But a synthesis is not possible if the two parts are not united in a third. This third is 'spirit'.[43] As the self emerges as free, so it becomes anxious.

Free selves are infinite insofar as they can think outside a particular temporal moment; they can imagine atemporal logical claims, for example; they can reflect on the future and shape it and they can be guided by ideals that transcend their finitude. They are also infinite insofar as they are grounded in a nature that ultimately culminates in God. This ontological reading is not all that Kierkegaard has to say on the subject but it is an important component of his thought. God, ontologically, is not, as I will note later on, to be understood as a fixed substance, but rather as a power, an infinite power that can be construed, in part, as the power of love and in terms of birthing metaphors.

Selves are finite insofar as they act, and, through acting, they contribute to shaping the natural world of which they are part. In other words, each free self is a self in process; it is a self in a process of becoming, but it is also a self that is capable of reflecting on itself and of imagining possibilities that transcend its immediate locus in time.

Whereas Kant's moral self strives to be a perfectly rational thing, Kierkegaard's moral self is, by contrast, at least in part, a finite, embodied being. Moreover, its freedom, grounded in its infinitude and, I will suggest, partially following Schelling, in its *ungrund*, is manifested in a fashion that allows it to act in good and bad ways. Partially following Schelling's *Freiheitsschrift*, Kierkegaard or Haufniensis sets out, in CA,

to explain how wrongdoing or sin is possible. Sin, to anticipate, is accounted for in ontological terms, as the self, here following Schelling,
taking itself as its own ground. By contrast, in order to act well, it ought
to recognize its shaping by intersubjective experience but also, as I will
argue in a moment, by a living and dynamic natural world outside that of
intersubjectivity. Ultimately it is shaped by a 'power' that remains incomprehensible to it. It is partially formed by a 'power that established it'.[44]
But, to note again, for Kierkegaard pure evil and pure goodness are both
impossible for beings like us.

Kierkegaard, as noted, was critical of all notions of the self as 'essentially' thought. He believed, to reiterate, that it is never possible to establish the truth of a view in the manner in which René Descartes, for
example, hoped for.[45] He writes of Descartes: 'If I am to emerge from
doubt into freedom, then I must enter in doubt in freedom'.[46] In other
words, for Kierkegaard, freedom cannot arise from thought but rather it
must be presupposed in order for thought to be possible. The self, to put it
differently, cannot consist merely in thought. This is true whether thought
is conceived as process or, as in Descartes' view, as presupposing a 'thing
that thinks'.

Although Kierkegaard often refers to the 'singular individual', and
although he wants to bring the individual back into central focus after
what he sees to be its overly derivative position in the work of Hegel (or
at least the work of the Danish Hegelians[47]) and Schelling, he nonetheless
does not wish to return to a Kantian view of the self as primarily a mind.
Either-Or, for example, begins with the fact of birth, suggesting that the
embodied finite natural being is of crucial significance for Kierkegaard.[48]
In CA, Kierkegaard writes: 'For ethics, the possibility of sin never occurs'. He also writes, 'Ethics and dogmatics became radically confused'.[49] There is no doubt that he has in mind here a critique of the
Hegelian (or, following Stewart, the Adlerian[50]) view that there are logical contradictions in reality. No doubt he is also sceptical of the view that
reason, as it is with Kant, is severed from its manifestation in the natural
world. He is, moreover, sceptical of the view that the Hegelian, or Adlerian, *Sittlichkeit* expresses the norms of a particular society. 'Actuality'
cannot be expressed through reason, or indeed, through reason as manifested in social norms.

But Kierkegaard is also concerned, throughout his works, although he
is no doubt hugely influenced by Kant, with chastising Kantian ethics. He

is, furthermore, sceptical about at least one of the Kantian notions of the self; for example, in the following formulation from *The Sickness unto Death*, 'the autonomous self is like a king without a country, actually ruling over nothing'.[51] Indeed, such a self is analogous to a fully determined self insofar as both are in despair. Perhaps he has in mind here not only the noumenal, purely rational Kantian self, but also the self as 'disposition', the self as neither phenomenal nor noumenal. The wording from SUD of the self 'striving to be itself'[52] suggests that it might be the latter Kierkegaard has in mind. Both Kantian notions deny the natural finitude of the self and its immersion in natural processes. They deny, furthermore, and importantly, the grounding of the self in the 'power that established it' that may be linked with the Schellingian *ungrund*, or the longing of the one to give birth to itself.

Kierkegaard, or Haufniensis, writes, in CA, 'One can see how illogical the movements must be in logic, since the negative is the evil, and how unethical they must be in ethics'.[53] He offers a critique of the Socratic notion of 'sin' that is at the same time a critique of Kant:

> In pure ideality, where the actual individual person is not involved, the transition is necessary—after all, in the system everything takes place of necessity—or there is no difficulty at all connected with the transition from understanding to doing. This is the Greek mind. . . . And the secret of modern philosophy is essentially the same: *cogito ergo sum*, to think is to be. . . . In the world of actuality, however, where the individual person is involved, there is this tiny little transition from having understood to doing.[54]

He writes further, 'One of the symbolical books declares the impossibility of an explanation. . . . [H]ereditary sin is so profound and detestable that it cannot be comprehended by human understanding'.[55] He continues, apparently with Kant in view, 'This feeling assumes the role of an accuser, who with an almost feminine passion and with the fanaticism of a girl in love is now concerned only with making sinfulness and his own participation in it more and more detestable'.[56] Once more, then, this may be a reference to the impossibility for us finite limited beings to exemplify pure evil.

Kierkegaard and Schelling on Process

Kierkegaard, like Schelling, adopts a 'process' ontology. There are other commentators on Kierkegaard who have emphasized his sympathy for a process ontology as opposed to one of static being. One important commentator, as noted, on this is Claire Carlisle,[57] whose work on this subject I came across after I had begun this text. She offers some telling commentary on Kierkegaard's conception of movement, of process, drawing particularly on the work of Aristotle on this subject. While her work, it seems to me, is significant in drawing attention to this aspect of Kierkegaard's work overall, she focuses on the influence of Aristotle on Kierkegaard, while it seems to me that the influence of Schelling is perhaps more immediate than that of Aristotle. Significantly, focusing on the influence of Schelling allows for the view that process applies both to thought and to activity, and, most significantly of all, to the two together. In fact, in Carlisle's view, which, as also noted, she shares with George Pattison, Kierkegaard is moving 'beyond philosophy' altogether. But this conclusion only follows if one restricts philosophy to 'reflection' or 'recollection' or, indeed, to a discipline that engages merely with thought, as opposed to engaging, additionally, with the natural world and, in turn, with these two in combination.

Kierkegaard not only offers a 'process' ontology, but also makes a number of remarks, throughout his writings, about how best to characterize this process, and he contrasts his own conception of process with one that conceives of it in terms of logical mediation. He also, however, characterizes it differently from a notion of fracture and chaos. He can be read as characterizing it, rather, I will suggest, in terms of metaphors of birth.

In the epilogue to *Fear and Trembling*, de silentio, the pseudonymous author of the text, refers, in a positive tone, to Heraclitus. He also mentions, in a critical manner, Heraclitus' follower Cratylus, who 'goes further'.[58] Cratylus 'went further' than Heraclitus and made the additional claim, in relation to the impossibility of stepping twice into the same river, that 'one cannot do it even once'.[59] Heraclitus offers an ontology of process, of movement. Cratylus, however, went too far in that he rendered both movement and stasis impossible and translated both into an Eleatic doctrine that denies movement altogether. In a note in his journal, Kierkegaard writes, in relation to this 'disciple' of Heraclitus: 'A disciple wanting to improve it said: One cannot even step into [the river] once. Thereby the nerve is cut; as far as making any sense, the statement becomes the opposite, an Eleatic sentence, and denies motion'.[60] In a commentary on Cratylus, David Sedley writes, 'Things change so rapidly that you cannot engage with them either by naming them or stepping into them'.[61] In a letter written in 1847, Kierkegaard refers approvingly to Diogenes' critique of the Eleatics. He writes, 'If anyone denies that movement exists I do as Diogenes did, I walk'.[62] (Diogenes simply walked up and down in refutation of the Eleatics' denial of the reality of motion.)

In *Repetition*, Constantin Constantinius writes that 'movement is dialectical, not only with respect to space . . . but also with respect to time'.[63] He refers once more, here, to the Eleatics as denying movement. Again, in CUP, Kierkegaard praises Heraclitus and criticizes the Hegelian notion of movement.[64] He writes, 'Everything that Hegel writes about process is illusory'.[65] In further confirmation of this view, in the introduction to CA, Haufniensis claims that there is only movement in 'existence' and that 'in logic no movement can come about for logic is and whatever is logical only is'.[66] This is clearly a critique of some notion of Hegelian logic—whether or not he is actually referring to Adolph Peter Adler (see Stewart[67])—and it could well be taken as a critique of the view that one can characterize movement and the ground of movement in terms of different conceptions of infinity. Logic, Haufniensis writes in CA, is concerned with necessity. Change, however, occurs contingently. Haufniensis notes that actuality, freedom and sin are contingent features of existence, whereas logic is the domain of necessity.[68] This parallels Schelling's concern with movement in existence.

Temporality is a process. Logic, which is concerned with necessity, cannot account for the dynamism of a process of change. To attempt to explain 'evil' or 'sin' in logical terms would be to render its qualitative character inexplicable. It would, moreover, make it difficult to account for the freedom that is required for the explanation of 'sin'. This freedom entails a 'leap' that cannot be accounted for in these kinds of logical terms. In SUD Kierkegaard claims that 'every moment that the self exists, it is in a process of becoming'.[69] An attempt to use logic would also make the natural aspect of the process system difficult to explain.

Kierkegaard, furthermore, in his journals, contrasts the ancient concern with 'actual' movement with the 'recent' (Hegelian) concern with mediation in logic. Moreover, *Fear and Trembling* is dedicated to the eighteenth-century philosopher Johann Georg Hamann, the founder of the *Sturm und Drang* movement, who influenced Schelling and Hegel, for whom God embodies himself in nature and history.[70]

Schelling Again

The process philosophies of both Schelling and Kierkegaard appear in their respective conceptions of the free self. The free self combines the ability to think outside a particular moment of time, when deploying logical laws, with its natural finitude shaped by the principle of causation. But these are not processes engaged in by different selves, as they are for Kant. For Kant, the free self, shaped by the moral law, is a noumenal 'person', while the finite self, shaped by the category of causation in the phenomenal world, is a phenomenal self. For Schelling, by contrast, there is only one self. This self is a natural living self just like all other natural objects. It is different from all other natural objects only through being 'more differentiated'—it has the capacity to reflect on its place in nature, to a degree that other natural living things do not. Yet, to reiterate, it is grounded in nature, and thus, in turn, in the ultimate 'ungrounded' nature of reality. It is, moreover, grounded in a living and active nature, one that might be conceptualized in terms of hylozoism or in terms of a natural system of purposes.

Schelling writes, to quote again a notion that will become vital for Kierkegaard, 'Spirit is therefore neither finite nor infinite, but rather in it is the *original unification of the finite in the* infinite'.[71] The free self, then, comes into existence, just as God comes into existence. The free self expresses the possibility of the emergence of the ungrounded whole. The free self is grounded in its own nature, but also in the nature in which it finds itself, which is itself, ultimately, ungrounded. When the self attempts, as noted above, to take itself as its own ground, this leads to evil or wrongdoing.

Kant's famous proof that existence is not a predicate is true if the sentence is read atemporally. However, as noted before, the same sentence, 'God exists', if read emphatically, can express both God's coming into existence and the realization, on the part of someone, that God exists. For Schelling, then, both thought and nature are active and productive, as they are for Haufniensis. Schelling's God, in fact, is made up of three potencies—the first potency, then the actualization of this potency, and finally the restoration of potency.[72] Humans, somehow, set these potencies in opposition with one another. Schelling deduces the possibility of evil from the distinction between ground and consequent. Both God's ground and its existence are, in some sense, really existent. Schelling uses the analogy of gravity and light. Both operate together although they are separable. Gravity, according to Schelling, is the 'eternally dark basis' for light. Similarly, it is possible to distinguish God's ground of existence from 'his' actual existence. He writes: 'God alone—as the one who exists—dwells in pure light since he alone is begotten from himself'.[73]

For Schelling, *Wesen*, or Being, has a dual character: it is being insofar as it is the ground of existence and being insofar as it is. There is, therefore, in *Deus sive Natura*, or God or Nature, both 'God or Nature's' ground of existence (what Schelling calls the dark principle) and that in God in which he exists (the light principle). Both are ultimately conceived in terms of birthing metaphors. Unlike Kant, then, he does not separate the rational 'will' from the sensuous nature of a person. The person, as contained in this nature, is a combination of its existence and its ground, in analogous fashion to the sense in which a baby is 'grounded' by its mother. Evil, or rather wrongdoing, to reiterate, then, is, for Schelling, the subject forgetting its grounding in these various processes, and ultimately in the *ungrund*, and instead taking itself as its ground. In CA, likewise, 'sin', after the emergence of freedom, is the self attempting to become its own ground, as it encounters the 'abyss' of freedom. I will return to CA and to the influence of Schelling on the text in the following chapter. But first I would like to examine what might be meant by these notions of process and particularly how Kierkegaard conceives of it.

COMMENTARY ON PROCESS

What might it mean to adopt an ontology of process? As Kant himself notes, we cannot fail to recognize that all experience occurs in time. Temporal apperception, as Kant writes, is simply a given for us. 'The manifold' in appearances, Kant writes in CPR, is 'always successive'.[74] According to Kant, though, we can apprehend this manifold in different ways. Experienced time allows us to distinguish temporal succession,

temporal simultaneity, and temporal duration. We can, as Kant puts it in
the Second Analogy, distinguish the successive perceptions of the parts of
a house from the successive perceptions of a ship moving down a river.[75]
Any given 'appearance' is subject to a rule 'that distinguishes it from any
other apprehension and that makes necessarily one kind of combination
of the manifold'.[76] Kant recognizes, in other words, that our experience is
of a temporal process, and yet he also recognizes that we are able to shape
this successive experience according to rules that enable us to draw a
distinction between the fact that it does not matter in which order our
perceptions occur in the case of the house and yet it does matter in the
case of the ship moving down the river. So far, then, it seems as though
Kant might be seen to be offering some sort of 'process' ontology as well.

Yet, on the other hand, Kant is also constrained by the Newtonian
physics he adopted, and perhaps also by other metaphysical assumptions.
So the conclusion of the First Analogy appears to be some version of the
principle of the conservation of energy: 'In all change of appearances
substance is permanent; its quantum in nature is neither increased nor
diminished'.[77] As Peter Strawson puts it, 'Kant was exposed to a very
strong temptation to identify whatever he succeeded in establishing as
necessary conditions of the possibility of experience of an objective
world with what he already conceived to be the fundamental, unquestion-
able assumptions of physical science'.[78] Indeed, Kant refers to 'substances' as the 'substrate of all determination of time'.[79] Strawson himself points to the discrepant thought into which his conflation of the
physics of his day with his metaphysical assumptions led him, in claiming
that while it is true, as Kant writes, that we need something abiding in
experience in order to account for change, this abiding 'thing' need not be
viewed in terms of what appears to be some principle of the conservation
of matter.

Where does this leave Kierkegaard, then? It seems to me that Kierkegaard, while he has a more thoroughgoing process ontology than Kant,
also accepts the point that we need some permanence in nature in order to
make sense of change. Many of his metaphors are of processes of change,
and yet he recognizes that we need some stability, in order to make sense
of this change. In a further dimension of the account, I will suggest, in
chapter 6, that he associates his view of time with the figure of woman,
the figure of a person who has a body that is capable of birthing.

Kierkegaard often writes about time and about the future. For example, in the first *Upbuilding Discourse*, he talks about the person who has a sense of the future as a noble being. The person who has a sense of the future 'has an awareness of their divine origin' because he or she has a sense of the self as being in time; such a person is aware of having a past as well. He or she is therefore aware of a dimension of existence that is denied to 'an animal [with] his head bowed to the earth, his soul captive to the service of the moment'.[80] This view of the future partly indicates that simple mechanical determinism cannot be true because if it were true then there would be no place for anxiety. It recalls Schelling once more: 'If the world were, as some so called sages have thought, a chain of causes and effects which runs backwards into infinity, then there would be neither past nor future in the true sense of the word'.[81] A true sense of the past and the future presupposes the capacity to reflect on the past and to have a sense of what might come to be.

Kierkegaard writes that, on the first day of the year, 'the past is finished; the present is not; only the future is, which is not'.[82] Only the future is, which is not. One thing he means by the self being a synthesis of the infinite and the finite, then, is this capacity to reflect on the past and the future, even though the past and the future extend beyond what a human being can think. Indeed, part of what he is referring to here is the ability, on the part of a subject, to distinguish the 'present phase' of a temporal process from a past phase as well as an anticipation of the future. All temporal experience, then, and here Kierkegaard moves beyond Kant, occurs in a temporal horizon, a temporal process, that contains past, present and future. There is a sense in which this 'retention' of the various temporal processes, in the apprehension of a temporal moment, is unlike 'recollection' of the past. The latter somehow fixes the past into a temporal memory that makes it appear present. It is this character of recollection specifically that leads Constantin, in *Repetition*, to believe that he is able to reproduce some aspect of the past. He finds, however, as I have noted, that he cannot do this. The trace of the past that occurs in the present, on the other hand, is different from this 'freezing' of memories. One could not have this notion of temporal process if one viewed time in terms of a series of 'nows'—a series of spatialized moments. Kant does not engage with the notion of process in this manner.[83]

The same kinds of point can be made about the anticipation of the future. The conception of the future that is presupposed here is not an image of some future event—the friends I am planning to visit tomorrow, the battle you will fight or the painting you might view. It is more like the continuous process of listening to a symphony or a drum roll. The future bars of the tune are anticipated but not in the sense in which a future event is imagined.

Sometimes, Kierkegaard writes, we act as though the future is clear-cut for us: we want to give something to a particular person about whom we care. But, as we think about the future, we recognize that there is nothing we can know about it. Elsewhere Kierkegaard—Haufniensis—refers to the lack of knowledge of the future as engendering anxiety: 'if a human being were a beast or an angel, he would not be in anxiety'.[84] One form of despair is the aesthetic and the Hegelian. This is a form of determinism, or fatalism. But there is a second form of despair—the Kantian form—that involves taking oneself to be self-legislating. This involves the consequence that the self is always guilty, that it always fails. It involves this, to reiterate, because the pure, perfectly rational, good self is an impossibility for finite, temporal beings like us.

If a human being were the kind of natural being that did not have the ability to reflect on its nature, then it could not be anxious; similarly, if it were a Kantian rational being, it could not be in a state of anxiety. The person reflecting on the future has a '"troubled soul"; he becomes perplexed'.[85] Kierkegaard, on the other hand, describes a person who is not yet aware of his capacity, which in its turn is connected to his freedom and his responsibility, as not yet being in a state of anxiety. This person gives presents, on the first day of the new year, 'lightly and effortlessly'.[86] This person is in a state of innocence prior to uncovering the responsibility that comes with the recognition of the undetermined nature of the future and therefore of his freedom.

In recognition of the need for some relative permanence in a process system, Kierkegaard offers a metaphor: 'When the sailor is out on the ocean, when everything is changing all around him, when the waves are born and die, he does not stare down into the waves, because they are changing. He looks up at the stars. Why? Because they are faithful; they have the same location now that they had for our ancestors and will have for generations to come'.[87] Adopting a process ontology, then, does not mean accepting that everything is changing all the time. If this were the case, we would not be able to make sense of our experience. It means, rather, that fundamentally, it is at least true that our perception of the world is and must be processual. Does it follow, however, that our ontology need be processual?

Just as Kant recognizes that the self that experiences this temporal flow must not itself be changing but rather must remain stable, so too does Kierkegaard, as we will see, outline the 'coming into being', with freedom, of a self that experiences temporality in this manner. This self is presupposed, in the fashion of the Kantian transcendental unity of apperception, although, as we will see, it is also very different from the Kantian notion, in order for temporal experience to be possible. Unlike the Kantian self, the Kierkegaardian self is an active and embodied one.

Importantly, the foregoing description of temporal flow for Kierkegaard is an account of the experience of time. This, one might argue, tells us nothing about time itself or about whether or not one's ontology is one of substances or processes. Yet it seems to me, from the foregoing, that, while Kierkegaard's ontology is very different from that of Kant, insofar as the subject does not itself constitute, in part through the forms of space and time, the objective world, it is nonetheless the case that the experience of temporal process occurs in a temporal horizon. This horizon, rather than being constituted in part by the substances of Newtonian science, is constituted rather through temporal flows, as exemplified, for example, in a musical refrain and significantly, as we will see in the remaining chapters, by natural birthing processes. Kierkegaard assumes, unlike Kant, partly reflecting the very different view of science, following Schelling, that the self is an active, passionate self, existing in a natural world that, in some way, preexists it.

The experienced world, both for Kant and for Kierkegaard, and for us too, is partly one of temporal flows, as outlined above. Kant describes, in his Analogies, ways in which some of these temporal flows become constituted as stable objects and others as moving objects or simply processes of some kind. Kierkegaard's metaphors, outlined above, are metaphors not only of experience of reality, but also of reality itself. Ultimately, though, to reiterate, this experience of temporal process, for Kierkegaard, unlike Kant, is grounded in a nature that is not fully comprehensible to the limited, finite, rational self.

I believe, furthermore, and I will argue this later, that Kierkegaard also accepted a process ontology in a different sense. While, in my view, Kant was limited in his conception of process by the science of his day, Kierkegaard, it seems to me, accepted a different ontology that was consistent with one that drew (without being derived from it) on a different conception of science, a science of powers, capacities and processes. Schelling, as we have seen, offers a view that both is in harmony with the science of electromagnetism of his day and anticipates later scientific developments. Nature comprises processes, as opposed to inert substances. Nature itself is active and living. All living beings, moreover, for him, exemplify some notion of freedom. Kierkegaard, as we will see, wishes to differentiate the form of freedom exhibited by 'human' beings from any freedom that might exist elsewhere in nature. Yet he also views nature as itself living and active. His notion of freedom can be seen to be both different from any freedom exhibited by, for example, a bacterium and yet also continuous with it.

RETURNING TO FREEDOM

Kant, as we saw in the last chapter, cannot prove the existence of freedom. He cannot provide an account of the way in which freedom comes into being. He cannot prove, from 'mere concepts a priori', 'the possibility of any real ground and its causality'.[88] For Kant, the law of identity reaches out to the domain of pure reason, where rational belief provides access to the laws of reason. The law of causality, by contrast, restricts knowledge to appearances. The schematized categories are constitutive—they unify the manifold of intuitions in the understanding. The ideas of reason, by contrast, are regulative only. Pure reason, for Kant, 'is not subject to the form of time'.[89] In the Transcendental Analytic of the first *Critique*, not being subject to time disallows logic from determining knowledge. In the Dialectic, this very same feature—the apparent independence from time—allows logical laws to open a way to freedom.

In this chapter, I have discussed the influence of Schelling on Kierkegaard. I have also begun to lay out both Schelling's and Kierkegaard's process philosophies. I have discussed some of the ways in which Kierkegaard is influenced by Schelling and some of the senses in which his 'process philosophy' represents a development over Kant's view of time. In the chapter that follows, I will begin to explore the way in which Kierkegaard responds to the difficulty experienced by Kant outlined in the previous chapter: the problem of explaining how it is possible freely to do wrong.

NOTES

1. Kierkegaard agrees with Leibniz that an 'indifferent will' is an 'absurdity and a chimera' (Kierkegaard, CA, viii). Kierkegaard is also critical of Descartes, writing, 'If I am to emerge from doubt into freedom, then I must enter in doubt in freedom'.

2. The interpretation of CA I will offer is not necessarily incompatible with readings, for example that of Hugh Pyper, to the effect that CA ought to be understood through biblical readings, in particular through Genesis 2 and 3 and the letter of James. Rather, I offer a different emphasis. See Hugh Pyper, *The Joy of Kierkegaard: Essays on Kierkegaard as a Biblical Reader* (Oakville: Equinox, 2011).

3. I am devoting a fair bit of discussion to *The Concept of Anxiety* and ascribing the views therein to Kierkegaard. I simply note that Kierkegaard originally published this text in his own name, switching to the pseudonym Haufniensis only at the last minute. Furthermore, Heidegger describes this work of Kierkegaard's as his most philosophical, along with the *Upbuilding Discourses*.

4. A view of the self as, in some sense, natural is obviously a highly controversial view to attribute to Kierkegaard. I am using the word 'natural' in a particular sense and I hope it will become clear that, understood in this way, it is not such a strange view to attribute to him.

5. CUP, 328.

6. CA, 122.

7. Ibid., 123.

8. Kant, CJ.

9. Friedrich W. J. Schelling, *Philosophical Investigations into the Essence of Human Freedom*, trans. Jeff Love and Johannes Schmidt (New York: State University of New York Press, 2006), 11; SW 338–339.

10. See George Stack, *Kierkegaard's Existential Ethics* (Tuscaloosa: The University of Alabama Press, 1977), x.

11. Alistair Hannay, *Kierkegaard: A Biography* (Cambridge: Cambridge University Press, 2001).

12. Ibid., 160.

13. Ibid., 162.

14. Ibid. From a letter to Emil Boesen, dated 14 December, letter no. 54, from PJ, 82.

15. Hannay, 163, quoting from PJ, letter no. 80. Patrick Gardner uses the expression 'woolly pretentiousness' to describe Kierkegaard's view of Schelling (see Patrick Gardner, *Kierkegaard* [Oxford: Oxford University Press, 1998]). Others, it should be noted, disagreed with Kierkegaard's assessment of Schelling's lecturing ability. Martensen, for example, thought he was a great lecturer

(see, for example, Joakim Garf, *Soren Kierkegaard, a Biography*, trans. Bruce H. Kimmse [Princeton: Princeton University Press, 2005]).

16. Neils Thulstrup, *Kierkegaard's Relation to Hegel*, trans. George L. Stengren (Princeton, NJ: Princeton University Press, 1980), 1972.

17. Alan White, *Schelling: An Introduction to the System of Freedom* (New Haven, CT: Yale University Press, 1983), 188.

18. Jon Stewart, *Kierkegaard's Relations to Hegel Reconsidered* (Cambridge: Cambridge University Press, 2003), 379.

19. Daphne Hampson, *Kierkegaard: Exposition and Critique* (Oxford: Oxford University Press, 2013), 106.

20. Hannay, *Kierkegaard: A Biography*, 212.

21. See, for example, Michael Burns, 'A Fractured Dialectic: Kierkegaard and Political Ontology after Žižek', in *Kierkegaard and the Political*, ed. Alison Assiter and Margherita Tonon (Cambridge: Cambridge Scholars Press, 2013), as well as Michelle Kosch. See also Markus Gabriel, *Transcendental Ontology: Essays in German Idealism* (London: Bloomsbury, 2013).

22. Reidar Thomte, historical introduction to CA, vii. Other sources noting the influence are V. McCarthy, 'Schelling and Kierkegaard on Freedom and Fall', in *International Kierkegaard Commentary, The Concept of Anxiety*, ed. Robert Perkins (Macon: Mercer University Press, 1985); and David Kangas, *Kierkegaard's Instant: On Beginnings* (Bloomington: Indiana University Press, 2007).

23. Michelle Kosch, *Freedom and Reason in Kant, Schelling and Kierkegaard* (Oxford: Oxford University Press, 2006).

24. See Kosch, *Freedom and Reason*, 124.

25. See Habib C. Malik, *Receiving Soren Kierkegaard: The Early Impact and Transmission of His Thought* (Washington, DC: The Catholic University of America Press, 1997), 22.

26. Søren Kierkegaard, *The Book on Adler*, ed. and trans. Howard V. Hong and Edna H. Hong (Princeton: Princeton University Press, 1998), 362.

27. Schelling, *Philosophical Investigations into the Essence of Human Freedom*, VII, 355.

28. Ibid., VII, 421.

29. Iain Hamilton Grant, *On an Artificial Earth: Philosophies of Nature after Schelling* (London: Continuum, 2006). I would like to thank Iain profusely again, not only for teaching me Schelling, but also for introducing me to a way of philosophizing that concerns itself with big questions and that is not restricted to ascertaining whether or not, for example, we know that the table is brown, or other technical epistemic or linguistic concerns. Any errors in the reading of Schelling are, of course, mine.

30. Bernard Freydberg, *Schelling's Dialogical Freedom Essay* (Albany: State University of New York Press, 2008), 23.

31. Schelling, *Philosophical Investigations into the Essence of Human Freedom*, 68; *Freiheitsschriff*, SW, 404–405.

32. I am grateful to Will Stronge for pointing out the distinction between *ungrund* and *abgrund*.

33. I am grateful to Barney Riggs for suggesting this wording.

34. Schelling, *Philosophical Investigations into the Essence of Human Freedom*; SW, 474–476, 54.

35. See Kant, RA, 31.

36. Schelling, SW, 408.

37. It is important to note that there are recent readings of Hegel that challenge this commonplace: see, for example, Maria J. Binetti, 'Kierkegaard's Ethical Stage in Hegel's Logical Categories: Actual Possibility, Reality, Necessity, Cosmos and History', *Journal of Natural and Social Philosophy* 3, nos. 2–3 (2007); and Catherine Malabou, *The Future of Hegel: Plasticity, Temporality and Dialectic*, trans. Lisbeth During (London: Routledge, 2005).

38. Schelling, *Philosophical Investigations into the Essence of Human Freedom*; SW VII, 360.

39. Schelling, *Philosophical Investigations into the Essence of Human Freedom*, 29; SW, 359–360.

40. CA.

41. Ibid., 85.

42. F. W. J. Schelling, 'I', in *Schelling Werke*, ed. Manfred Schroder (Munchen: E.H. Back, 1959), 367. Kosch, *Freedom and Reason*, documents Schelling's influence on Kierkegaard. She argues that it is true that Kierkegaard attended Schelling's lectures in 1841–1842 to hear Schelling and was at first very enthusiastic and then hugely disappointed. But she points to a very strong influence of the *Freiheitsschrift* on *The Concept of Anxiety*.

43. CA, 43.

44. SUD.

45. In *Philosophical Fragments*, Johannes Climacus represents doubt as inherent in thought.

46. JP, vol. 4, chapter 11; and CA.

47. See Jon Stewart, *Kierkegaard's Relations to Hegel Reconsidered* (Cambridge: Cambridge University Press, 2003).

48. EO I, 19.

49. CA, 12.

50. Stewart, *Kierkegaard's Relations to Hegel Reconsidered*.

51. SUD, 69.

52. Ibid.

53. CA, 13.

54. SUD, 93.

55. CA, 26.

56. Ibid.

57. Claire Carlisle, *Kierkegaard's Philosophy of Becoming, Movements and Positions* (New York: State University of New York Press, 2005). It is important to note that, in a letter of 1847, no. 5978, Kierkegaard writes: 'There is no modern philosopher from whom I have profited so much as from Trendelenburg' (JP, vol. 5, 1839–1848, 1978, p. 367).

58. Søren Kierkegaard, epilogue, in FT.

59. FT, 152.

60. From JP, vol. 3, no. 3290, p. 511.

61. David Sedley, *The Cambridge Companion to Greek and Roman Philosophy*, 1st ed. (Cambridge: Cambridge University Press, 2003), 19.

62. JP, vol. 5, 1829–1848, no. 6063 (1847).

63. Kierkegaard, *Repetition and Philosophical Crumbs*, trans. M. G. Piety, with an introduction and notes by Edward Mooney and M. G. Piety (Oxford: Oxford University Press, 2009).

64. When I write 'the Hegelian' here, I realize that this is a hostage to fortune. There are many readings of Hegel, and Jon Stewart has argued, as noted before, that Kierkegaard is not responding to Hegel himself but rather to the Danish Hegelians, particularly Adler. It is also the case that there are readings of Hegel that make his work out to be similar, in some respects, to the view attributed here to Kierkegaard.

65. CUP, 307.

66. CA, 12–13.

67. Stewart, *Kierkegaard's Relations to Hegel Reconsidered*.

68. Gordon Marino, 'Anxiety in the Concept of Anxiety', in *The Cambridge Companion to Kierkegaard*, ed. A. Hannay and G. D. Marino (Cambridge: Cambridge University Press, 1998), 308–328.

69. SUD, 30.

70. See Johan Georg Hamann, *Sämtliche Werke Historisch-Kritische Ausgabe*, ed. J. Nadler (Vienna: Herder, 1949); and Frederick Beiser, *The Fate of Reason: German Philosophy from Kant to Fichte* (Cambridge: Harvard University Press, 1987).

71. See Freydberg, *Schelling's Dialogical Freedom Essay*, 38.

72. These are written in strange mathematical terms—A1, A2 and A3.

73. Schelling, SW, 359–360.

74. Kant, CPR, 261, B234.

75. See Ibid., A190/B235, A192/B237.

76. Ibid., 262, A191, B236.

77. Ibid., B224.

78. Peter Strawson, *The Bounds of Sense: An Essay on Kant's Critique of Pure Reason* (London: Methuen, 1966), 129.

79. Kant, CPR, A188–189/B231–232.

80. EUD, 17.

81. WA, 11. This is from Andrew Bowie's translation of *Die Weltalter* (Ages of the World) (Manfred Shröter: Münich, Biederstein, 1946), quoted in Andrew Bowie, *Schelling and Modern European Philosophy* (London: Routledge, 1993), 102.

82. EUD, 8.

83. There are those who have doubted, in relation to the discussion of this kind of temporal process in the phenomenological literature, that experience is actually like this. See, for example, Barry Dainton, *Stream of Consciousness: Unity and Continuity in Conscious Experience* (London: Routledge, 2000), 159. However, if one thinks, again, of a musical refrain as opposed, for example, to looking at a table, then one is more likely to be able to conceptualize experience in this manner.

84. CA, 4, 42; Kosch, *Freedom and Reason*, 210.

85. EUD, 9.

86. Ibid.

87. Ibid., 19

88. CPR, A558, B586.

89. Ibid., A551–552.

5

THE CONCEPT OF ANXIETY AND KANT

In this chapter, I will outline the beginnings of Søren Kierkegaard's or Haufniensis' solution to Immanuel Kant's problem. I will first present Kierkegaard's view of the origin of freedom and I will follow that with my reading of his response to Kant.

The Concept of Anxiety, as suggested, displays the influence of Friedrich Wilhelm Joseph Schelling. In CA, Haufniensis refers to Schelling a number of times. Kierkegaard additionally wrote a detailed collection of notes on Schelling's lectures that are collected together in his *Notes on Schelling's Berlin Lectures*. There, he writes, 'Kant took pure reason only in the subjective sense, not as the infinite potency of cognition, as is done here. . . . The content of the infinite potency of cognition is the infinite potency of being'.[1] Moreover, he continues, 'the first content of reason is not something actual; its content is the opposite of actuality. That this word reason [*vernuft*] is *foemini generis* [feminine gender]'.[2]

I should like, first, to comment briefly on this notion of 'actuality'. It is a concept frequently deployed by Kierkegaard. 'Actuality', as Jon Stewart carefully explains, is a concept in Adolph Peter Adler's Hegelian philosophy that is critiqued by Haufniensis.[3] Stewart argues that Haufniensis was unhappy with Adler's notion because the latter treated it as an abstract logical category rather than an existential one. But there is more than one alternative reading of the notion that Kierkegaard might be adopting. For Stewart, and he reads it this way also in his article 'The Notion of Actuality in Kierkegaard and Schelling's Influence',[4] the alternative to Adler's notion is the existential anthropological category. It is read this way also by many commentators on Kierkegaard. As George Pattison puts it, to give one example, Kierkegaard, unlike Heidegger after him, at least in the voice of Climacus, is concerned with '*my own*' (italics in the original text) existence, and not Dasein's existence.[5] But there may be a difference, and Kierkegaard or Haufniensis may have seen this difference, between Adler's concept of actuality and Schelling's. Stewart sees Schelling as treating actuality, like Adler, as merely an abstract notion. But one can read the Schellingian notion differently. One may instead see Schelling's notion of 'actuality' as implying something that is the effect of a system of forces that ground its being. Nature naturing—*natura naturans*—or, using the metaphor of mother and child, the mother giving birth—is contrasted with *natura naturata*, or the fact of the independently existing child. This is not necessarily incompatible with Kierkegaard's evident concern with first-person experience.

Returning, in light of this, to CA and to the story of Adam and Eve, Adam is supposed, according to the Christian tradition (and Kant also reads the story this way), to be the reason everyone else does wrong. Adam brought sin into the world. Strictly, however, it is not Adam but Eve who did this. Moreover, if we try to explain the story in the terms that speculative reason accepts, 'every attempt to explain Adam's significance for the race confuses everything'.[6]

Kierkegaard asks: 'Is the concept of hereditary sin identical with the concept of the first sin, Adam's sin, the fall of man?'[7] In this reading, the existence of Adam doesn't explain anything. If Adam is inside the history of finite limited beings, then his sin is just like the sin of everyone else. If, on the other hand, he is placed wholly outside history, then he has no relation to everyone else's sin precisely because he is placed outside this world. Adam's sin does not explain the sin of others if his sin is seen either as a first cause in a series of mechanical causes or as a certain kind of rational explanation for sin. However, Adam's sin explains the sin of others in a different way. In a criticism that is probably directed at Hegel but also at Kant, he writes: 'Let mathematicians and astronomers save themselves if they can with infinitely disappearing minute magnitudes, but in life itself it does not help a man obtain his examination papers and much less explain spirit'.[8]

Kierkegaard or Haufniensis writes that the difficulty for the understanding is precisely this, 'that sin presupposes itself'.[9] With his brilliant wit and prose, Kierkegaard compares Kant's claims about Adam to 'the counting rhyme in which children delight: one-nis-ball; two-nis-balls . . . up to nine-nis-balls and tennis balls'.[10]

Instead, Kierkegaard writes that 'by the first sin, sinfulness *came into Adam*'.[11] The position is the same, indeed, for every other human being. The concepts with which Kantian speculative reason deals belong in logic, while the notion of sin lies in ethics. Innocence is a natural state of the natural being that may continue in existence. Innocence is ignorance. One can, according to Kierkegaard, no more give a psychological explanation of the fall than one can give a logical or a mechanical causal explanation. But one can offer another kind of causal account.

Kierkegaard's account, I believe, drawing on the reading of Schelling above, can be reconstructed to run as follows: In the biblical story, Eve and Adam, as natural beings, in a world of similarly constituted natural beings, existed. Adam and Eve, in other words, were part of a living and active natural world that preexisted the domain of the free and thinking being. Adam, at that point, was neither free nor not free. Adam had no awareness of the possibility of choice. Eve—in some way a derived person—came into being later. She, via the serpent, seduced Adam. At that point, Adam became aware, through sensuality, of good and evil. Through the first sin, sinfulness, or the capacity to reflect on our passions and desires and to enact some and not others—in other words, human freedom—came into Adam. Adam may have existed alongside other natural objects. These natural objects possessed powers and capacities that were akin to our human conceptual apparatus, but they were also different. The natural objects existing alongside Adam were not, in other words, purely inert mechanical things. Strictly, freedom emerged first in Eve, rather than Adam. 'The woman was the first to be seduced, and that therefore she in turn seduced the man'.[12] Sin, then, in Eve and Adam, is grounded in nature, the nature of which both were part before they became free. Yet the science that explains the grounding of each individual in its precursor cannot completely account for sin and for freedom.

Adam, as well as each subsequent individual, is responsible for his own sin. The explanation, according to Haufniensis, of Adam's sin must also explain the sin of every other person. Adam and Eve, as the first individuals, represent both themselves and 'the race'. 'With sinfulness, sexuality was posited. In that same moment the history of the race begins'.[13] Adam and Eve, prior to the act of eating the fruit, are in a dream-like state of innocence. 'Innocence is ignorance. In innocence, man is not qualified as spirit, but is psychically qualified in immediate unity with his natural condition'.[14] Freedom 'enters into' Eve via a 'qualitative leap'.[15] In other words, Eve existed alongside all other natural beings, and she emerged, as they did, from her ground. If Eve and Adam are placed outside history then the story cannot explain anything. Haufniensis writes, 'As soon as Adam is placed fantastically on the outside, every-thing is confused'.[16] What happens to Eve and Adam is reflected in the emergence of freedom subsequently in each individual who sins. The qualitative leap brings about anxiety and the awareness, in Eve and Adam, of right and wrong, good and bad.

There are two points Kierkegaard is making, then, in response to Kant. First, the free will cannot be wholly outside time because it would be unable to operate if it were so placed. But secondly, although Kierke-gaard accepts Kant's point that the notion of freedom of the will cannot be explained in either logical or mechanical causal terms, he does not accept the conclusion that this means that it cannot be explained at all. For Kant, either Adam is wholly outside history or he is wholly inside history. But there is a third alternative: namely that Adam is partly inside and partly outside history—the history of beings like us. He is outside it as an innocent and natural being and inside it as a being that has become rational and free.

In language reminiscent of Schelling, Haufniensis writes: 'The annul-ment of immediacy is therefore an immanent movement within immedia-cy, or it is an immanent movement in the opposite reaction within media-cy. Innocence is something that is cancelled by a transcendence'.[17]

Kant's difficulty in explaining the notion of freedom to do wrong stems from his radical separation of the free will from the finite natural phenomenal being. It stems, furthermore, in Kierkegaard's view, from Kant's restriction of nature to that which can be accessed by human phenomenal experience. Nature, for Kierkegaard, then, by contrast, must be understood in two ways: first as human nature—natural intersubjective embodied experience as well as the nature that can be accessed by ration-al and finite beings. But there is also a second sense of the notion—the living dynamic nature that includes plants, bacteria and other animals and that, according to this reading, included Adam and Eve prior to the emer-gence in them of freedom. This nature must preexist Adam and Eve, must constitute some sort of 'great outdoors', to return to Meillassoux's ex-pression, in order for it to ground the possibility of freedom in beings like us. This does not, I accept, constitute the kind of proof that a sceptical epistemologist might want, that there is such a nature, but it is, nonetheless, a speculative hypothesis that offers the possibility of explaining the origin of freedom in beings like us.

Haufniensis argues that sin or evil results from the self taking itself as its own ground. Kant, as we saw, was forced to look for the ground of evil either in our own nature, in which case we are not really free, or in some external and wholly evil source. For Kant, when the individual acts from the moral law, a law that she herself, at least according to many readings of Kant, prescribes, she is approximating as closely as she possibly can a 'holy will' or a perfectly rational being. Even if one does not adopt the very strong reading of the relation between the moral law and the free self, the latter is still strongly shaped or grounded in reason. Indeed, in the third *Critique*, as we have seen in chapter 3, Kant deploys the notion of the holy will.

But, according to Schelling and Kierkegaard, it is not possible for the self ever to be a perfectly rational being or a holy will or even closely to approximate these notions; thought cannot ground itself. There will always be a remainder when the epistemologist attempts to gain certain knowledge or when the ethicist attempts to ground morality. No law prescribed to a human being can be perfectly or even approximately perfectly rational. But the other side of the coin is that pure evil is also impossible for us finite limited beings. The difficulty Kant faced of accounting for the freedom to do wrong arose because of the way in which he set up his morality. Acting well is construed in a very strong sense. He therefore had to offer an account of the freedom to do wrong in terms of the person being given over wholly to self-love. But *pure* self-love is not possible, Kierkegaard is claiming, for finite limited beings like us. However hard we try, none of us will ever exemplify 'pure evil'.

It may seem, despite the qualifications, that I am suggesting here that Kierkegaard is responding only to a very strong reading of Kant's Categorical Imperative and of the relation between the free will and the moral law. But Kierkegaard would, I think, claim that it is very difficult, given Kant's separation of the natural and phenomenal self from the self that acts morally, for him to escape something like this strong reading.

Given, then, the impossibility of perfect rationality, the self might imagine that it is following Kantian rational moral laws when in fact it is following either the norms of a particular society, which may be wrongheaded, or worse, norms set by a dictator like Hitler. In other words, for Schelling and Kierkegaard, in the very attempt to attain perfect rationality, to follow a law prescribed by the finite being itself, the self may actually be adhering to norms that are likely to be wrong. The world of the finite limited being—the actual—involves contingency,[18] while the attempt to speak in terms of a perfectly rational will does not recognize this.

When the self takes itself as its own ground, then, it is lost in finite grounds, such as those that may be expressed by the 'norms' of a society or, in Kierkegaard's outlook, by the banalities of the 'present age'. Some of these norms may not, of course, be directly evil, but in precisely the sense Arendt took from Kierkegaard, they are 'unthinking' and they might, as they did in the specific case of Adolf Eichmann, become evil by default.[19]

Freedom, then, for Haufniensis, involves the possibility of committing acts that are morally wrong. This Haufniensis refers to as 'anxiety about evil'.[20] The only way that this anxiety can be replaced by the alternative—a concern with the good—is through faith: 'The only thing that is truly able to disarm the sophistry of sin is faith'.[21] In other words, sin involves failing to recognize the grounding of the self in something external to it, while acting well involves a recognition of this grounding. For Haufniensis, though, if one goes a step further than simple evil, into the demonic, freedom is somehow curtailed.[22] Haufniensis describes the demonic as 'anxiety about the good' and as 'unfreedom'.[23] This is a state where the individual has been taken over and consumed by evil. Again we can see a critique of Kant here.

Alenca Zupancic[24] makes the point that Kant needs an infinitely existing body to be able to explain moral conversion, and she refers to the Marquis de Sade. But Kierkegaard suggestively implies that the two notions—an imaginary infinitely existing body and a perfectly rational will—stem from the same problematic assumptions: that the will and the body are radically separate. De Sade seeks out more and more pleasure and yet he can torture his victims only until they die. Seeking out endless pleasure, then, would be possible only if the seeker had an infinitely existing body. But this is impossible, of course, for us finite limited beings. It parallels the Kantian rational will, insofar as such a will, as well, imagines an infinite rationality. These two notions, then, exemplify pure rationality on the one hand and pure evil on the other. Both, to reiterate, are actually impossible for us.

In *Either-Or*, Eremita describes Don Juan and the Kantian rational self as each embodying a form of determinism.[25] The Kantian self is shaped and determined by its autonomy and Don Juan by being pure body; pure sensuality. Freedom is, for Kant, separation of the autonomous free self from the pathological; from embodied desire; from the phenomenal.

Importantly, then, freedom, for Haufniensis,[26] 'came into' Eve through sexuality. It is appropriate, indeed, for freedom to emerge, initially, into a body that can birth. For birth, or procreation, is the means by which species reproduce themselves and the means by which one species emerges from another. It is also, as we will see later in the book, the metaphor Schelling uses for the *ungrund*—the yearning of the one to give birth to itself. This yearning, in its turn, is characterized as love. The yearning, or the power, is, for him, infinite love. It is appropriate for freedom to emerge into a body that can birth, because the process of the emergence of freedom, in this speculative naturalist account, mirrors the natural process of birthing. Freedom is 'born' in an individual who initially lacked this capacity or power.

Sexuality, therefore, and then subsequent birth, is appropriate as a metaphor for the process of producing the capacity to be free.[27] Freedom, in this speculative naturalist theory, then, emerges in finite beings in analogous fashion to the emergence of one species from another, although there is a crucial difference. It cannot be fully explained in the way in which the emergence of a body from its ground may be 'scientifically' accounted for.

Haufniensis writes, in CA, that 'woman is more sensuous than man'[28]: 'That woman is more sensuous than man appears at once in her physical structure . . . aesthetically her ideal aspect is beauty. . . . Then I shall introduce her ethically in her ideal aspect which is procreation'.[29] Eve is 'more sensuous' and therefore more anxious than Adam partly, and importantly, because she has the capacity, or potency, to give birth. Indeed, perhaps it is because of the latter that she is the former. It is well known that a greater degree of anxiety, for Haufniensis, signifies strength rather than weakness. 'Although anxiety belongs to her [Eve] more than man, anxiety is by no means a sign of imperfection'.[30] Insofar as she has the capacity to give birth, she illustrates in bodily form, as well as in 'spirit', the self in process, the self both as organic process and as free being, a potentiality capable of becoming a number of possible selves—of taking up and believing a number of possible ideas and of acting in a multiplicity of ways. The emergence of freedom, in Eve, to reiterate, is itself like a birth. Eve is effectively reborn as a free self capable of good and bad actions. Moreover, as Anti-Climacus puts it in *The Sickness unto Death*, in 'willing to be itself, the self is transparently grounded in the power that established it'.[31] The 'power that established it' can be read, at least in part, in the Schellingian sense of a grounding of the self in an original event of creation of the whole and in a process of 'ejecting love', a process that 'yearns' to give birth to itself. Haufniensis uses language reminiscent of Schelling, when he writes that when sin comes into the world, sin 'acquired significance for the whole creation. . . . The meaning of this I can indicate by calling attention to the Scriptural expression ἀποκαραδοκία τῆς κτίσεως (the eager longing of creation) (Romans 8.9)'.[32] Haufniensis continues: 'Inasmuch as one can speak of an eager longing, it follows as a matter of course that the creation is in a state of imperfection'.[33] The free self is capable of receiving a norm from a transcendent source. Each time it exercises its freedom, it reenacts its grounding in the source of the whole of nature.

But it is also grounded in the 'dark ground', or a further potential, that leads to anxiety. The 'dark ground' is the potentiality in the ground of God for evil. Subjective anxiety, then, is anxiety in the face of the recognition of the potential that lies at the heart of the human being. The deity is born out of the opposing forces that constitute its ground. In a footnote, in CA, when discussing the creation, Haufniensis refers to these metaphors of Schelling. He writes: 'By these expressions he signifies, if I may say so, the creative birth pangs of the deity'.[34]

The reading I am offering of the Eve story is consonant with a Schellingian influence on Kierkegaard. It is consistent with a picture according to which 'matter itself becomes, in some manner difficult to conceive, capable of participation in the form of the understanding'.[35] For Schelling 'subjectivity arises in nature'.[36] In *Ages of the World*, Schelling writes, 'Necessity is before freedom'.[37] For Schelling, to reiterate, human beings are derived creatures, emanating from a pantheistic Absolute, which can be construed as God or Nature. But Schelling's nature, as noted, is a living nature; it is an active and dynamic nature. His pantheism is not a deterministic and dead form. Nor is it necessarily incompatible with conceiving of God as, in a sense, transcending nature because God's ground is different from his actuality. The word 'nature', it is important to register, comes from the Latin *natura*, meaning 'birth' or 'character'. Freedom, in his system, is 'in' all of nature, for it simply means the emergence of the self or the entity from its ground. Its form in beings like us, however, is different from its character in trees or rocks.

I am suggesting, here, that Kierkegaard accepts the broad parameters of this ontology but that he adds a further dimension—the 'leap' whereby the consciousness of freedom emerges in a being like Eve as well as in all subsequent finite rational beings.

Once freedom has 'emerged' in natural living beings, they acquire the capacity to reflect on their place in nature and on their own particular kind of being. They can think, and when they think, they express the conception of logic outlined earlier. For Schelling, 'God can only become revealed in that which is similar to him, in free beings acting from themselves. If all beings (*Wesen*) in the world were only thoughts of the divine mind, they would have to be living just because of it'.[38] All thinking, for Schelling, is primarily a form of acting. Freedom, moreover, for him, must be the capacity for both good and bad. Idealism, for Schelling, if it does not 'preserve a living realism as a basis becomes as empty and abstract a system as the Leibnizian'.[39] Idealist thinking, in other words, if it presents thought in a 'dead' form, as many logicians have done, will become 'empty and abstract'. The same thing happens, on the other hand, when naturalism or materialism is conceived as theorizing dead matter. One needs, therefore, a living matter, a living thought, and a living initiator of the whole process, whatever form this takes. As Bernard Freydberg puts it, 'the task of solving the problem of evil is the task of conceiving and articulating a living god'.[40] What is required, then, is a 'god of flesh and blood, a god willing to get dirty'.[41] Schelling implicitly likens the ideal principle to the 'masculine' and the real, mediating basis or ground to the feminine. The ideal principle needs to find a living basis.

KIERKEGAARD'S RESPONSE TO KANT

For Kierkegaard, then, contrary to Kant's view, nature can function as the causal ground of freedom because nature is not exclusively constructed

by beings like us. Moreover, nature itself, following Schelling, is conceived of as living and active and as preexisting beings like us.

Adam and Eve, then, to reiterate, prior to the emergence of freedom
may have been simply part of a preexisting nature. The existence of
Adam and Eve in this fashion fits with a metaphysic that has nature
operating as the ground of human action. An active nature, with powers
and capacities, in this account, preexists human reflective capacity.

In innocence, for Kierkegaard in CA, 'man' is not qualified as spirit.
Man is neither a beast nor an angel. 'If he were a beast or an angel, he
could not be in anxiety'.[42] He is neither animal nor rational. Kierkegaard—or rather the pseudonymous author Haufniensis—outlines how
the state of innocence in the Garden of Eden is precisely that. There is no
knowledge of good and evil. Eve cannot understand the prohibition.
There is peace and repose. But what else is there? Nothing. Nothing has
the effect of producing anxiety. Anxiety is 'freedom's actuality as the
possibility of possibility'.[43] Man is a synthesis of the 'psychical and the
physical'. Anxiety 'passes into Adam as the possibility of possibility'.

When Kant writes, as he does in his work *Conjectural Beginning of
Human History*, about the origins of freedom, he prioritizes, as one would
expect, reason. Freedom comes about, according to him, from someone in
the Garden, seeing two fruits and choosing between fruits. But this version of the story presupposes the very thing it is setting out to explain—
freedom—which is, no doubt, why Kant ultimately came to regard the
origin of sin as inexplicable. The notion of freedom based on reason also
makes the idea of acting well on the part of finite rational beings too
strong and difficult a notion and it further makes the contrary, acting
badly, impossibly strong as well. For Kierkegaard, instead, the moment
'spirit' enters into Adam it must posit also—since the human is the synthesis of the psychic and the bodily—its antithesis in the sensual, and the
most extreme form of the sensuous is the sexual. Adam was beguiled by
Eve, who was 'more sensuous', and therefore more anxious, than him.
Without sin there is no sexuality; the moment Adam becomes man, he
does so by becoming animal as well. The difference, in my reconstructed
account of Kierkegaard, then, is that Adam existed, prior to the realization of his freedom, as part of a dynamic nature, with its own powers and
capacities. The awareness of his freedom evolved in him. Conceptual
capacities, and specifically the capacity for freedom, therefore, evolved

out of a nature that contained, in some sense, analogous powers to those Adam came to acquire.

It might be argued, however, in an objection to this account, that in Haufniensis' account as well, the capacity to choose must already have existed in Adam. After all, Eve and Adam knew about the prohibition. But the reading I am offering suggests that Eve was not, prior to the eating of the fruit, a fully free being. The prohibition, at that time, functioned as a limit on the extent of her world. A lioness in the wild has limits on her world, but she does not have the capacity to choose evil. A fence in a zoo prevents the lion from roaming outside his cage, but this does not give him the freedom required to attribute responsibility for his actions. Eve, as Haufniensis reports, in the Garden, is neither beast nor angel. She is not quite like the lion nor is she a Kantian holy will. Importantly, though, and additionally, she is not yet free to make choices.

So Kierkegaard's response to Kant's problem outlined in chapter 3 is as follows. First, in order to be in possession of something analogous to the strong notion of freedom Kant wants, the future must be wide open for the individual agent. According to the account I have offered of Haufniensis' reasoning, for Kant the future is not fully wide open because the self is strongly shaped by her reasoning power. So despite Kant's desire to offer a strong conception of freedom, the freedom to engage in acts that are good or bad, his account does not allow for this. The future is, for Kant, grounded in the moral law that shapes how the self is to act. In Kierkegaard's view, however, this means that the self is not fully free. For Kierkegaard, the self becomes anxious because of her awareness of this wide open character of the future.

But secondly, it is the nascent awareness of the prohibition, which awakens anxiety, that itself constitutes, for Kierkegaard, the source of free norms. These norms are grounded in the processes outlined in this and the previous chapter, and ultimately in a God, or in a Schellingian *ungrund*. This is the infinite aspect of the self. The finite aspect of the self, furthermore, is shaped by a nature that is not a Newtonian deterministic one. This nature itself displays some degree of freedom.

Metaphorically, then, the freedom of Eve comes about through her developing awareness of the 'prohibition' that brings about the feeling of anxiety. Like every natural being, but in a stronger sense than many of these others, Eve is partially independent of her ground and this is what allows for the possibility of wrongdoing. So, to reiterate, the freedom to do wrong, for Eve as well as for all finite and partially rational beings, is the self taking itself as the ground of its actions, rather than taking as its ground norms that stem in the way outlined from a source outside it.

In a Kantian view, by contrast, the burden of guilt becomes debilitating. Kant finds difficulty explaining free but wrong actions partly because of his over-separation of the rational from the sensuous but also because of his restriction of nature to the phenomenal, mechanical nature experienced by finite and limited beings. He eventually, as we have seen, explains 'sin' as innate in all of us and as constantly tempting us away from the moral law. For Kierkegaard, though, as free and finite rational beings, we are continually both rational and sensuous; we are free to choose to do good in terms of the love that comes from sensuality and from the *ungrund*, but that can be generalized beyond this into the moral domain. Or we are free to choose the bad. For him, freedom is conceived partly as the spontaneous capacity of the natural and rational being in the face of the undetermined nature of the future but also as the shaping of this being by a norm that stems from an external nature. This external nature transcends the experience of this limited being but is simultaneously simply part of the natural world. It 'appears' to the finite being through 'revelation'.

The terms of the above explanation are not open to Kant. For him, any explanation will be either rational or mechanical causal or no explanation at all. Ronald Green suggests, as we have seen, that sin is inexplicable for both Kant and Kierkegaard. However, Kierkegaard, I am suggesting, has open to him a form of explanation that arises, if you like, from his recognition that in some way, a human being is a paradox—a synthesis of two opposing notions. But this paradoxical nature of the human being does not suggest nonsense. Rather, it suggests that explanations in ethics must take a different form from explanations in logic or in those domains of thinking that are governed by mechanical causation. If there is, as Iain Hamilton Grant's reading of Schelling implies, a naturalistic explanation of ideas, 'a physical explanation of idealism',[44] there may be a natural grounding of the mind and of mental phenomena. This natural grounding cannot be a purely mechanical one, for such a ground would not have the capacity to give rise to human mental abilities. Although the myth of Eve and Adam is just that—a myth—it is a myth that provides an explanation for something, the origin of freedom, that otherwise remains inexplicable. My reading of Kierkegaard's explanation, then, fits with a deep form of metaphysical naturalism, which sees mental phenomena as grounded in a powers-based and active nature.

However, while the influence of Schelling is important, there is one caveat to this that I would like to mention, and it is a point I take from Michelle Kosch. She argues that Schelling tries too hard to explain freedom in quasi-scientific terms. Kosch points out that Schelling 'turns an ethical point into a cosmological one'.[45] Schelling claims that there is freedom in the whole of nature. In a sense, as I have outlined, I take this point. Nature as a whole manifests some degree of freedom. Even the bacterium can make rudimentary choices. But this kind of freedom is not equivalent to the freedom of human agents that goes along with responsibility for action. This kind of freedom cannot be fully explained in the way both Kant and Schelling attempted. Schelling offers a radically different view of the natural world from that of Kant and yet he, also, wants to explain human freedom in quasi-scientific terms. Kant wanted to explain what freedom is and in his case, his explanation took, on Kierkegaard's view, an overly rational form. Schelling sets out to eliminate the distinction between the Kantian noumenal and the phenomenal, but his picture of human freedom remains a cosmological one rather than an ethical one. Instead, as Kierkegaard notes, the character of the kind of freedom had by finite rational beings like us is, in some sense, inexplicable. It is partially inexplicable because a crucial component of freedom is that we do not know what the future will bring. We experience this lack of knowledge as anxiety. This does not mean, however, that a partial explanation cannot be provided, but it must incorporate concepts, like anxiety, and like birthing, that cannot be wholly explained in scientific or in logical terms.

The explanation for wrongdoing, as well as for good behaviour, lies in the simple fact that human beings are natural beings with passions and desires but they also have the capacity to reflect on these. Freedom is a condition of being human and freedom involves the capacity to act in good or bad ways. It specifically arises, however, out of the awareness of sexuality. Adam and Eve, I am suggesting, were embodied sexual beings in the Garden.

Kant sees freedom as arising rationally out of thoughts' capacities. Freedom, according to Kierkegaard, though, is the 'anxious possibility of being able' crucially formed through sensuality and through a growing awareness of the 'prohibition'. It is ultimately grounded in a Being that, like Schelling's Absolute—or his *ungrund*—contains the ground of both good and evil. As Schelling puts it in *Ages of the World*, 'necessity and freedom are in God'.[46] The ground of both good and evil may be nature, but crucially nature understood as being active and dynamic and as existing outside the limits of possible human experience. Nature, in this sense, cannot be made commensurate with the finite and knowable. There can be no empirical marks of this nature. J. P. Lawrence, writing about Schelling, describes the 'unborn God', the heart of pure freedom, as 'awakening the craving to be from the abyss of what absolutely is not'.[47] This is also conceptualized, to reiterate, in terms of a process that longs to give birth to itself.

Kierkegaard rewrites some of this in a phenomenologically more persuasive manner, but also in what is ultimately a more naturalistic vein, in terms of the story of Adam and Eve. Adam and Eve were 'fleshy' living beings both before the emergence of freedom and after. The craving 'to be' emerged from a capacity in Adam that he was not aware he had. I will move, in the next few chapters, to consider both Kierkegaard's view of woman and this ontological ground itself in more detail and depth.

Michelle Kosch quotes David Hume on miracles, which, as she argues, inspired Kierkegaard, through his reading of Hamann. Hume writes: 'So that upon the whole we may conclude that the Christian religion was not only at the first attended with miracles, but even to this day cannot be believed by any reasonable person without one. Mere reason is insufficient to convince us of its veracity. And whoever it moved by faith to assent to it, is conscious of a continued miracle in his own person'[48] . Kierkegaard upholds this 'miracle' in our own person. For Kierkegaard, there is a continued miracle in his own person, for the self is the 'synthesis of the infinite and the finite'.[49] But the whole of nature may be miraculous in similar, though not identical, ways. Natural objects are interlinked with one another as well as with human beings. Natural objects, moreover, have powers and capacities, as Kant himself spelt out so carefully in his discussion of teleological causation in relation to a tree, in the third *Critique*.

Arising out of this reading of Kierkegaard is a further advantage over the Kantian theory of freedom and wrongdoing, and that is the possibility of a form of wrongdoing—like that of the suicide bomber—that may have nothing to do with the principle of self-interest. This is one respect in which I disagree with Kosch, who has inspired some of this. She suggests that 'sin', following Schelling, is characterized 'as selfish-ness'.[50] As Lawrence again puts it—on Schelling—'the pain and horror of being pushes spirit, already at its deepest and still unconscious levels, beyond the animal quest for feeding appetites'.[51] Sin may not be selfish-ness, but it is rather the self taking itself—perhaps its purported 'rational-ity'—as its ground.

Overall, the attempt to provide a complete explanation for ethical notions, in the way that Kant sets out to do, is, Kierkegaard argues, bound to fail. Human beings have agency precisely insofar as they are not per-fectly rational—determined by their reason—or determined by their de-sires. Rather, they are a combination of the infinite in the finite. While, therefore, Kierkegaard argues that acting well and acting wrongly ought not to be construed as Kant does, he nonetheless allows for a strong sense of freedom that is ultimately grounded in a 'God' that, in the sense de-scribed, transcends the natural.

In these opening chapters of the book, I have outlined a couple of readings of the difficulty faced by Kant of explaining how it is possible freely to do wrong. I suggested that this is connected with the problem he has in accounting for the origin of freedom. I then moved to argue that Kant's difficulties stem partly from the limited notion of nature with which he operates. Kierkegaard, by contrast, can offer an account of the origin of the freedom to do wrong. He also has a view of freedom that crucially allows that evil acts, as well as good acts, can stem from free-dom.

The account I have offered, deriving from my reading of Kierkegaard, rests on a picture of the human being that is, as many phenomenologists have argued, both a rational and an embodied thing—a lived body. But it also rests on a speculative naturalism that postulates a living and active nature existing outside the domain of limited and finite beings. Further-more, the notion of nature presupposed by this account might be precisely what is required in order to make sense of both natural capacities and human conceptual powers. I also believe, and I have argued this else-where,[52] that Kierkegaard's moral theory, based on love, has much to commend it. This will not convince committed Kantians but it may, I hope, provoke some thought.

FREEDOM TO DO WRONG: KIERKEGAARD'S RESPONSE TO KANT

So, to conclude this chapter, Kierkegaard's response to Kant is as follows: Haufniensis does not face the difficulty that befalls Kant's theory since he does not separate, in the fashion of Kant, the 'rational' self that follows a norm from the sensible, natural self. Moreover, for Haufniensis, unlike Kant, selfishness and sinfulness, as well as the capacity for good, come into being with freedom. Prior to the act of eating the fruit, these characteristics of an actual person were nonexistent. Kierkegaard, moreover, differs from Kant insofar as, for him, sin and evil are contingent on freedom and not, as Kant suggests, innate. Kierkegaard, then, can make sense of the Augustinian distinction between *pecatum originale*—the first sin—and actual sin—the sin as realized by an actual, existing individual. It is difficult for Kant, however, to make sense of this distinction, since he argues that sin is innate.

Instead, as I noted above, the self of CA is a combination of these two things—it is a synthesis of 'body and soul', 'temporality and eternity', 'finitude and infinitude'[53] and necessity and freedom. Further, since, as I have argued, freedom arose in humans through the first sin—Eve's sin—there was no awareness of goodness or evil until after this point. When people sin, they are taking themselves as the origin of the norm, while when they act well they are following a transcendent norm. Kant wants, in *Religion within the Limits of Reason Alone*, to hold the view that when people do wrong they are choosing to subordinate the moral law to a sensual desire, but as I argued in chapter 3, this conflicts with some of his other claims about freedom. The transcendent norm, when the self acts well, for Haufniensis, by contrast, consists in divine grace. It stems, indeed, ultimately from the *ungrund*.

Much of the discussion in this chapter and in the chapters that follow uses metaphor. The story of Adam and Eve is just that—a story. But it is important to note that scientists, as well as artists and storytellers, use metaphor. As Mary Hesse puts it, 'The world does not come naturally parcelled up into sets of identical instances for our inspection and description'.[54] Rather, scientists need to use models and metaphors. In fact, she argues that metaphor is primary over literal meaning. Indeed, as Evelyn Fox Keller writes, highly complex processes 'pose particular challenges for the meaning of understanding'.[55] In the sciences of life, or the biological sciences particularly, 'the core of [Keller's] argument is that much of the theoretical work involved in constructing explanations of development from genetic data is linguistic—that it depends on productive use of the cognitive tensions generated by multiple meanings, by ambiguity, and, more generally by the introduction of novel metaphors'.[56]

In the following chapters, I would like to pursue the theme begun here, of the birthing body as a metaphor for the nature that can ground the freedom of individuals. But before doing that, I will consider in more detail and depth Kierkegaard's view of women and his process philosophy.

NOTES

1. Søren Kierkegaard, *Notes on Schelling's Berlin Lectures*, in *The Concept of Irony with Continual Reference to Socrates and the Notes*, ed. and trans. Howard V. Hong and Edna H. Hong (Princeton: Princeton University Press, 1989), 337.

2. Ibid., 338.

3. Jon Stewart, *Kierkegaard's Relations to Hegel Reconsidered* (Cambridge: Cambridge University Press, 2003), 378–414.

4. Jon Stewart, 'The Notion of Actuality in Kierkegaard and Schelling's Influence', *Ars Brevis: Anuario de la Càtedra Ramon Llull Blanquerna* 17 (2011), 237–253.

5. George Pattison, *The Philosophy of Kierkegaard* (Chesham: Acumen, 2003), 86.

6. CA, 29.

7. Ibid., 25.

8. Ibid., 31.

9. Ibid., 32.

10. Ibid., 32.

11. Ibid., 33 (italics mine).

12. Ibid., 47.

13. Ibid., 52.

14. Ibid., 41.

15. Haufniensis distinguishes his own understanding of this 'leap' from Hegelian logical understanding. 'Hegel's misfortune is exactly that he wants to maintain the new quality and yet he does not want to do it, since he wants to do it in

logic'. CA, 30, footnote. Hegel's conception of the leap is contrasted there with that of Schelling.

16. CA, 28.

17. Ibid., 37.

18. See Ibid., 10.

19. Arendt sees Kierkegaard as offering the 'deepest critique of Descartes'. Later, in *Eichmann in Jerusalem*, she describes the banality of evil as arising in this way, through the absence of thought. Eichmann, she argues there, substituted belief in the Fuhrer for belief in Kant's Categorical Imperative (Hannah Arendt, *The Human Condition* [Chicago: University of Chicago Press, 1989], 275).

20. CA, 131.

21. Ibid., 117.

22. See Ibid., 118–136.

23. Ibid., 123.

24. Alenca Zupancic, *Ethics of the Real: Kant and Lacan* (London: Verso, 2000), 80–82.

25. See Michelle Kosch, *Freedom and Reason in Kant, Schelling and Kierkegaard* (Oxford: Oxford University Press, 2006), for a very useful discussion of this.

26. I am using the pseudonymous author of CA. However, I believe that there are continuities in the various pseudonymous texts of Kierkegaard as well as between these and the works written in Kierkegaard's own name.

27. A commentator who notes the connection between the emergence of freedom, anxiety and sexuality is Pattison, although he does not spell this out in the way I am suggesting. Zupancic (*Ethics of the Real*) also writes, offering a different but related interpretation to mine: 'How did innocence as innocence come to take this step (into evil and freedom)? It was of course *seduced*, incited to do it' (88).

28. CA, 64.

29. Ibid., 65.

30. Ibid., 47, footnote.

31. Kierkegaard, SUD, 14.

32. CA, 57–58.

33. Ibid., 58.

34. Ibid., 59.

35. Iain Hamilton Grant, *Philosophies of Nature after Schelling* (London: Continuum, 2006), 37.

36. Schelling, SW, 162.

37. F. W. J. Schelling, *Ages of the World*, trans. Frederick de Wolfe Bolman Jr. (New York: Columbia University Press, 1942), 44.

38. Schelling, SW, 347.

39. Ibid., 356.

40. See Bernard Freydberg, *Schelling's Dialogical Freedom Essay* (Albany: State University of New York Press, 2008), 29.

41. Ibid., 29.

42. CA, 155.

43. Ibid., 42.

44. See Schelling, *Ages of the World*; and Grant, *Philosophies of Nature after Schelling*, 61.

45. Kosch, *Freedom and Reason*, 214.

46. Schelling, *Ages of the World*, 5.

47. J. P. Lawrence, 'Schelling's Metaphysics of Evil', in *The New Schelling*, ed. Judith Norman and Alistair Welchman (London: Continuum, 2004), 180.

48. Kosch, *Freedom and Reason*, 185–186.

49. SUD, 13.

50. Kosch, *Freedom and Reason*, 213.

51. Lawrence, 'Schelling's Metaphysics of Evil', 182.

52. See Alison Assiter, *Kierkegaard, Metaphysics and Political Theory* (London: Continuum, 2009).

53. CA, 155.

54. M. Hesse, 'Tropical Talk: The Myth of the Literal', *Aristotelian Society* 61 (1987, supplement), 297–310, 311.

55. Evelyn Fox Keller, *Making Sense of Life, Explaining Biological Development with Models, Metaphors, and Machines* (Cambridge: Harvard University Press, 2003), 299.

56. Ibid., 117.

6

KIERKEGAARD ON WOMEN

I would like to begin this chapter by noting that, among those who have previously written about Søren Kierkegaard on women, many of them characterize his view of women negatively. Kierkegaard is seen by, for example, Robert Perkins, Wanda Warren Berry and Celine Leon[1] as an extreme misogynist.

My own reading of Kierkegaard is very different. It is possible, of course, that there is no 'correct' reading of his brilliant and haunting texts.[2] Yet there does seem to me to be sufficient evidence at least to justify the view that this alternative interpretation ought to be given some weight. It is not so much, indeed, that I disagree with what these commentators say about Kierkegaard's male and female heroes; I disagree, rather, with how to read what they write.

Celine Leon,[3] in her beautifully written book, confesses both her love for the works of Kierkegaard and her belief that he is deeply sexist. She writes:

> If I had unquestioningly accepted the views proffered on women, woman/sexual difference, the feminine, and male-female relation, it was because I had embraced as my own the male paradigm they privilege. Only by imagining my sex as it was portrayed in the aesthetic works and also in the journal on which my early readings had concentrated, had I been able to glance, without being offended at the Elviras, the Margarettes, all the secondary beings, whom the arbitrary fact of an entirely male direction had excluded from the banquet table where, once again in the history of philosophy, had gathered the seekers of

heady delicacies, their moods heightened by the effervescence of drink
and the hubbub of conviviality *inter pares*.[4]

Women, Leon writes, 'are the objects of a double mediation by means
of which are paired essentialist characterisations and stereotyped, degrad-
ing, and patriarchal comments on their sex'.[5]

I quote these two passages at length because they give such a forceful
and strongly negative picture of Kierkegaard's overall view of women. I
believe that the views are not unrepresentative of opinion on Kierkegaard
on women. However, I read Kierkegaard very differently. My own love
of Kierkegaard's deeply engaging writings is not in spite of his picture of
women, but partly because of it. When Leon notes that woman represents,
for Kierkegaard, 'a creature whose existence, assimilated to biology, culminates in the act of procreation',[6] I concur. When she writes that 'a male
"explains" that a woman cannot assert herself as an autonomous individual without threatening the feminine ideal',[7] I also agree. However, where
I differ, not only from the work of Leon on this subject but also from
Robert Perkins[8] and from several of the contributors to the volume Leon
edited with Sylvia Walsh,[9] is how to read this association of woman and
biology, woman and procreation.

I agree with the sentiments of both Leon and Berry, who claim that
women are beings who exist, in Leon's words, 'for the sake of another';
women focus, unlike men, on 'bodily immediacy', and they have a contingent 'and relative nature' as opposed to 'man's transcendent and absolute self'.[10] From *Fear and Trembling*, a woman's labour consists 'in
reproducing the species in pain'.[11] There is one context in which I hesi-
tate to agree with Kierkegaard, and that is when, in extremis, now writing
in his own name in *Works of Love*, he argues against women's liberation
and claims that 'he is proud to have fought for no emancipation what-
soever'.[12]

Berry, offering a similar picture of Kierkegaard's women to that of
Leon, writes that women appear 'only as shadows'.[13] Women are derived
from dramas written by men. Woman, taking Marie, for example, in
'Silhouettes', is denied the 'full experience of humanity'.[14] Man, again,
for Leon, is the 'universal', while woman 'is only specific'[15]; 'man is a
totality, a complete individual, an autonomous whole'.[16] 'Woman differs
from man as body does from intellect'.[17]

Leon expresses a concern, which I think is important to note, that valuing the qualities she believes Kierkegaard associates with women, as inherently positive qualities, in itself risks denigrating women. So, to take one example, she writes: 'Kierkegaard has not escaped a recent tendency of feminist theory to re-examine in a positive light texts in which a male thinker privileges the feminine for both sexes'.[18]

To give another example, she writes, in a footnote: 'Already in his dissertation, *The Concept of Irony*, published in 1841, Kierkegaard, intending this characterization as a praise, reflects on the "specificity" *foemini generis* [of the feminine gender], a phenomenon he equates with the ability to "surrender [*at hengive sig*] to the stronger on account of its feminine [*qvindelige*] nature"'.[19] Leon is understandably worried about associating such qualities with women, since she believes that doing so may reflect gendered cultural assumptions that operate to women's disadvantage. She writes: 'It seems, however, difficult, if not impossible, to envision the extension onto all human beings of qualities traditionally seen as feminine'.[20] If it is read this way, as, indeed, it has been read by some postmodern-influenced feminists, then I concur with her point. If Kierkegaard were to be read, overall, as valuing cultural assumptions about women that operate to our, or their, disadvantage, then I would concur with her reading. Indeed, the point she makes is very important. Those feminists, to make a parallel point, who have associated 'caring' qualities with women and who have seen these as intrinsically valuable may have contributed to a cultural imperative for women to exhibit such qualities, and, moreover, they may have contributed also to a failure to analyze what constitutes effective and good care for others.

However, there is another way of viewing the matter. As Edward Mooney notes, in a discussion of Kierkegaard's various references to silence, and his sometimes associating silence with women, this should not mean that 'voiceless women were preferred to disquisitional ones, Christianly speaking'.[21]

I am suggesting in this book something different from Leon's reading of Kierkegaard. I am certainly not supposing that the qualities Kierkegaard associates with some women should be valourized by all women. I am not suggesting that, for example, all women ought to be caring mothers. Rather, I am drawing attention, and suggesting that Kierkegaard also does this, to the deep denial, at the ontological level, in ways I will go on to outline in more detail and depth, of certain qualities that happen to be associated with women. This, I am suggesting, has led to a distorted view of the way reality is and ought to be understood. I will spell out further what I mean by this in the following chapters.

According to Leon, while on the one hand it is true that Anti-Climacus offers the feminine mode of relating as the pattern for human life, on the other hand, it is also true that this very same pseudonym[22] suggests that woman and man are equal before God. For Anti-Climacus, the pseudonym that she writes, is 'closest to Kierkegaard',[23] the basic structure of selfhood is the same for both sexes. In relation to God, writes Anti-Climacus, 'the distinction of man-woman vanishes'.[24] The self only becomes a self, Anti-Climacus writes, in relation to the power—God—that established it. Leon, however, doubts that such a positive view, for Kierkegaard, of the equality between men and women in relation to God also applies to the relation between men and women in marriage, for example.

I would like only to note, at this point, that there is one commentator who has contested the ready association, demonstrated in these works, of Kierkegaard with deep misogyny. This is Christine Battersby. Unlike Leon and Berry, Battersby sees the female as coming to occupy centre stage for Kierkegaard. Battersby suggests that Kierkegaard deeply understood how 'paradoxical it is to exist as a woman'.[25] She writes that the 'self-other divide is [for Kierkegaard] established relationally, via repetitive iterations that mark out time'.[26] Kierkegaard, she notes, 'posits a self that is shaped by forces outside it'.[27] As I have written elsewhere,[28] Kierkegaard is critical of the model of the self as an autonomous moral person. Such a self is 'a king without a country'.[29]

Rather than denigrating 'woman' for being relational, for being closer to nature than 'man' and intertwined with others to a greater extent than the male, Kierkegaard, I believe, values these qualities to a greater extent than he does the 'myth' of a perfectly autonomous, perfectly rational and whole 'person'. It is possible to accept this point while also recognizing that he is not claiming that all women, or all men either, should forgo their autonomy. This is not the point. The point, rather, is that Kierkegaard challenges the Kantian image of the self—the transcendental unity of apperception, that has no qualities of its own but that unifies sensible intuitions under concepts and then under categories.[30] In other words, he challenges the role played ontologically, in Immanuel Kant's thought and in that of many subsequent philosophers as well, by this kind of a self. In its turn, he also questions the particular conception of the 'object of knowledge' constructed by this Kantian self. This need not involve a literal denial of the importance of respecting a person's autonomy in political and ethical relations with others. Yet it does suggest that Kierkegaard recognizes that the importance attached to freedom and autonomy in the thought of Kant, and of others influenced by Kant, may be overrated. Hopefully these notions will become clearer as we move through the book.

KIERKEGAARD ON TIME

One indication of Kierkegaard's overall view on this subject is illustrated by his view of time. Once again, we can find an association of the 'male', albeit a rather extreme version of the male, with a notion of temporality that is viewed, by the above commentators, positively. Women, by contrast, are connected with an opposing picture that is negatively perceived. So Leon, again, writes that 'the concept of man [for Kierkegaard] corresponds to the idea of man. Therefore one needs only one man in existence and no more'.[31] Man 'equates his specificity with the universal',[32] while woman is 'multiple'. In a telling quotation, furthermore, Leon, referring to the 'unbounded' energy of Don Juan and of Johannes the Seducer, describes the former, in a quote from *Either-Or*, as a 'hero, who can become epic only by continually finishing and continually being able to begin all over again . . . the man whose life is the sum of discrete moments as well as moments that have no coherence as the moment is the sum of moments and as the sum of moments is the moment'.[33]

Leon implies that Kierkegaard, or Eremita, valourizes this view of time. Frequently, however, Kierkegaard, sometimes writing in his own name, but also in the pseudonymous works, critiques this spatialized model of time, associated here with the seducer. The Danish word *tiden*, George Pattison[34] has pointed out, which is translated appropriately as 'the age', can also mean 'time'. Pattison refers to Haufniensis' discussion of time in CA, chapter 3, where Haufniensis critiques a spatialized model of time.

Typically we see time, as Pattison points out—and many philosophers, from Zeno onwards, have seen it this way—as a series of 'nows'— a series of spatialized moments. Haufniensis, however, points out how no moment is ever really present, because 'every moment is a process,—a passing by—no moment is a present, and there is in time neither present nor past nor future'.[35]

In fact, Kierkegaard uses visual metaphors in CA when it seems that the visual locks one into the spatialized model of temporality and the spatial ontology that Kierkegaard is critiquing. Pattison suggests, however, that the expression 'the glance of the eye' is actually figurative. When Ingeborg looks out to the sea after her departing lover[36] she is looking at a 'vanishing object',[37] something in the process of disappearing from her field of vision. She is looking at a vanishing object and she knows that Frithiof fails to understand that she will be married off to another while he is away. Pattison suggests that the 'pure moment of vision' is the unqualified, because unarticulated, apprehension of the eternal in, with and under the incognito of a temporal moment.[38] The eternal image is inexpressible but, if it can be expressed temporally at all, it is a moment when the eternal 'comes into time'.[39]

It is important to note the influences upon the Kierkegaard of the text of CA here. Haufniensis, as previously noted, emphasizes an ontology of process, where each spatialized moment contains elements of past and future. In this respect, as I have noted many times in this book, one important influence is Friedrich Wilhelm Joseph Schelling. But Kierkegaard is also, throughout his writing, as David Kangas, in his brilliant work *Kierkegaard's Instant*,[40] has pointed out, responding to a teleological model of time whereby a subject is, as he puts it, 'a self-mediating drive toward the realization of its being'.[41]

As Kangas points out, a teleological reading presupposes a continuous temporality defined by the movement of self-consciousness in coming to itself. The 'highest' stage would be the one that best expresses its principle. But Kierkegaard does not accept this kind of Hegelian system. Kierkegaard's self holds itself open not to absolute being but to nonbeing. The final chapter of CA articulates the relation between faith and anxiety, 'anxiety being a relation to the nothing of possibility. Faith is sinking into what absolves itself from being, a relation to what cannot be gathered into presence'.[42]

Christine Battersby has written on this subject: 'Access to the noumenal and the infinite comes, instead, from a different relation to time'.[43] According to Battersby, it is woman who gives access to infinity 'by being excluded from Kantian serialized time'[44] and also from the 'onward march of Hegelian serialized history'.[45] Constantin, in *Repetition*, thinks about a mode of time that would proceed by echo and repetition 'and which is non-linear in the Kantian sense'.[46]

'A' in EO uses music to illustrate this kind of process. 'Only music', he writes, 'occurs in time'.[47] This contrasts with 'the other arts'. 'That which the other arts produce suggests their sensuousness precisely by having its continuance in space'.[48] 'Music does not exist except in the moment it is performed', and this indicates, he writes, that it is 'a higher, a more spiritual art'.[49]

POSITIVE COMMENTARY ON WOMAN

In my reading, then, rather than overvaluing the Kantian autonomous mind and denigrating 'woman', Kierkegaard challenges this Kantian picture of the self and offers a positive characterization, by contrast, of 'woman'.[50]

One illustration of this occurs in 'Silhouettes', in *Either-Or*, where the pseudonymous author, 'A', continues a theme that is expressed earlier in EO. In 'The Immediate Erotic Stages', 'A', through a discussion of the music of Mozart, emphasizes hearing as opposed to sight. Hearing, as many philosophers have noted (see, for example, Bergson and Strawson), offers an experience of a continuous flow, as opposed to one of discrete items. Hearing, as Battersby points out, can be used by philosophers to emphasize the 'flow' of time.[51] Many philosophers prior to Kierkegaard relied predominantly on vision to develop their view of the world. 'A', however, writes about the limits of vision. He refers to the difficulty of 'seeing' a person through a discussion of joy and sorrow. Joy is 'communicative, social, open and wishes to express itself'. Sorrow, by contrast, 'is inclosingly reserved, silent, solitary and seeks to return into itself'.[52] To quote 'A': 'It is this reflective sorrow that I aim to single out, and, as far as possible, have emerge in a few pictures'.[53] 'A' calls these pictures 'silhouettes', 'partly to suggest at once by the name that I draw them from the dark side of life, and partly because, like silhouettes, they are not immediately visible'.[54] He uses illustrative material from stories, material that concerns women. The first character presented is Marie Beaumarchais, taken from Goethe's *Clavigo*.

Kierkegaard appears to be identifying with Marie here. She cannot be seen and she is also, in some sense, powerless. She is subservient and she has been wronged. Kierkegaard, as Battersby puts it, often refers to 'vertical' relationships; he refers to the powerful and the powerless and he often adopts the perspective of the latter. But the 'victim' (this is my word rather Battersby's)—and this is illustrated in the case of his discussion of Marie—is never 'merely' a victim. If unhappy love is due to a deception, then its pain and suffering occur because the grief cannot find an object.[55] For love, according to Kierkegaard (or 'A'), 'a deception is indeed an absolute paradox, and therein lies the necessity for a reflective grief'.[56] Whatever love is, he continues, 'a deception is a paradox that thought cannot think'.[57] This recalls the discussion in *Philosophical Fragments* about a human thinker who is interested in the boundaries of her thought. Here the ultimate paradox of thought is the infinite—or God: 'the ultimate paradox of thought: to want to discover something that thought itself cannot think'.[58] The unknown that thought cannot think is 'the god'.[59] It recalls also, of course, Abraham, who believes 'the absurd'.[60] Abraham 'expresses the sublime in the pedestrian absolutely'.[61] Furthermore, in his work *The Woman Who Was a Sinner*, Kierkegaard writes, 'Piety or godliness in its essential nature is femininity'.[62]

Marie loves passionately and yet she knows that her love involves a deception. Marie's love for Clavigo is a perception that thought cannot think. An engagement that is broken is a possibility, not an actuality. One might imagine that the effects of a broken possibility are not as great as a broken actuality, but, according to 'A', 'when a possibility is shattered, the momentary pain may not be as great, but frequently it leaves a little ligament or two whole and undamaged, which remain a constant occasion for continued pain. The destroyed possibility appears transfigured in a higher possibility'.[63] If Marie were to enter a convent, then, 'reflection' would have triumphed; she no longer would have the passion that was previously present. If she were, in those circumstances, to be asked what she was sorrowing over, she would have nothing to say. In this respect she is just like the sage who, when asked what religion is, asked for more and more time to think. In other words, in the moment of her love, when her passion is at its greatest, she signifies the relation between a human being and God: she feels something that thought cannot think, just like the relation of love, for Kierkegaard, expressed in *Works of Love* and in the *Upbuilding Discourses*, as well as elsewhere, between a human being and God.

Kierkegaard, then, as Battersby notes, writes from the perspective of woman, of the female. He sometimes, to reiterate, takes the point of view of the victim—of the person who has been wronged. There are no doubt resonances of his own life here. But these perspectives are uncannily parallel to the relation that Kierkegaard advocates between God and human beings. In his journals, he writes: 'Woman's consciousness is far more universal or at least far less subjectivised and therefore more a community-consciousness (an Amen)'.[64] Marie, then, importantly, exemplifies an alternative ethic as well as an alternative ontology to that of the Kantian rational self. As Kierkegaard puts it in *Works of Love*, 'In erotic love, preserve love for the neighbour'.[65] For Pattison, 'a decisive motivation at work in the discourses [the religious *Upbuilding Discourses*] is the need to develop an ethical and religious transubstantiation of erotic love'.[66] 'Silhouettes' suggests a veil drawn across appearances, but the passion of Marie can recall the struggle engaged in by the religious person coming to terms with faith. Marie also represents, ontologically, the 'actuality' of process as opposed to a logical idea conceived in terms of mediation. 'Actuality', here, is to be understood, then, neither in the logical terms suggested by G. W. F. Hegel nor as referring merely to the particular person. It is rather, I am suggesting, a metaphor for Kierkegaard's process ontology.[67]

'WOMAN' AS A CHALLENGE TO A KANTIAN AUTONOMOUS 'MIND'

In *Stages on Life's Way*, I believe, Johannes the Seducer extends Kierkegaard's positive commentary on woman and on process. Johannes, first of all, accuses his fellow interlocutors of '[being] possessed by the devil'.[68] Many of them, as Robert Perkins writes,[69] had spoken in strongly derogatory fashion about women. I would like to discuss the subject of the devil in more detail and will do so in the following chapter.

Johannes, in *Stages*,[70] however, after comparing his compatriots to the devil, speaks, in a slightly convoluted way, 'in praise of woman'.[71] We read:

Just as the person who is supposed to talk about the divine must be inspired by the divine in order to be able to talk worthily and there is taught what he is to say by the divine itself, so it is also with speaking about woman. Woman, even less than the god, is a whim from a man's brain, a daydream, something one hits upon all by oneself and argues about *pro et contra*. No, only from her herself does one learn to talk about her. And the more one has learned from her, the better.[72]

Furthermore, in the case of the story of Tobias and Sarah, in *Fear and Trembling*, 'Sarah is the heroine'.[73] If we had 'let Sarah be a man . . . the demonic would not be far away'.[74] Each of these characters, Sarah, Faust and Abraham, represents a character that cannot be conceived in terms of a Kantian autonomous, self-sufficient and self-subsistent 'substance'. Each of them, in his or her own fashion, is incomprehensible from that perspective; from within that perspective, their actions are incapable of explanation. But 'woman' is closer to the divine than is the devil. A further illustrative example is the case of Antigone, discussed by Kierkegaard, through 'A', the aesthete, in the essay 'The Tragic in Ancient Drama Reflected in the Tragic in Modern Drama'.[75] Antigone bears a dreadful secret—her knowledge of the relation of her father, Oedipus, to her mother (her father killed his father and married his mother)—which she can never disclose.[76] She is, therefore, like Abraham, condemned to silence. Like his, her actions would be incomprehensible within the 'ethical universal' both of Kant and of Hegel. Hegel does consider Antigone to draw a distinction between types of law, but it is the silent aspect of her predicament that is incomprehensible within his system as well as within that of Kant.

One more illustration of this is the characterization of despair and of the different forms of despair in SUD. There is the 'feminine despair', which is the despair of 'not willing to be oneself', and then there is the 'masculine despair', which is the despair of failing to recognize one's own grounding in the process of creation, and taking oneself to be one's own ground. This is, again, the source of evil or wrongdoing for Schelling and for Haufniensis, in CA. 'Masculine despair', then, could be construed either as the despair at taking oneself to be the source of one's own norms, as Kant may have believed one did, or perhaps as the despair at having society as the origin of one's norms, as Hegel did. As Kierkegaard puts it, 'And thus, perhaps, live a great multitude of people—they work away so minutely at dimming their ethical and ethic-religious awareness'.

An extension of this would be imagining that it is possible to sell one's soul, as Faust did, in the legend, to some personification of evil.[77]

In this chapter, I have begun to illustrate Kierkegaard's positive commentary on women. I have outlined the views of some who have taken a rather different perspective on Kierkegaard on women and suggested that there may be a different way of viewing at least some of his works. I have also noted and acknowledged some of the concerns of feminist commentators on Kierkegaard who view him as a misogynist. I have argued, however, that the reading I would like to give of the role of women concerns a deeper ontological matter than some of the critics have acknowledged. In the following chapter I will outline a reading of his works that suggests a role for metaphors of birth in his ontology.

NOTES

1. See Celine Leon and Sylvia Walsh (eds.), *Feminist Interpretations of Søren Kierkegaard* (University Park: Pennsylvania University Press, 1997).

2. Roger Poole (*Kierkegaard: The Indirect Communication* [Charlottesville: University of Virginia Press, 1993]) argues that there is no correct way to read Kierkegaard, although he draws the conclusion, like others cited in this text, that it follows that Kierkegaard is not a philosopher.

3. Celine Leon, *Neither/Nor of the Second Sex: Kierkegaard on Women, Sexual Difference and Sexual Relations* (Macon: Mercer University Press, 2008).

4. Cf. SLW, 24, 535–536; JP, paper V, B 187:9, in Leon, *Neither/Nor*, 2.

5. Leon, *Neither/Nor*, 3.

6. Ibid.

7. Ibid., 124.

8. Robert Perkins, *Woman-Bashing in Kierkegaard's 'In Vino Veritas': A Reinscription of Plato's Symposium*, in Leon and Walsh (eds.), *Feminist Interpretations of Søren Kierkegaard.*

9. Leon and Walsh (eds.), *Feminist Interpretations of Søren Kierkegaard.*

10. Leon, *Neither/Nor*, 260.

11. FT, in Leon, *Neither/Nor*, 121.

12. See Leon, *Neither/Nor*, 10. It is important to note, however, that, in this same work, Kierkegaard writes: 'People have foolishly busied themselves in the name of Christianity to make it obvious to the world that women have equal rights with men—Christianity has never demanded or desired this' (WL, 139–140). In other words, he is not strictly, here, arguing against equal rights but simply saying that Christianity does not require their existence.

13. Wanda Warren Berry, 'The Heterosexual Imagination and Aesthetic Existence in Kierkegaard's Either-Or, Part One', in Leon and Walsh (eds.), *Feminist Interpretations of Soren Kierkegaard*, 32.

14. Ibid., 35.

15. Leon, *Neither/Nor*, 40.

16. Ibid., 41.

17. Ibid.

18. Ibid., 191.

19. Ibid., 211, footnote 23, partially quoting CI, 9.

20. Leon, *Neither/Nor*, 199.

21. Edward F. Mooney, *On Soren Kierkegaard: Dialogue, Polemics, Lost Intimacy, and Time* (Aldershot: Ashgate, 2007), 236.

22. Ibid., 191.

23. Leon, *Neither/Nor*, 191. Note, however, that the journal entry where Kierkegaard refers to this is a little more ambiguous than Leon's reading suggests. The full entry reads as follows:

> Johannes Climacus and Anti-Climacus have several things in common; but the difference is that whereas Johannes Climacus places himself so low that he even says himself that he is not a Christian, one seems to be able to detect in Anti-Climacus that he regards himself to be a Christian at an extraordinarily high level, at times also seems to believe that Christianity really is only for geniuses, using the word in a non-intellectual sense. His personal guilt, then, is to confuse himself with ideality (this is the demonic in him), but his portrayal of ideality can be absolutely sound, and I bow to it. I would place myself higher than Johannes Climacus, lower than anti-Climacus. (JP, vol. 6, no. 6433)

24. SUD, 85, quoted in Leon, *Neither/Nor*, 193.

25. Christine Battersby, *The Phenomenal Woman: Feminist Metaphysics and the Patterns of Identity* (London: Routledge, 1998), 149.

26. Ibid., 183.

27. Ibid.

28. See my *Kierkegaard, Metaphysics and Political Theory* (London: Continuum, 2009).

29. CA, 69.

30. It is important to note that while this picture is most certainly present in Kant's CPR, Kant is also critical, as noted previously, using some of the same arguments Kierkegaard himself deploys throughout his works, of Descartes' arguments for the 'thinking self' being a substance, as demonstrated through his

doubt that he exists as a *thing* (my italics) that thinks. It is, however, also Kant's image of the self as a purely rational 'person' as demonstrated in his moral philosophy of which Kierkegaard is critical.

31. Leon, *Neither/Nor*, 40.

32. Ibid.

33. From EO I, 101, quoted in Leon, *Neither/Nor*, 38.

34. George Pattison, *The Philosophy of Kierkegaard* (Chesham: Acumen, 2003).

35. CA, 85.

36. See Ibid., 87.

37. Pattison, *The Philosophy of Kierkegaard*, 17.

38. Ibid., 18.

39. George Pattison, *Kierkegaard's Upbuilding Discourses: Philosophy, Literature and Theology* (London: Routledge, 2002), 18.

40. David Kangas, *Kierkegaard's Instant: On Beginnings* (Bloomington: Indiana University Press, 2007).

41. Ibid., 7.

42. Ibid., 8.

43. Battersby, *The Phenomenal Woman*, 172.

44. Ibid.

45. Ibid.

46. Ibid., 173.

47. EO I, 68.

48. Ibid.

49. Ibid.

50. If one takes Kierkegaard's norm to be some notion of Kantian autonomous reason and if one then sees this notion as encapsulated in the male, then Kierkegaard's remarks about woman can be read as critical. However, as I am suggesting, I read these remarks differently.

51. Battersby, *The Phenomenal Woman*, 179.

52. EO I, 169.

53. Ibid., 172.

54. Ibid., 173.

55. Ibid., 178.

56. Ibid., 179.

57. Ibid.

58. PF, 37.

59. Ibid., 39.

60. FT, 54.

61. Ibid., 70.

62. See notes to JP, vol. 4, 773.

63. EO I, 180.

64. JP, vol. 3, no. 2386, 33.

65. WL, 62.

66. Pattison, *Kierkegaard's Upbuilding Discourses*, 193.

67. Further support for this view can be found in CA, footnote on the moment.

68. SLW, 71.

69. Perkins, *Woman-Bashing in Kierkegaard's 'In Vino Veritas'*.

70. As will be obvious, I read *Stages* differently from the piece by Robert Perkins in Leon and Walsh's edited collection (Perkins, *Woman-Bashing in Kierkegaard's 'In Vino Veritas'*, 83–103), although I accept, as he ably points out, that there is much in the text of *Stages* that could clearly be read as misogynist.

71. SLW, 73.

72. Ibid.

73. FT, 129.

74. Ibid.

75. In EO I.

76. Margherita Tonon, in her piece 'Suffering from Modernity', in *Kierkegaard and the Political*, ed. Assiter Alison and Margherita Tonon (Cambridge: Cambridge Scholars Press, 2012), describes the depiction of Antigone by 'A' as implicitly offering a critique of the Hegelian notion of modernity. The ancient tragic hero (although Antigone is an exception here—see Tina Chanter, *Whose Antigone? The Tragic Marginalisation of Slavery* [Albany: State University of New York Press, 2011]) is, in Tonon's words, 'intrinsically determined by those relations to which it fundamentally belongs,—the family, the state or the lineage of generations—the modern tragic hero has lost his connection with the above elements, and is hence understood as a figure of silence, isolation and solitude' (88).

77. Such personification may simply be an extension of the former point, that the person believes in some purportedly perfectly rational self, which, since it can exist and it is, in effect, a belief in the power of one's self-produced norms, becomes the personification of evil. An illustration of the way in which this kind of thing might happen is the example mentioned earlier in the book, of Hannah Arendt's Eichmann. Eichmann, she argues, substituted duty to the Fuhrer for duty to the Categorical Imperative. There is, Kierkegaard would argue, no absolute Categorical Imperative, since there cannot be, in finite limited beings like us, a perfectly rational will. Therefore, it is not difficult for belief in such a will to be transferred over to some 'sovereign' who seems to personify this absolute will if we combine this with Agamben's brilliant work illustrating how 'the sovereign' constitutes himself as both the initiator of the law and outside the law. In tandem

with this, in Agamben's reading, the sovereign constitutes himself as able to legitimate the power to kill certain individuals without the 'murderer' being held responsible for their murder, and, alongside this, without the individual concerned being able to be sacrificed. In other words, the finite rational self cannot himself create a perfectly rational will, and attempts to do so might be corrupted into these 'evil' personifications, since—it is possible to hypothesize—they are able to delude themselves into believing that they are indeed the personification of rationality.

7

METAPHORS OF BIRTH IN KIERKEGAARD

In his *Notes on Schelling's Berlin Lectures*, Søren Kierkegaard (noting Friedrich Wilhelm Joseph Schelling) describes the emergence of freedom in humans alongside the process of the creation of the universe. The creation, he notes, was 'built upon moving ground'.[1] This stands in stark contrast to G. W. F. Hegel's perspective, which seems to claim that logical relations existed in the mind of God prior to creation.[2] In CUP Kierkegaard challenges a version of the Hegelian starting point of his system. He writes, '*How does the system begin with the immediate? That is does it begin with it immediately?*'[3] He may be referring here to what is immediate epistemically, for the self. Yet CUP is also making the general point that 'immediacy never simply is, but is transcended as soon as it is'.[4]

Only Being or God, Schelling argues in his *Freiheitsschrift*, has its ground within itself. This ground, to reiterate, Schelling expresses in the following terms: 'The first beginning for the creation is the yearning of the one to give birth to itself or the will of the ground. The second is the will of love whereby the word is spoken out into nature and through which God first makes himself personal'.[5] These metaphors are the expression of the opposing forces that are required for generation. Living nature is the expression of mutually opposing forces. Willing, for Schelling, 'is primal being'.[6] Any activity that is not conditioned by some difference becomes the unconditioned.

Schelling's 'will of love' is reflected in Kierkegaard's focus, throughout his works, on love. In *Philosophical Fragments*, when Climacus discusses the Incarnation, he writes, 'What could move God to make his appearance?'[7] He continues that God becomes a human being because he is moved by love. This directly reflects a claim of Schelling's to the effect that the 'human will is the seed—hidden in eternal yearning—of the God who is present still in the ground only'.[8] Again, moving back to Kierkegaard or Climacus, the latter writes: 'When the God becomes teacher, his love cannot be merely seconding and assisting, but is creative, giving a new being to the learner, or as we have called him, the man born anew; by which designation we signify the transition from non-being to being'.[9] In his *Upbuilding Discourses*, as well, Kierkegaard describes love as a power of revelation.

In this chapter, I will articulate Schelling's view of nature and his use of metaphors of birth. I will also begin to describe Kierkegaard's appropriation of some of these ideas. In the chapter that follows, I shall continue outlining Kierkegaard's use of birthing metaphors.

KIERKEGAARD AND SCHELLING ONCE MORE

Form, for Schelling, emerges from this process of opposing forces working together. 'The understanding' for Schelling 'is born from that which is without understanding'.[10] In his *Notes*, Kierkegaard offers a metaphorical or mythological description of this process, a process that is beyond human understanding, as 'the feminine, as something attracting the will, as the alluring'.[11] Kierkegaard continues:

> This element is depicted in mythology by a feminine being, Persephone, who corresponded also to the *duas* of the Pythagoreans. Yet Persephone is only a reflection of the beginning of the beginning of this condition. The beginning itself is a surprise; only in the conclusion does consciousness become clear.[12]

Now referring to a subject he will take up again in CA, Kierkegaard writes, 'Something similar is taught in Genesis. Three elements in particular should be noted: (1) man's first sin is beguilement; (2) the accessible side is woman; (3) the seductive principle is the serpent'.[13]

In 1786,[14] in his *Metaphysical Foundations of Natural Science*, Immanuel Kant expresses concerns about 'hylozoism'—the notion of living matter. Matter, he writes there, 'has no absolutely inner determinations'.[15] We have seen, in an earlier chapter, how this view of Kant's was partly shaped by his picture of what constituted a legitimate and scientific conception of causation and of nature. Schelling, by contrast, was not limited in the same fashion by Newtonian science. Perhaps prefiguring later science to a greater extent than Kant, he rather sees nature as, in the words of Andrew Bowie, 'a living organism'.[16]

In Schelling's system, there is a constant process of production. For Schelling, the capacity to give birth—the ground—could be construed as the 'becoming' of which the being that is born is the consequent. In most cases, the capacity to give birth itself presupposes a being that has this potency. But nature as a whole creates itself and therefore creates the creative force that gives rise to other dependent beings. Underlying all this, in order to avoid an infinite regress, there must be something that precedes all Being—Schelling's *ungrund*. The series, then, must ultimately culminate in a being that gives birth to itself—a being—the *ungrund*, that has its ground within itself. At the outset of the process is a capacity or a power, or, to repeat, the 'yearning of the one to give birth to itself'.[17] At the other end, as particular things, human beings, as the 'most differentiated', emerge from previous grounds: from parents and grandparents, from other species, and then from non-animal creatures.

To quote Schelling's 'On the World Soul':

> Now if in general the negative presupposes the positive . . . then our philosophy must not begin with mechanism (as the negative) but rather with the organics (as the positive). . . . [W]here there is no organism there is no mechanism. Rather than the other way round. Unrestricted mechanism would destroy itself—the world is only infinite in its finitude. Therefore it must be an organisation. Every motion presupposes a positive and a negative force. These two conflicting forces lead to the idea of an organising principle—perhaps the ancients wished to intimate this with the world soul'.[18]

He writes further, 'The essence of life does not consist at all in a force, but rather in a free play of forces'.[19]

Self-organization, according to one commentator on Schelling, Marie-Louise Heuser, is 'not just an ephemeral, marginal phenomenon in a course of nature which is otherwise determined, but contains the "primal ground of all reality", for mechanisms, (such as that of genetic inheritance) can be created by organising processes, whilst organising processes, on the other hand, cannot arise mechanically'.[20] Nature, then, on the model, in its early stages, evolves unconsciously and then, at a certain stage of development, becomes conscious productivity.

It is perhaps noteworthy that, to my knowledge, while the word 'birth' appears in Schelling's works, commentators have not particularly noted its significance and its value for Schelling's overall system.[21] One reason for its value is that the capacity to give birth, as well as the birthing body, is a natural notion. It is thus consonant with a naturalist reading of Schelling. The capacity to give birth is a natural force that requires no thought on the part of the birthing body. It is, to return to Luce Irigaray, less hylomorphic than a model that has the 'potency' depicted as a soul or an idea. It is less likely, therefore, to picture matter itself as inert.

In a further dimension of this process, I have suggested that Kierkegaard, in CA, adds the evolution of the capacity, in finite beings, for rational thought and the evolution of the freedom to do right and wrong. But there is also, in Constantin Constantinius' *Repetition*, for example, a reference to Leibniz's *Theodicy*,[22] which refers to God's power of creation and to divine activity, which is repeated in individual monads. This directly recalls Schelling's free differentiated beings expressing, through their freedom, the *ungrund*, or the creative potential of the universe.

In Schelling's system of thought, then, 'thought' and 'being' are not divided. Yet ordering in general—willing or unfolding—presupposes something that 'can never be made comprehensible to reason'.[23] This is the longing of the 'one' to give birth to itself.

METAPHORS OF BIRTHING FOR NATURE AS A WHOLE

I would like to begin this section with a comment pertaining to Kierkegaard's appropriation of some of this, which was no doubt intended as an aside, but which seems to me to be crucial and to support some of the claims I would like to make. In his book referred to earlier, *The Philosophy of Kierkegaard*, George Pattison discusses Kierkegaard's view, articulated in CUP, that 'truth is subjectivity'.[24] Pattison, throughout his text, outlines what he describes as Kierkegaard's conception of actuality, in its Aristotelian sense, as containing potentiality or possibility within itself. 'Being a human being', Pattison writes, 'is not, according to Kierkegaard, something we can ever finally actualise'.[25] The world is, as Pattison puts it, 'permeated by temporality or becoming'.[26] Becoming, or possibility, includes 'the leap' of faith. In the context of this discussion of process or becoming, Pattison mentions Schelling and the fact that Kierkegaard attended the latter's lectures in 1841–1842 on 'The Philosophy of Revelation'. He notes that Kierkegaard famously wrote, after attending Schelling's second lecture: 'I am so pleased to have heard Schelling's second lecture, indescribably. . . . The embryonic child of thought leapt for joy within me as in Elisabeth, when he mentioned the word "actuality" in connection with the relation of possibility to actuality. I remember almost every word he said after that. Here perhaps clarity can be achieved'.[27]

Pattison points out that Kierkegaard is referring here to 'the moment in the gospel story when Elisabeth, pregnant with John the Baptist, is visited by Mary, herself pregnant with Jesus. According to St. Matthew's gospel, Elisabeth reports that the moment she heard Mary's voice, the baby in her womb leapt for joy'.[28] Pattison comments: 'Is Schelling then the philosophical Messiah whose prophet Kierkegaard perhaps imagines himself becoming?'[29] But an alternative reading is possible. Is Kierkegaard implicitly conceptualizing the Schellingian 'creation' story, in terms of the 'unprethinkable' giving birth to itself, as the epitome of a process ontology? This would be an ontology that reads both thought and nature as in process; an ontology that sees the active self that each of us can become as itself part of an active nature. It would also be an ontology that reads the free self, the human being attempting to become truly subjective, as attempting to internalize, or 'actualize', to use the Aristotelian terminology, in its freedom, its grounding in the 'unprethinkable'. When Kierkegaard writes in CUP that he wants the subject to be 'infinitely concerned about himself'[30] he must mean that the subject must be concerned with something beyond his or her own finitude. Furthermore, he writes in his *Journals and Papers*, 'It is true in only one sense that a human being owes his existence to the act of procreation; there is also present a creative factor which must be attributed to God'.[31] While he is partly referring to the idea that the human being owes his or her existence partly to God, he may also be referring to God's creative power.

Throughout his works, indeed, Kierkegaard, through his various pseudonyms, emphasizes the first-person nature of faith and the fact, which de silentio particularly stresses in *Fear and Trembling*, that faith is an 'infinitely difficult' task for the individual that, indeed, involves an element of paradox. His own 'present age', he believed, had devalued faith.

Schelling's ontology, as articulated throughout this book and as deployed, as suggested in previous chapters, by Kierkegaard, of an active living nature that extends to the whole, makes some kind of sense of these ideas. Freedom involves recognizing one's own potential to actualize many possibilities, including ethical requirements on the singular individual. It also involves appreciating the grounding of the individual self in an active nature, one that involves many processes of actualization of potentialities, processes that can be metaphorically understood in terms of processes of birthing. In its turn again, it involves recognizing its own ground in the whole. The fall, in initiating the possibility of evil, through, in Schelling's terms, seeing itself as its ground rather than recognizing its ground in the whole, brings about the possibility of the self being cut off from its ground, severed from its source in the whole. Paul Tillich reads the fall in this way.[32]

THE ALTERNATIVE 'DEAD' NOTION OF THOUGHT OR BEING

Kierkegaard, in his doctoral dissertation, *The Concept of Irony*,[33] discusses a text that expresses a version of the 'dead' notion of thought or being. He engages there with Plato's *Symposium*. Kierkegaard notes that Plato writes that those who love the soul love the male sex. Kierkegaard comments:

> In these words there is already an adequate description of the intellectual love that is bound to be present in a people so esthetically developed as the Greeks, where the individuality was not infinitely reflected in itself but instead was what Hegel so significantly calls 'beautiful individuality' in which the conflict in the individuality was not split so deeply as to allow the true love to be the higher unity. But when this intellectual love preferably seeks its object among the youths, it is thereby suggested that it loves possibility but avoids actuality.[34]

In other words, those who love the soul or reason, expressed here in terms of the love of the male sex, are concerned with possibility rather than actuality. Those who love the soul forget the type of love that involves both embodiment and mindedness. Schelling, writing along similar lines, laments the loss of love and life from both 'dead' pantheist theories and from pure idealism. According to Bernard Freydberg, reading Schelling, 'in Plato's *Symposium*, Diotima's teaching of Socrates concludes with an ascent from eros of beautiful bodies to pure, perfect disembodied beauty. So entrancing is this prospect that in the very ascent the soul forgets itself as embodied'.[35] We find a similar theme in Constantin Constantinius' *Repetition*, where we find expressed a contrast between 'recollection' and 'repetition'. Recollection in some way typifies both Constantin's view of the Platonic epistemology that sees the truth as fixed and eternal, and the Hegelian notion of movement that, at least according to Kierkegaard's Hegel (or at the very least his Adler), is characterized in terms of logical relations. The Hegelian notion of 'mediation' does not depict real movement, because it is concerned with a logical relation between concepts. Repetition, by contrast, is a movement of becoming: a movement that is concerned with the future. It seems to me that there is evidence here of Constantin, despite his drawing on the Greeks and his emphasis on the importance of the Greeks, offering a different notion of movement from that of Aristotle. Aristotelian *kinesis* is, as noted previously, a movement from potentiality to actuality, whereas the notion with which Constantin concerns himself is a movement both from potentiality to actuality and from actuality to becoming. In other words, he is concerned with the production process not only from, for example, the seed to the plant, but also from the plant to future plants and to the propagation of the species. Aristotle, of course, was also concerned with these matters, and yet there is no doubt that the ontology he primarily offers is one of substances rather than one of processes. 'When the Greeks said that all knowledge is recollection, they affirmed that all that is has been; when one says that life is a repetition one affirms that existence which has been now becomes'.[36] This directly recalls Schelling's process system wherein the actuality—the mother, to take an example—only becomes an actuality because of its future potentiality. The mother only becomes a mother when she has a child.

Plato's *Symposium* is, of course, more complex on this very matter. The men are taught about love by a woman—Diotima. She, indeed, refers to love as giving birth, in respect to both body and soul.[37]

Yet in *Stages on Life's Way*, a text that is modelled on Plato's *Symposium*, Kierkegaard, through the mouthpiece now of Johannes the Seducer, speaks of woman in a different way from Plato. Woman, he writes, 'pleases me just as she is'.[38] Woman is the most seductive thing, for Johannes, and yet he 'speaks in praise of woman'.[39] Woman and the erotic, for Johannes, represent finitude and change. Woman is a 'power weaker than his own and yet stronger'.[40] Finitude and change, in other words, in the natural world, are preferable to the pretence of autonomy and independence. The gods, Johannes writes, created woman but they did not let her know how beautiful she was. They created her as an innocent being. She is like a 'display fruit'. She is inviting and alluring precisely by being elusive. Woman, then, represents the natural; she depicts the finite and the innocent. Yet Johannes does not have a picture of the natural as inert. Woman, for Johannes, represents a lived body that relates to others. But she also represents a lived body, after the emergence of freedom and with the awareness of sexuality, that emerges from a preexisting nature that is itself living and active.

In *Stages*, Johannes speaks of the gods creating women. In *The Concept of Anxiety*, this metaphor is transformed into a natural process. Woman and man, as free beings, free to do right or wrong, evolved out of a purposive nature. Specifically, the awareness of freedom evolved out of a sexual capacity; the sexuality of a woman, of a being that has a body that can give birth.

Writing on a similar subject, much later than Kierkegaard, Irigaray, in her work *Speculum of the Other Woman*,[41] has suggested that theorizing a body that is capable of birthing can create new ontological possibilities. Moreover, extending Irigaray's thought, if one thinks from the perspective of the foetus, in the prenatal phase of its development, there is no separation between subject and object, subject and world. The prenatal is genuinely a capacity; it is a power. It is the capacity to become an independent self-substance. This capacity, in its turn, is akin to Schelling's 'ground' that gives rise to its consequent, which takes the form of particular beings.

Plato, as Rachel Jones has argued in her reading of Irigaray,[42] by focusing on the eternal Forms as the only true reality, 'displaces our actual beginnings in birth. The ideal "father" of visible offspring supplants birth from the mother'.[43] Physical birth is relegated to the sensible inferior world of becoming, while the soul—freed from the shackles of the body—is 're-born' through the unchanging world of the Forms.[44]

Irigaray writes, therefore, that in a topsy-turvy distortion, the Forms substitute for our maternal origin, and set in train a logic of thinking that is expressed throughout the history of Western philosophy. One of the most extreme expressions of this is in René Descartes, whose thinking self gives birth to itself by means of a process of thought. As many have argued, Descartes does not make a clean break with his Aristotelian heritage; rather, he extends this heritage. Irigaray suggests that the subject, for Descartes, becomes its own 'other' 'in such a way that it gives symbolic birth to itself'.[45] Irigaray borrows from Descartes' *Optics*, and the title of her chapter in *Speculum* on Descartes, 'And if, Taking the Eye of Man Recently Dead', is derived from an experiment in this work.[46]

Rachel Jones,[47] in her powerful reading of Irigaray, traces this picture through Kant's work. Reading Kant, she suggests that, although the subject, for him, is active in constituting knowledge, it must be given the matter of sensation if it is to process this into form. The subject is dependent on this outer matter. Until it is organized by the forms—space and time and the Categories—this matter is chaotic and disorganized. Moreover, nature, for Kant, is specularized. It is nature as 'seen' by the mind. There is a similarity, then, for Irigaray, between Descartes and Kant. Descartes separates the 'thinking I' from any materiality, but so too is the Kantian self constructed against a chaotic matter that it orders into objects.

Kierkegaard's view is very different. The 'sexual', in Johannes' reading referred to earlier, resonates with Maurice Merleau-Ponty's notion of the 'flesh' as the 'lived' body. For Kant, the 'flesh' would no doubt have been 'mere' flesh. But for Kierkegaard, the sexual, or the 'flesh', involves both a relation to a human other and an immersion in the nonhuman natural world. Iris Young[48] and Irigaray[49] have criticized Merleau-Ponty's notion of the flesh partly for failing to recognize sexual difference. Kierkegaard, however, through the mouthpieces of Johannes and Haufniensis, recognizes the power of sexual difference, sexuality, and birth in his metaphysic.

Indeed, there is a further significant dimension here. Irigaray also concerns herself with the *Symposium*. Reading Plato, she reclaims Diotima, from the *Symposium*, the wise woman who teaches Socrates about love. In Irigaray's reading, Diotima sets out to recover the traces of the maternal from Plato's Cave metaphor.[50] This metaphor can be read as suggesting a transcendent reading of the forms, with the cave as the inert matter containing the deceptive world of the senses from which 'man' has to move into the transcendent realm of the Forms—the world of light and truth.

Irigaray seeks to destabilize this version of the Cave myth by demonstrating a blind spot in this reading of the journey of the prisoner en route to truth. As Jones puts it, 'the ideal father of visible offspring supplants birth from a mother. In this way, the horizon of metaphysical thought obscures the more primordial horizon that orients human beings in the world, namely our relationship to our maternal origins'.[51]

No doubt there is more in Plato's works, as many have argued recently,[52] that suggests an immanent reading of the forms. But it is Irigaray who has painted a picture of the morphological resonance between the cave and the womb—*hystera*. Again, as noted by Jones, 'ground, dwelling, cave—all these terms can be read as equivalents of the *hystera*. Men are living in a place shaped like a cave or a womb'.[53] Just as the cave is like a womb, so is the journey from ignorance to wisdom like a birth. But, at the same time, for Plato, according to Irigaray, the Cave metaphor turns the womb into an inert object.

A further dimension, in Jones' reading of Irigaray, is the double meaning of the Greek word *hystera/hysteron*: the men in the cave are chained so that they cannot turn towards the light. *Hysteron*—what is behind—is also what comes later. In Jones' words again, 'what is behind us (spatially) lies ahead (temporally) while that which came first stands before us (spatially) even though it is temporally behind us'.[54] The forms, then, are temporally first but farthest away spatially. This means that the cave is an example of a *hysteron proteron*, which translates as 'putting the cart before the horse'—that which comes later, the shadows, has mistakenly been put up front.

In Kierkegaard's revisiting of the myth, this topsy-turvy account is turned the 'right' way up. Instead of the process of generation being both implicitly in the cave, as womb, and in the 'father' or the form of the Good, the process lies in the natural world—a natural world that is partially conceptualized in terms of a body that can birth.

In *Stages*, Johannes makes some very strong claims about woman in the context of comments about creation. Indeed, he develops a view that can be read both along the lines of Schelling's picture of nature and as sympathetic to Irigaray's outlook. He writes, 'I rejoice that the female sex, far from being more imperfect than the male, is more perfect'.[55] He refers to the 'Greeks telling us' that 'originally there was only one sex; it was the male sex'.[56] Moreover, this comment is made in the specific context of a comment about 'the very famous Limping God [who] formed of earth the likeness of a shy maiden, Pandora'.[57] He writes further that

> necessity teaches even the gods to surpass themselves in inventiveness. They searched and pondered and found. The power was woman, the wonder of creation even in the eyes of the gods a greater wonder than man, a discovery on which the gods in their naiveté could not help congratulating themselves. What more can be said to her honor than that she would be able to do something of which even the gods did not think themselves capable, what more can be said than that she was capable of doing it; how wonderful she must be to be capable of it![58]

Woman, then, is a greater wonder than man, even in the eyes of the gods. She is a greater wonder because she is capable of birth, because she has the capacity or the power to give birth. She is able to do something of which the gods did not even think: she does not need to think about her capacity or her power; it is a capacity or a power she simply has. There may be other ways of reading this passage, but it certainly, in the context, implies a process of creation—the capacity or the power to give birth.

The text, however, changes. The woman becomes an enchantress who is full of deceit, and she casts her spell on man and makes him a prisoner of all the 'prolixities of finitude'.[59] The male seducers are the only ones able to withstand her devilry. Such men place an infinite value on the female 'bait'. Yet Johannes returns, nonetheless, to the idea of woman as 'not exhausted by any woman'.[60] Now his illustrative quotations are from Genesis. Woman is a part of man and yet more perfect than he. Woman is 'finiteness but finiteness raised to the highest power'.[61]

Woman, moreover, contains the forces, the powers, or the capacities to produce another; she is 'a play of forces . . . united in the invisible center of a negative relationship in which she relates herself to herself'.[62] Woman is like Schelling's 'yearning' or the play of forces that constitutes the *ungrund*. The one thing 'she' does not have is the Kantian knowledge that he believed 'mother nature' would have to have in order for her to play the role I am attempting to attribute to her. She does not have knowledge of her power. She is ignorant, innocent, and modest. She is 'but a dream and yet the highest reality'.[63]

It is important that these remarks are made in a context where, according to Thomas Laqueur, the one-sex model of birth was in the process of being challenged. This view, according to Lacquer, was still accepted in the eighteenth century, and it certainly appears that Hegel accepted it.[64] This was the view according to which woman acted merely as the receptacle for the male seed. Given this predominant view of the processes of birth, it is not surprising that Kant was unable to see the capacity, within the female body, to produce another from within itself.

Might this recent change in the view of the role of woman in procreation not have been part of the source of Kierkegaard's wonder at the power of the female body? In the eighteenth century and following the French Revolution, there was considerable debate about sex and procreation, partly motivated by a desire to ascertain whether or not women were suited to be equal to men, as the French Revolution proclaimed.[65]

Moreover, Carl Linnaeus, the botanist, physician, and zoologist, who laid the foundation for modern biological naming, was a major influence on Goethe. The latter, a well-known influence on Kierkegaard, writes of Linnaeus, 'With the exception of Shakespeare and Spinoza, I know of no one among the no longer living who has influenced me more strongly'.[66] Plants, for Linnaeus, had male and female organs. One commentator, George Connell, writes of Kierkegaard that 'much of SUD shows a passion for taxonomy' drawing from Linnaeus.[67] In an entry in his *Journals and Papers*, Kierkegaard writes: 'Even Plato assumes that the genuinely perfect condition of man means no sex distinction'.[68] Given the above comments about woman, one might read it, in a different way from that intended by Plato, as implying instead that an ideal being might be androgynous.

RETURNING TO CA

Returning to CA, we saw, in chapter 5, that Haufniensis writes that woman is 'more anxious' than man, yet the 'greatness of anxiety' is 'a prophecy of the greatness of the perfection'.[69] Woman also is 'more sensuous' than man and 'the proportion of sensuousness corresponds to that of anxiety'.[70] Moreover, Haufniensis introduces her 'under her ideal aspect which is procreation'.[71] Anxiety, he writes, 'is always conceived in the direction of freedom'.[72] Moreover, 'what has often been said about her, that she is the weaker sex, is something entirely indifferent to me'.[73]

Kierkegaard did not develop a relational sense of self by reference to human others, but rather he saw the self as relating itself to itself through the medium of God. For Anti-Climacus, the self is itself only when it is related, in Walsh's words, 'in total dependency to the power that established it'.[74] One can, then, become a self 'only through the relationship to God'.[75]

Yet it is well known that Kierkegaard was critical of many aspects of the established church in his lifetime and also that he was critical of some aspects of what presents itself as Christian belief. So, for example, when it comes to sexuality and the erotic, he chastises some aspects of church teaching. He writes:

> Is a person is to be told every Sunday that he is born in sin and that his mother conceived him in iniquity, and thereupon learn for the poets that their heroines had a naiveté the like of which not even Eve possessed? To my way of thinking this is nonsense, and when for a long time no alarm was raised, this must have been because our time has acquired a remarkable thoughtlessness in relation to what it means to live, and a concern for everything else, especially that which is loudly proclaimed; when each person should be concerned about himself and about transforming his life into a beautiful, artistically finished whole.[76]

He is also strongly critical, in his work *Practice in Christianity*,[77] of the 'Church triumphant' as opposed to the 'Church militant'. The former group believe themselves to be in possession of absolute theological truth—a notion Kierkegaard constantly challenges. Instead, Christianity is a matter for each individual—it is about the subjectivity of each one of us, and about a choice to live and act in certain ways. It stands directly in contrast to the established order.

In the same note, he argues that 'the single individual who is capable of it should apply himself to studies of a scientific nature, but in such a way that such study would have its validation in an education whose ultimate expression is to impress the idea upon his own life'.[78] He mocks the idea that a child is basically wicked. He suggests that a child who is accused of being wicked might 'make fools not only of its parents but of all human speech and thought'.[79] Interestingly, in light of the view I am attributing to him, he compares this to the 'rana paradoxical' (the para-doxical frog) that 'mocks and defies the naturalists' classifications of frogs'.[80] Might he not here be accusing those Christians who insist on believing in the inherent wickedness of a child at birth of denying the process of evolution and of saying something akin to a paradox in the context of his contemporary biology?

Is it not possible, given the above, then, to attribute both views to him—a belief in some kind of transcendent God and a belief in nature in the sense outlined? There would be transcendent power—a longing to give birth to itself—as a metaphor for the ground of nature as a whole or the Absolute. The Absolute would be the whole process, and this process is necessarily incomplete. For God, writes Anti-Climacus, in SUD, 'everything is possible'.[81] This notion of possibility need not entail that everything is simply wide open—there is no restriction on what might happen (although indeed it is this way, as argued in chapter 5, for the individual finite being). Rather, God is that which sets the process in train and, in order to be capable of doing this, God must contain attributes that enable 'him' to ground the rest of nature. This necessarily means that God is a capacity or a power and that the rest of nature shares something of the same characteristics. God would, then, in line with Kierkegaard's de-scription in SUD, be the 'power'[82] that sets the process in motion.

One cannot account for the emergence of one being from its ground, and in its turn that ground from its ground, in a way that suggests onto-logical necessity or epistemic certainty. Indeed, bringing the process to completion, one will arrive at a groundless being or a being that cannot be accounted for in terms of ground and consequent—an 'unprethinkable' being—or in the terms I am using here, a capacity or power that, to quote Schelling again, 'longs to give birth to itself'.

Haufniensis, in CA, writes that 'the sexual as such is not the sinful'.[83] But, he continues, 'in Christianity, though, the religious has suspended the erotic not merely as sinful, through an ethical misunderstanding, but as indifferent, because in spirit there is no difference between man and woman'.[84] When we are concerned, as Haufniensis is in this text, with freedom and the 'generation' of freedom in subsequent individuals, the sexual difference, and the significance of the body that can birth, be-comes apparent. '[A] woman in childbirth is in anxiety'.[85] Haufniensis writes of procreation; he notes the generation of one individual from another: 'In the moment of birth, anxiety culminates a second time in the woman, and in this moment a new individual comes into the world'.[86] Indeed, in the early draft of CA, Haufniensis refers to Johannes the Seducer from *Stages*, writing that 'the seducer's secret is simply that he knows that woman is anxious'.[87]

Haufniensis refers to Luke: 'A perfect spirit cannot be conceived as sexually qualified'.[88] He writes that there is no mention of sexual temptation in relation to Christ, and yet, in contradistinction to those 'dogmatic' Christian views that describe Christ as being without semen, instead Haufniensis writes that he 'withstood temptation',[89] suggesting that Christ is, indeed, human in this respect. He writes, also, of the importance of love, which can lead, in humans, to the forgetting of the sexual and to the transformation of sensuousness into spirit. In these circumstances, he writes, 'anxiety is driven out'.

What Haufniensis is offering here, then, is a process system, beginning somewhere and continuing through generation and procreation. He is also describing, as we saw in chapter 5, the process of the evolution of freedom and the beginnings of the identification of sensuality with sin. This only occurs at a stage in the process of evolution. Initially, sexuality was an innocent power of Eve and Adam, a potentiality in them.

Freedom, returning again to CA, arises in Adam, through his relationship to Eve. In its turn, his anxious capacity to act is brought about through sensuality. Sensuality, for Kierkegaard, is a 'most abstract' idea expressed through music.[90] The sexual contains both spirit and sensuality. The link between the two notions of nature—human nature and the speculative notion—therefore lies in sexuality. It is through the lived bodily experience of sexuality that freedom comes into being for finite beings like us. Freedom, for Kierkegaard, arises out of a speculative nature that preexists the human and human conceptual capacities, but it also stems from a distinctly embodied human capacity.

Moreover, not only Haufniensis, in CA, but also Victor Eremita, in *Either-Or*, recognizes the significance of the act of birth, for the latter begins EO with a reference to this.[91] In CA Kierkegaard, or Haufniensis, writes, directly reflecting the Schellingian-inspired view of human beings outlined above but also making a specific point about woman, 'The creation of Eve outwardly prefigures the consequence of the relationship of generation . . . in a sense, she signifies that which is derived'.[92] 'God is tempted by no-one'.[93]

Freedom is, following Schelling, 'the intelligible essence of each thing, and especially of each human being'.[94] Reason is, for Schelling, no longer disembodied, emasculated from nature. Rather, it reveals itself in nature. Freedom is also, in CA, the intelligible ground of a human being's activity. This intelligible ground, though, is manifested in time, through action. The intelligible ground, moreover, when it manifests itself in human beings, finite limited beings, cannot appear as it would if God manifested 'itself' all at once and in pure form. Rather, God manifests 'itself' or 'himself' in humans at the point at which they are free, or become free, and yet, because they are limited manifestations of the whole, this freedom appears in humans as the possibility of both evil and good. Haufniensis' account of freedom, therefore, unlike that of Kant, allows for the freedom to do good and bad.

The notion of freedom that arises first of all in Eve, moreover, is a conception that allows for the paradoxical notion of the human as the 'infinite in the finite'. The human is finite precisely insofar as he or she is immersed in a natural world; he or she is embodied and exists in time. Yet she also, in the 'instant' (to use David Kangas' word) she becomes free, has the capacity to think about possibilities that may transcend her immediate situation, and these possibilities, at least for some beings like her, include 'actualities' that are paradoxical from the point of view of her own limited finitude. They are paradoxical partially because they reflect the grounding of the person in the *ungrund*. There are Kierkegaardian individuals—Abraham, for example, and the figure of Christ—that exemplify, in a more immediate fashion, the 'paradox'. They encapsulate the limits of finitude and allow, through their dependence on the ultimate ground, which is God, or, I am suggesting here, the 'longing of the one to give birth to itself', for a self whose 'being' or whose processual becoming may be literally incomprehensible from the point of view of certain rational systems of thought. These are the exceptional individuals, who become 'holy wills' not in Kant's fashion, through becoming perfectly rational, but rather through becoming entirely comfortable in the paradoxical character of their nature.

In this chapter, I have begun to articulate the metaphor of the body that can birth, in Kierkegaard's works, as a metaphor for nature as a whole and for the grounding of this nature. I will continue this theme in the following chapter, returning initially to the text of *Fear and Trembling*.

NOTES

1. Søren Kierkegaard, *Notes on Schelling's Berlin Lectures*, in *The Concept of Irony with Continual Reference to Socrates and the Notes*, ed. and trans. Howard V. Hong and Edna H. Hong (Princeton: Princeton University Press, 1989), 401.

2. George F. W. Hegel, *The Science of Logic*, trans. A. V. Miller (New York: Humanity Books, 1969).

3. CUP, 112, his own emphasis.

4. 9.95 CUP, 112. Perhaps this is not actually Hegel's view. Stewart has argued that the real targets here are H. L. Martensen and J. L. Heiberg. See Jon Stewart, *Kierkegaard's Relations to Hegel Reconsidered* (Cambridge: Cambridge University Press, 2003). But Kierkegaard is contesting the view that any kind of starting point is 'given' or logically clear. Whether this applies to an assumed Hegelian starting point, as is supposed here, or a Cartesian one, that begins from knowing the self with certainty, Kierkegaard will challenge the possibility of any of these kinds of starting point.

5. F. W. J. Schelling, *Philosophical Investigations into the Essence of Human Freedom*, trans. Jeff Love and Johannes Schmidt (New York: State University of New York Press, 2006).

6. Schelling, *Philosophical Investigations into the Essence of Human Freedom*, SW 7:350.

7. PF, 30.

8. Schelling, *Philosophical Investigations into the Essence of Human Freedom*, 32, 437–439.

9. PF, 38.

10. F. W. J. Schelling, *Freedom Essay*, SW VII, 359–360, p. 29.

11. Kierkegaard, *Notes on Schelling's Berlin Lectures*, 402.

12. Ibid., 402.

13. Ibid.

14. Immanuel Kant, *Metaphysical Foundations of Natural Science*, ed. and trans. Michael Friedman (Cambridge: Cambridge University Press, 2004).

15. Ibid., 120.

16. Andrew Bowie, *Schelling and Modern European Philosophy* (London: Routledge, 1993), 33.

17. Schelling, *Philosophical Investigations into the Essence of Human Freedom*, 59, VII, 395.

18. F. W. J. Schelling, 'On the World Soul', trans. and with an introduction by I. H. Grant, *Collapse VI: Geo/Philosophy* (6), Urbanomic (2010), ed. R. Mackay, 58–95.

19. Ibid., 56.

20. Marie-Louise Heuser, 'Schelling's Concept of Self-Organization', in *Evolution of Dynamical Structures in Complex Systems*, ed. R. Friedrich and A. Wunderlin, Springer Proceedings in Physics (Berlin/Heidelberg/New York: Springer, 1992), S. 395–415.

21. I would like to mention two of our undergraduate students—Heather Nunney-Boodan and Rosie Massey, *A Feminist Reading of Schelling's Metaphors of Birth* (both graduated in 2012), who carried out, for their UG dissertations, some very interesting work on this. Heather continued this work in her MA dissertation.

22. Gottfried Leibniz, *Theodicy: Essays on the Goodness of God, the Freedom of Man and the Origin of Evil*, ed. Austin Farrer (Chicago: Open Court, 1985).

23. F. W. J. Schelling, *The Philosophy of Art* (Minneapolis: University of Minnesota Press, 1989), 101.

24. CUP, 189.

25. George Pattison, *The Philosophy of Kierkegaard* (Chesham: Acumen, 2003), 41. Kierkegaard's journal entry refers to Schelling's second lecture, Papirer III, A 179, JP, 5355.

26. Pattison, *The Philosophy of Kierkegaard*, 40.

27. CI, xx1–xx11, quoted in Pattison, *The Philosophy of Kierkegaard*, 44.

28. Pattison, *The Philosophy of Kierkegaard*, 44.

29. Ibid.

30. CUP, 130.

31. JP, vol. 1, p. 31, note 78.

32. Paul Tillich, *Systematic Theology*, 3 vols. (Chicago: University of Chicago Press, 1951).

33. CI.

34. Ibid., 192.

35. Bernard Freydberg, *Schelling's Dialogical Freedom Essay* (Albany: State University of New York Press, 2008), 21.

36. Søren Kierkegaard, *Repetition*, trans. Walter Lowrie (New York: Harper and Row, 1964), 149.

37. Plato, *Symposium*, trans. A. Nehamas and P. Woodruff, in *Complete Writings*, ed. J. M. Cooper and T. S. Hutchinson (Indianapolis: Hackett Publishing, 1997), 206b.

38. SLW, 72.

39. Ibid., 73.

40. Ibid., 74.

41. Luce Irigaray, *Speculum of the Other Woman*, trans. G. C. Gill (Ithaca: Cornell University Press, 1985).

42. Rachel Jones, *Irigaray* (Cambridge: Polity Press, 2011), 224; Freydberg, *Schelling's Dialogical Freedom Essay*.

43. Jones, *Irigaray*, 47.

44. It is possible that there are closer connections between my argument here and that of Plato's *Timaeus*. As Barney Riggs has put it, 'the Platonic χώρα, which contains nothing but a "swirling sea of chaos"' (from Plato, *Timaeus*, trans. Donald J. Zeyl [Cambridge: Hackett Publishing, 2000]), bears some resemblance to Schelling's *ungrund*. But, as Riggs also points out, there cannot be an identity between Plato's concept and Schelling's since, at least for the latter, the notion precedes all identity (see Barney Riggs, 'The Surging, Billowing Sea: The Concept of "Beginning" in F. W. J. Schelling's Freiheitschrift and Plato's Timaeus' (essay submitted for undergraduate degree in philosophy, UWE, Bristol, 2014), 19.

45. Irigaray, *Speculum of the Other Woman*, 100.

46. Irigaray, *Speculum of the Other Woman*.

47. Jones, *Irigaray*, 224.

48. Iris Marion Young, *On Female Body Experience: 'Throwing Like a Girl' and Other Essays* (New York: Oxford University Press, 2005).

49. Luce Irigaray, *An Ethics of Sexual Difference*, trans. G. Gill and C. Burke (London: Continuum, 2004).

50. See Rachel Jones' reading of Irigaray on Plato, in Jones, *Irigaray*, chapters 2 and 3.

51. Jones, *Irigaray*, 47.

52. See, for example, the work of Iain Hamilton Grant and also Jeremy Dunham, Iain Hamilton Grant, and Sean Watson, *Idealism: The History of a Philosophy* (London: Acumen, 2011).

53. Irigaray, *Speculum*, 243.

54. Jones, *Irigaray*, 54.

55. SLW, 74.

56. SLW.

57. Ibid., 691, footnote 211.

58. Ibid., 75.

59. Ibid.

60. Ibid., 76.

61. Ibid.

62. Ibid., 77.

63. Ibid., 80.

64. See Tina Chanter, *Ethics of Eros: Irigaray's Re-writing of the Philosophers* (New York: Routledge, 1995), 84–85.

65. Thomas Laqueur, *Making Sex: Body and Gender from the Greeks to Freud* (Boston: Harvard University Press, 1992).

66. Uppsala University, 'What People Have Said about Linnaeus', *Linné On Line*, retrieved 3 October 2011.

67. George Connell, 'Knights and Knaves of the Living Dead: Kierkegaard's Use of Living Death as a Metaphor for Despair', in *Kierkegaard and Death*, ed. Patrick Stokes and Adam Buben (Bloomington: Indiana University Press, 2011), 26.

68. JP, vol. 1, p. 18, note 45.

69. CA, 64.

70. Ibid.

71. CA, 65.

72. Ibid., 66.

73. Ibid.

74. Sylvia Walsh, *Living Christianity: Kierkegaard's Dialectic of Christian Existence* (University Park: Pennsylvania State University Press, 2005), 29.

75. It is important to note, however, as Walsh herself pointed out to me, that, if one carefully reads WL, which preceded SUD, Kierkegaard emphasizes the importance of loving others as neighbours and this being commanded by God.

76. JP, in CA, 192.

77. Søren Kierkegaard, *Practice in Christianity*, trans. Howard V. Hong and Edna H. Hong (Princeton: Princeton University Press, 1991).

78. CA, 193.

79. Ibid., 76.

80. Ibid.

81. SUD, 40.

82. Note that David Wood emphasizes the word 'power' here. In 'Thinking God in the Wake of Kierkegaard', in *Kierkegaard: A Critical Reader*, ed. Jonathan Ree and Jane Chamberlain (Oxford: Blackwell, 1998).

83. CA, 68.

84. Ibid., 70.

85. Ibid., 72.

86. Ibid.

87. Entry from JP, paper V, B 53:26, taken from *Selected Entries from Kierkegaard's Journals and Papers Pertaining to the Concept of Anxiety*, in CA, 189.

88. Luke 20:34–36, in CA, 79.

89. CA, 80.

90. See EO I, 54–56.

91. EO I, 19.

92. CA, 63.

93. Ibid., 64.

94. Schelling, SW, 383.

8

MORE ON BIRTHING

In the previous chapter, I began to derive, from Kierkegaard's writings, a model of a body that can birth, as a metaphor for the whole of nature. This, in its turn, I have been suggesting, is grounded in a process that is not thinkable for us humans, but that can be metaphorically outlined in the language of Friedrich Wilhelm Joseph Schelling in terms of the longing of the one to give birth to itself. This latter, then, may be construed as being both about the beginnings of the world and also the beginnings of Being, or time, itself. I would like, now, to return to *Fear and Trembling*, to continue the story.

Pure evil is, as we have seen, an impossibility for us limited finite beings. But Søren Kierkegaard imagines it, in its extreme form, in terms of the self being grounded in the devil. I would like, in the next section, to discuss the similarities and differences between de silentio's devil, Abraham, and certain female characters in order to illustrate further the significance of metaphors of birthing. I will then move to consider the weaning metaphors deployed in *Fear and Trembling*.

Haufniensis, in CA, as I have suggested in previous chapters, is concerned, in part, with moral evil and with responsibility for wrongdoing. *Fear and Trembling*, 'Problema 3' is also concerned with this issue. De silentio's illustrative examples of characters who exemplify moral evil, in *Fear and Trembling*, are Faust and the merman, from the legend of Agnes and the merman. Faust, like Abraham, although of course he is also very different, 'stand[s] in an absolute relation to the absolute'.[1] The former, in FT as well as in the classic German legend, has made a pact with the devil. Kierkegaard also, in *Practice in Christianity*, describes the 'church triumphant'—the church that simply follows the crowd, that imagines 'it' can know God and that is the church of 'the world'—as one where 'the gates of hell have prevailed'.[2] This could be another direct reference to the probable corruption of Kantian reason.

The Devil and the Divine share this in common, then: each is 'beyond' the universal ethical, the sphere of the spoken word, the realm of Kantian and Hegelian ethics. 'The demonic has that same property as the divine'.[3] Agamemnon, in FT, who represents the universal ethical—who, as the 'tragic hero', is comprehensible within the ethical—must speak.[4] He ought to explain to his wife, Clytemnestra, why he has been forced, by the gods, to sacrifice their daughter, Iphigenia. His actions are comprehensible within a Kantian or, of course, not strictly a Kantian but a Hegelian ethical system. The Hegelian rewriting of the Categorical Imperative removes the purely 'formal' element of it but also removes its 'absolute' content in terms of an approximation to the holy will. Hegel rewrites it as expressing the norms of a particular type of society.

Agamemnon sacrifices his daughter in order to save his people.[5] But Abraham, by contrast, believes 'by virtue of the absurd'. Abraham 'cannot speak'.[6] Abraham 'is sublime'.[7] Close to the sublime, however, is 'madness', and Faust, once he has sold his soul to the devil, is unable to return to the universal ethical—the domain of Kantian autonomy and Kantian reason. Indeed, evil, to reiterate, involves taking oneself as the source of one's norms, as opposed to recognizing this source as lying outside the self. The Kantian rational self becomes an evil self, since it is not possible for limited beings like us to be perfectly rational. Imagining that we are able to be perfectly rational, therefore, is effectively selling ourselves to a devil, since it presupposes something that cannot be perfectly rational setting itself up as though it could become close to this.[8]

Abraham, too, as de silentio puts it, 'offers him [de silentio]' 'a paradox'.[9] Abraham is entirely comfortable in his belief and goes about his daily business, despite being 'in' a paradox. He believes both that God will require him to kill his son Isaac and that he will get Isaac back. He believes that there is an 'infinite power', although he recognizes that he cannot know this power.

Abraham, while he has made the 'double movement' into infinite resignation and then to faith, would be perfectly capable of returning to the ethical. Faust, by contrast, has sold his soul to the devil, and thus he cannot return to the ethical.

Clearly there is a question, which has been much commentated upon in the literature, as to what this all means. There is one commentator on the subject of Abraham whose view I would like to mention. In his excellent guidebook on de silentio's *Fear and Trembling*,[10] John Lippitt mentions a number of different ways, outlined by different commentators on the subject, of reading the characteristics of the knight of faith. After discussing these interpretations, he offers his own view, which is that Abraham simultaneously holds the two beliefs—that Isaac will die and that he will not die. He believes both things simultaneously and continuously. In other words, Abraham does not merely hold these two incompatible beliefs at one moment; rather, the two beliefs 'co-exist at every moment'.[11] Lippitt argues, and here I concur with him, that it is important to take head on that this is what the text is saying, and that any interpretation that refuses this is failing to note the central claim. How, for Lippitt, are the two incompatible beliefs possible? He claims that while the belief that Isaac will die is the belief that 'human reason' dictates, and the belief the evidence supports, 'Abraham's faith is such that he believes the latter'.[12]

It seems to me that this is important. However, I would like to offer an addition to it. It may be that the claim can be read not solely as a contrast between 'reason' and 'faith', with 'faith' effectively lying outside philosophy and 'reason' within it, but rather there may be two different ontological views coexisting here. There may be a way of reading the claim, in other words, that suggests that, from the perspective of the Kantian reasoner, Abraham believes that Isaac will die, but from a different philosophical perspective, one that I am developing here, Isaac will live.

In order to develop this explanation, I should like to return to Kant. Abraham, according to de silentio, expresses 'the sublime in the pedestrian absolutely—that is something only the knight of faith can do—and it is the one and only marvel'.[13]

What might this reference to the sublime mean here? Returning for a moment to Immanuel Kant, and to the Kant of the *Critique of Judgment*, the mathematical sublime, for Kant, is the moment when appearances in nature bring with them 'the idea of infinity. Now the latter cannot happen, otherwise than through the inadequacy of the greatest effort of our imagination in the estimation of an object's magnitude'.[14] In the experience of both the mathematical and the dynamical sublime, the imagination and reason appear to be pulled apart. Imagination, in the case of the mathematical infinite, strives to experience the infinite and ultimately fails; reason desires a whole, a complete idea. 'Our imagination strives to progress towards infinity, while our reason demands absolute totality as a real idea, and so the imagination, our power of estimating the magnitude of things in the world of sense, is inadequate to the idea'. [15] While the two cannot be reconciled in the manner of the harmony of imagination and understanding in the appreciation of beauty, there is nonetheless a form of reconciliation. As Wicks writes, one's imagination is 'brought to a frustrating tread-mill like activity that fails to comprehend the object fully'. [16] The frustration, though, he continues, is 'answered' by reason in its apparent capacity to comprehend infinite totalities. One might hypothesize, then, by analogy, that when he deploys his reason, Abraham believes that Isaac will die, as that is what is dictated by the evidence. But, by stretching his imagination, he could think of Isaac alive and well, at the same time that he knows he will die. This explanation, while plausible, is not quite satisfactory, however, since, on the hypothesis, the two beliefs of Abraham pull apart. Perhaps, then, we can find a better account if we look at the dynamical sublime.

Turning, then, to Kant's notion of the dynamical sublime, he suggests that we experience naturally powerful events—a raging thunderstorm, an erupting volcano—as fearsome, yet when these phenomena are considered from the perspective of our reason, or specifically in terms of the individual acting for a moral purpose, they are made small and the fear subsides. The warrior who has a moral conscience exemplifies a dynamically sublime character for whom nothing stands in his way in carrying out his ideals. [17] It is, indeed, 'man', acting as a moral agent, who is the exemplary manifestation of the dynamical sublime. Using the dynamical sublime as our analogy, we might read the case of Abraham differently. From one perspective he believes he will lose Isaac and he is fearful, but seen from the perspective of his reason, he believes Isaac will live.

In this case, if we view Abraham by analogy with the warrior, we can see him overcoming his fear of losing Isaac and coming to believe he will get Isaac back. Both the fear and the overcoming of it would be continuously present.

Once again, however, this explanation does not yet quite work. Abraham is supposed to have overcome Kantian reason, and yet this explanation would have him using Kantian reason. There is, as I have been suggesting throughout the book, something odd about the suggestion here that it is 'man' following the Categorical Imperative who best exemplifies the sublime. It is precisely, Kant argues, the inability of the human mind to reach pure infinity that characterizes the dissonance between imagination and reason in the case of the experience of the mathematical sublime. He also believes that nature itself is unable to express the ideas of reason: 'It is precisely nature's inadequacy to the ideas'.[18] Yet Kant also suggests that it is the human being, instantiated as the pure exemplification of the moral law, that provides the best illustration of the supersensible aspect of our awareness of the sublime. The human being acting in this manner illustrates the ideal of reason that is stimulated in the feeling of the sublime. Given this reference to the supersensible, though, it is not surprising that, in the end, for Kant, it is not our reason that grounds our morality; rather, it is God. Kant offers a moral argument for God's existence: 'From this so called principle of the causality of the original being, we must think of it not merely as an intelligence and law-giver for nature, but also as the law-giver in general in a moral kingdom of purposes. In relation to the highest good that is alone possible under such a sovereignty, namely the existence of rational beings under moral laws, we can think of this original being as *all-knowing* . . . ; as *all-powerful* . . . ; as *all-good* and at the same time *just*. In this way moral teleology supplements the deficiency of physical teleology and first grounds a theology'.[19]

Kant himself, as I have noted a number of times, rejects the metaphor I have been outlining in this book. Yet Kant is searching for something that grounds both the view of the natural world as seen by reflective judgement in terms of purposes and, also, the self, acting as a moral agent. The metaphor of a body that can birth provides a more consistent view of the teleology for which Kant is searching here. A pure, perfectly rational self, of whatever kind, is not well suited to grounding a teleological natural system. A series of birthing bodies, culminating in a power that 'ejects love', is a better metaphor for this, for it itself exemplifies the very purposiveness Kant is describing, in his account of the experience of teleology and of beauty. Although Kant, as we have seen, ultimately rejects the notion of teleology in nature because he is not persuaded that causal powers in nature are scientific, he nonetheless accepts that living things acting in accordance with plans display a close similarity to living

things that are causes and effects of themselves. When he looks for an
account of the origin of these two notions, he locates the unconditional
ground of the whole in a transcendental or a supersensible source. Kant
argues that, in order to formulate causal laws in general, we need to
regard nature as if it were the result of an intelligent design. The same
applies, indeed, to purposiveness in general:

'It is impossible to conceive or make the purposiveness that must
reside at the basis of even our cognition of the inner possibility of many
natural things comprehensible, otherwise than by representing those
things and their world in general as the product of an intelligent cause (a
God)'.[20] God is both a 'wise being' and a 'cause of things that is distinct
from nature'.[21]

But Kant himself was well aware of the arguments against this that
had been formulated by David Hume in his *Dialogues*.[22] Hume, through
Philo, argues that the argument only proves an architect, not a creator of
the world, and that it is reasoning to a cause on the basis of only one
instance. Moreover, Kierkegaard, in CUP, satirizes the idea of the existence of God stemming from thought alone. 'Existence', he writes, 'is
motion'.[23] Kant's argument, unlike the one Hume is critiquing, is explicitly intended not to be a 'scientific' one. It is supposed to offer an
intelligible ground not for the whole of nature but rather only for the
intelligible aspects of nature and specifically for morality.

Kant is quite explicit here that he is not offering a new proof of the
existence of God that contradicts his refutations of all rational proofs of
God's existence outlined in the *Critique of Pure Reason*. Kant's argument
in CJ is not designed to form such a proof or to show that we know that
there is a God. Indeed, he is clear that we cannot know of God's existence. He rather sets out to outline a presupposition, based on faith, of
morality. The argument is that we must assume God's existence in order
to explain both natural purposiveness and morality. Kant might claim that
he is not committing the error described by Hume for he is reasoning
rather from the moral and free aspects of the natural world and the suppo-
sition of natural purposiveness in the world to the idea of a supreme cause
of this world. But, to reiterate, the argument form is so similar to the one
Hume is critiquing that it is difficult to see how Kant's version can be
exempt from Hume's critique. It is as though Kant believes that, by
labelling his argument as grounded in faith, rather than making a determi-

native and cognitive judgement, he can escape Hume's criticisms. But it is doubtful that he really can.

The model I am suggesting, of a birthing body, grounded in a process of longing to give birth to itself, in contrast to Kant's model, is one that is consistent with the teleology it is setting out to explain: it simply extends the model of self-causation to the whole. It also hypothesizes a power, or a capacity, as the underlying cause, which is, again, consistent with, for example, the power of the tree to produce itself and to produce its species.

To return to Abraham, then, he is sublime, extending Kant's notion in the above fashion, insofar as he knows that he is finite and limited and yet has also transcended his finitude through his belief in an infinite power that, through its power of love, can enable him to find happiness in this world, despite his being required to commit the ultimate sacrifice. Abraham's 'sublimity' lies in the notion that, although he cannot comprehend the infinite power of the ultimate force that gives rise to the world, he is not afraid to believe that it will not be an evil force. Rather, it will be a force of love. Such a force would not require him to lose his son. Isaac, then, to use the words of Giorgio Agamben, may be sacrificed but not killed, and Abraham's power of love for Isaac will remain. Insofar as he is finite and limited and he exists purely as a natural being, Abraham believes that Isaac will die. Insofar, on the other hand, as he recognizes his grounding in a force that cannot be made comprehensible to reason, he believes that he will get Isaac back. He believes both things simultaneously and continuously.

This interpretation, indeed, is not incompatible with the claim that Abraham believes one thing by virtue of his faith and another through the evidence, although it is transposed into his believing one thing through the finitude of his imagination and another through his capacity to see nature in terms of a series of processes of birth.

I should like to add to this by referring once more to David Kangas' reading of *Fear and Trembling*. He writes: 'In various ways the "Problemata" expose a demand upon the subject, an absolute duty, which cannot be formulated as an ethical demand. It is a duty that violates the ethical in that it violates the presuppositions of the ethical: pre-eminently, the notion that the subject is, originally, in possession of it-self'.[24] Kangas continues by suggesting that the subject, any subject now, is not self-positing, or grounded in itself, but is rather, at least in part, constituted by faith. The subject—any subject—is partially grounded in something that cannot be made comprehensible to reason. In a further development, however, Kangas draws attention to a phrase in *Fear and Trembling* that is not often noted or quoted. This is Johannes' claim that the one who has faith 'will give birth to his own father'.[25] Faith gives birth to that from which it is supposed to derive. Kangas suggests that this is a metaphor for the production of time itself. Here he refers to the influence of Meister Eckhart on Kierkegaard. In sermon 22, in the words of Kangas, Eckhart aims at 'thinking the event whereby presence is first given—an origin, but not a principle (or sometimes a principle without principle). . . . He articulates a movement of entering into time as an event, time as birth or becoming, rather than as presence'.[26] Giving birth to one's own father is impossible. It is not logically contradictory, but it is temporally impossible. But (this is now my own interpretation rather than that of Kangas) suppose Kierkegaard is attempting to think, through the story of Abraham, the birth of temporality and of subjectivity. Schelling, remember, suggests that the antecedent, for example the mother, only becomes antecedent at the point at which the consequent—the child, in this case—comes into being. The mother is not a mother until she gives birth to her child. A son, at the beginning of time, cannot come into being unless there are both a mother and a father. But, at the beginning of time, metaphorically, the birthing process—the *ungrund*—must give birth to a father and to a mother. The one who has faith—expressed as Abraham—recognizes his own grounding in something that is not comprehensible to reason. Through faith, then, he reenacts this grounding and accepts it.

Perhaps the story of Abraham, as expounded by de silentio, is itself metaphorically attempting to express this grounding, in terms of a paradox that makes some sense to us finite beings. Imagining Abraham giving birth to his mother and father would make no sense to us as a moral requirement. Transposing this paradox into the one about Abraham and Isaac transforms it into one that almost makes sense to us; it becomes a paradox about loss and gain rather than pure gain. Giving birth to a new mother and father would be pure paradoxical gain. Losing one's son (or daughter) is the most extreme form of loss for us finite beings. Getting him (or her) back again would be pure joy.

We will find further support for this interpretation by examining the 'weaning' metaphors that are offered in *Fear and Trembling*.

WEANING IN *FEAR AND TREMBLING*

Fear and Trembling contains mother-child imagery. In the 'Attunement', there are four narratives of Abraham and Isaac that, according to de silentio, fail to measure up to 'the' Abraham, and yet each one carries out God's command. The description of each of these four 'sub Abrahams', to use Lippitt's words,[27] is followed by an account, variously flawed, of a child being weaned by a mother. The act of birth depicts an enactment of love. Birth ought to be followed by care or nurturing or love. In the cases of the various 'sub Abrahams', however, something goes awry.

Each 'sub Abraham' represents, in Lippitt's words, 'an Abraham whom Johannes considers not to be worthy of the title "knight of faith"'.

The first 'sub Abraham' does not 'conceal from Isaac where this way is leading him'.[28] Isaac pleads for his life and Abraham then changes tack and cries out, 'I am an idolator. Do you believe this is God's command? No, it is my own desire'.[29] When Isaac sees this Abraham's face, 'his [Abraham's] gaze was wild, his mein one of horror'.[30] This Abraham, unlike the true knight of faith, believes that he really will have to kill Isaac, but he does not believe that he will also get Isaac back. The metaphor offered here of the weaning of the child reads as follows: 'When the child is to be weaned the mother blackens her breast, for it would be a shame were the breast to look pleasing when the child is not to have it. So the child believes that the breast has changed but the mother is the same, her look loving and tender as ever. Lucky the one that needed no more terrible means to wean the child!'[31]

The body that can birth has here produced her offspring. Someone must nurture her child—the consequent to her antecedent, to return to the language of Schelling. Here, then, Kierkegaard is deliberately offering a metaphor for the knight of faith in terms of the model of a birthing body, although now from the perspective of the progeny of this birthing body and his or her needs. The metaphor is offered, moreover, in a discussion of the highest point of the system of faith Kierkegaard advances, that of the knight of faith, and what, it is assumed, such a knight requires in order to be such.

Edward Mooney and Dana Barnea write, 'The scene on Moriah horrifies us. A degree of that horror leaks down to the weaning. The scene on Moriah is momentous. A degree of that momentousness leaks down to the weaning. If faith is measured by a mother's compassionate weaning then by osmosis that tenderness rises up and the intensity of Moriah is lowered a notch'.[32] Mooney and Barnea further write that the weaning metaphors make the events on Moriah, because of the implied love that must be present, somehow less horrific but, in its turn, the weaning itself, with a blackened breast, becomes more horrific.

Mooney and Barnea's comments are important. The events on Moriah are, indeed, horrific. But it is important to remember that not one of the 'sub Abrahams' is the real Abraham, as described by de silentio.

The second 'sub Abraham' is joyless. He carries out everything that God requires of him, but he becomes 'old'. He loses his happiness in life. 'Abraham's eye was darkened, he saw joy no more'.[33] The weaning metaphor here is of a mother who covers her breast, so the child 'no more has a mother'.[34] The very young child needs its mother. A process system in the terms I have been describing requires processes of birth, but also processes of ensuring that the offspring of the various births are cared for and nurtured.

It is very important to note that each of these two 'sub Abrahams' has done exactly what Abraham was required to do by God. Neither disobeyed the injunction. But, on the other hand, neither of these corresponds to the knight of faith. Being sublime, and acting in accordance with the absurd, as 'the' Abraham does, requires that someone care for each body that has been born. Indeed, the whole living system, culminating in the *ungrund*, needs to be cared for and nurtured, and each offspring, if it requires this, must be ready to be moved off the breast. The true Abraham is comfortable and happy in this life, believing both that he will be required to kill Isaac—the manifestation of the u*ngrund* in him— and that he will get Isaac back. This Abraham would be metaphorically one where the breast is full of milk and available to the child and then, when the child is ready, he or she will be weaned from it.

The third 'sub Abraham' has Abraham believe that his duty to Isaac overrides his love for God, so that he appears to remain a tragic hero, in the Kantian or Hegelian ethical sphere. The third weaning metaphor sees the mother suffer sorrow at the loss of her child from the breast so that they grow apart. Finally, in the fourth case, Isaac loses his faith. In the corresponding weaning metaphor, the mother has solid food available. De silentio writes, 'Lucky the one who has more solid food at hand'.[35] The weaning process here results in solid food, but the question is, what if there is no solid food available?

To reiterate, each of these characters representing Abraham is prepared to go through with God's command. Each of them is prepared to
draw the knife and do as God requires. Yet none of them represents 'the'
knight of faith. None of them really encapsulates what it is about Abraham that makes him so great. Therefore, it follows, of course, that none of
the above weaning metaphors represents what weaning really ought to be
about. Johannes does not offer a weaning metaphor for 'the' Abraham
perhaps because it ought to be obvious to us what each of the above
descriptions leaves out.

Clearly no mother weaning her child in a loving and caring way will
blacken her breast. Nor will she cover her breast or sorrow in such a way
that she and the child grow apart. Each of these mother/child pairs lacks
something of the love that is and ought to exist between a mother and her
weaning child. The fourth metaphor lacks something as well: the emphasis is simply on the solid food. The child, in this scenario, has plenty of
food and so no longer 'needs' the breast. But there does not appear to be
the loving care that is required to make the child feel at home in this new
state of enjoying solid food *while continuing to enjoy the mother*. In other
words, just as 'the' Abraham believes 'the paradox' that he will lose Isaac
and get Isaac back, so, too, in the case of an ordinary loving relationship
between mother and child, will the child lose her mother (her mother's
breast) and also get her mother back (her mother's love).

Can we not, in the light of this reading of the weaning metaphors, see
the story of Abraham and Isaac as being at least in part about the love
between a father and a son? Every parent-child relationship involves
transformation and continued loss—from the loss of the breast for both
child and parent, through the first mornings spent away from the parent,
to the point where the child becomes fully an adult. None of these stages
is anything like the requirement God places on Abraham. Yet they depict
the power of love. The love between parent and child transcends the
losses experienced at each stage. The love for a child, in a sense, represents a love of a continuity of the family, and a reaching back into the
past, to past generations. The love a parent feels for his or her child
transcends the relationship between the two people.

Of course this cannot be all that the story tells. *Fear and Trembling* is
about faith in God. Yet the weaning metaphors, combined with the birthing body metaphor for the whole, allow us to give an account that makes
sense of the text. It makes sense, in the ways outlined above, of what is

meant by 'paradox' and it brings in the power of love—a vital Kierke-gaardian trope—in a range of ways.

Is it not plausible to suggest, furthermore and additionally, that while these metaphors speak in part about Kierkegaard's relationship to Regine Olsen,[36] the 'mother' here represents God, the breast, Abraham, and the baby, Isaac? If it were so, would it not make sense to suggest that the 'mother' also represents the Schellingian 'yearning' of the one to give birth to itself? The yearning, here, would have been altered and would be represented in terms of a body, rather than a capacity or a power. Yet the metaphor clearly concerns one who has just recently given birth and whose body is depicted in terms of its powers—its power to give birth and its power to care for the baby. The metaphors are offered, after all, in the context of a discussion of various representations of the knight of faith, each of whom fails fully to carry out his role.

These weaning metaphors seem to me to be, as Mooney and Barnea note, although in different ways than I, highly significant both for the message of *Fear and Trembling* and for Kierkegaard's authorship as a whole. Yet they are rarely mentioned in the voluminous body of com-mentary on Kierkegaard. Is the reason for this, perhaps, as Mooney and Barnea put it, that 'to talk of beginnings, of birth, is to talk of women, wombs and nursing and many have thought that these are hardly fit topics for philosophical discussion'?[37]

In *The Sickness unto Death*, its author, Anti-Climacus, claims the self to be a reflexive relation between the infinite and the finite. The human being is able to understand itself as a relation that encompasses this relation between the infinite and the finite. The finite self, relating this now back to Abraham, is the self that is comfortable and happy in the finite world. But this self is already different from a Kantian reasoner, for the latter thinks ontologically in terms of substances with properties and in terms, as we have seen, of time as a series of separate 'nows'. Such a reasoner, at least the Kantian reasoner of the first *Critique*, thinks in terms of causal powers that are separate and distinct from their effects, and he further thinks in terms of a causally determined world. The Kierkegaar-dian finite self, by contrast, is a temporal self, where its present, in the fashion outlined earlier, contains elements of past and future. It is a self that is inseparable, given the Schellingian influence, from its ground. For example, the child is dependent upon its mother, or the being that gave birth to it. The 'mother' only, however, becomes a mother at the point where her consequent has come into being. So the 'finite' natural Abraham is in nature in a different sense from that in which the Humean billiard ball is 'determined' to move off (barring a change in the course of nature) when it is hit by another ball.

The infinite aspect of the self can also be construed in a number of ways—the mind is free to think about a range of possible norms or possible futures. We can also imagine a God making a demand on us that we may find unfathomable, if only because we cannot fully comprehend the infinite. If we think, though, that the infinite, as well, is conceived somewhat differently from the way in which Kant sees it, then the apparently contradictory beliefs of Abraham are themselves seen in another light. For Schelling, a claim such as 'The body is a body', as we have seen, is a claim that the subject grounds the predicate. Additionally, for him, to say, for example, that freedom is grounded in necessity means that freedom is grounded in a natural world that contains necessity. It is grounded in a nature that precedes it, but that itself is ultimately ungrounded. The finite self is grounded in something outside it—it is grounded in a nature that precedes it—so the self in its finitude does not fully comprehend its environment; it does not understand the demands placed upon it. There is not, then, in this reading, such a stark contrast between the infinite and the finite. Abraham believes that he will have to kill Isaac—this is a belief that is grounded in his immediate surroundings, which include the influence of Kantian modes of reasoning. But he also believes that will get Isaac back, and that belief is grounded ultimately in a being that 'ejects love'.

The figure of the devil, by contrast, who forgets his grounding in an infinite and ultimately incomprehensible source, and takes himself as his ground, effectively becomes confused. It is not accidental that it is the figure of Faust that de silentio chooses as an illustration of pure evil. Faust illustrates the confusion into which a self that attempts to be pure evil is led. Faust seeks to become the Kantian rational will, or the 'holy will'; he seeks to be all-knowing and all-powerful. But this, to reiterate earlier points, is impossible for us finite limited beings, and he thus becomes confused and unable to speak. Yet even Faust, for de silentio, despite being the 'supreme doubter' has still preserved his 'love for humanity'.[38] Kant himself, paradigmatically, of course, is the philosopher who illustrated the impossibility of being 'all knowing'. Yet, as I have illustrated throughout this text, when the self acts as a moral agent, for

Kant, matters are different. Here, the self seeks to approximate the holy will.

The other characters described by de silentio—the merman, for example, from the legend of Agnes and the merman—fail to exemplify pure evil in the way Faust does. The merman appears to be a pure Don Juan character engaged in the seduction of Agnes. Yet he falls in love with her and he cannot exemplify pure seduction.

Faust and the female characters, Sarah and Marie, for example, are like Abraham in the respect that they do not express the imaginary, Kantian rational, autonomous self. They rather express the finitude of human beings, their grounding in nature, specifically in the nature I have been outlining in this book. Marie loves passionately and yet she knows that her love is a perception that thought cannot think. Her passion cannot be expressed in terms of the Kantian reasoner. But she, unlike the reasoning autonomous character, is closer than he is to Abraham, to the sublime. These various characters, then, while each of them is 'outside' Kantian or Hegelian reason, are nonetheless not equivalent. Abraham, in FT, is happy in this life, at the same time that he is aware that he is living a 'paradox'. He 'admits the impossibility and at the same time believes the absurd'.[39] Sarah, though, expresses, for de silentio, a 'higher' level of morality than the devil. As we have seen, de silentio notes that if she had been a man, she would have been a devil.

In the twentieth century, Victor Frankl kept himself alive and happy in the concentration camps through the power of his love for his wife. Love, he wrote, 'goes far beyond the physical presence of the beloved. It finds its deepest meaning in his spiritual being, his inner self. I did not know whether my wife was alive, and I had no means of finding out; but at that moment it ceased to matter'.[40] Frankl did not mind whether or not his wife was actually alive. It was his love that mattered and this kept him going. Similarly, Abraham loves Isaac and his love for Isaac enables him to be happy in this world. This love, I am suggesting, is grounded in a power that is itself a power of love—the yearning of the one to give birth to itself or the power of love.

Isaac, therefore, returning to Agamben's language, is radically different from those humans reduced to 'bare life' who can be killed but not sacrificed.

Abraham is comfortable in his version of the paradox, and, moreover, it is perfectly possible for him to return to the position of the tragic hero—to the 'universal ethical', represented by Kantian or broadly Hegelian ethics. Faust, by contrast, cannot return to the ethical. There is a direct reference to Kant's position here—Kant, too, argues that once a person has sold his soul to the devil, he cannot return to the ethical. Yet while for Kant, the respective 'grounds' of good and evil are radically separated, by contrast, in Kierkegaard's account of God and 'its' grounding, in the reading I am offering, they are not separated. The ground of the whole of nature, God, is, I am suggesting, at least partly conceptualized in terms of a body that can birth—and this, in turn, is conceptualized in terms of some 'groundless ground'.

Abraham stands outside the domain of Hegelian 'reason'. He is not able to explain, in a fashion that would be comprehensible to the Hegelian, why he acted as he did. But this is ultimately, as I have noted, because, according to Kierkegaard, one cannot explain truly moral behaviour in these terms. Truly moral behaviour is grounded in something that remains incomprehensible to the finite rational self, and that therefore cannot be expressed in the terms of that rationality. There is no doubt that Kant himself recognizes this, in his *Critique of Judgment*, when he writes about the ultimate grounding of morality in God, in a God who is exemplified, in Kant's terms, through the ultimate expression of beauty for beings like us, which is the person acting perfectly as a moral agent. While I think Kierkegaard would argue that it is not possible to act morally if this is conceived, as we have seen, in terms of a rational law, Kant's ultimate grounding of this law in God suggests that he too recognizes this.

SOME POSSIBLE CRITICAL REACTIONS TO THIS

I would like, at this point, to consider some possible criticisms of the view I have been attributing to Kierkegaard. There will, of course, be many more criticisms, some of which will not have occurred to me. However, there is a particular set of responses I would like discuss. I mentioned earlier that there have been some critical reactions to Luce Irigaray, in particular. Irigaray herself, in response to Maurice Merleau-Ponty's notion of the 'flesh'—his conception of the feature that connects the mind to the body—has argued that implicit in his notion is a concept of a birthing body. Like Kierkegaard, Merleau-Ponty, in his work *The*

Visible and the Invisible,[41] notes the role of embodiment in perception and experience. Body and mind are not, for him, separable. It is 'flesh' for him that both interlinks body and mind and constitutes the visibility of things outside the embodied self. Irigaray, however, argues that Merleau-Ponty remains in thrall to a visual model of the subject's relation to the world.[42] She further argues that Merleau-Ponty fails to acknowledge the role of the maternal body that is implicit in his thought. According to Irigaray, what is not visible is the origin of the human that takes place in the womb. In a gesture to the view I have been articulating here, she claims that the eye must be created in order for it to do its work of seeing the world.

Judith Butler, however, has argued that focusing, in the way I have been, and in the way Irigaray does, on the role of birthing in the female body does not offer a neutral description of a biological process, but rather imposes on women a norm.[43] Through doing this, it effectively ostracizes those women who do not choose to or who cannot give birth. Furthermore, it leaves no room for 'inter-sexed' people. I have not, in this work, considered the view that there are more than two sexes. However, I do not think that the claims made here, while they have been metaphorically associated with women, need fall foul of Butler's objections. The notion of the body that can birth is a metaphor and one that need not be associated with any particular sexed body. It is an image that shapes a perspective of nature as living and active. It is, I have been suggesting, associated, in Kierkegaard's conception, with the bodies of women, but the connection between the two is contingent and it could be otherwise. The metaphor derives from a facet of some women's bodies. But it need not imply that all females can or do give birth, nor that birth must be associated with female bodies. Furthermore, there need not be a claim to the effect that all bodies must be divided between male and female.

Furthermore, it seems to me important to accept, contrary to Butler's view, that there are biologically female and biologically male bodies. There is a tendency in her work and in that of other recent feminists influenced by postmodern and poststructuralist theory[44] to deny the biological and the natural altogether. Furthermore, as Lena Gunnarsson[45] and Carrie Hull[46] have pointed out, Butler's claim that 'a good 10% of the population has chromosomal variations that do not fit neatly into the XX-female and XY-male categories'[47] has strong affinities with positivism insofar as it assumes 100 percent accuracy in the prediction of categories.

Moreover, as Elisabeth Grosz[48] has forcefully argued, in her defence of Irigaray, sexual difference is of a different ontological order from other differences. Sexual difference is that from which the transition from nature to culture is effected. Irigaray, Grosz argues, does not downplay differences of sexual orientation, of class or race; rather, she suggests that each of these simply functions in a different manner both from all of the others and from sexual difference itself. Sometimes oppression arising from race or from sexual orientation will prevail over any form of oppression arising from other differences. But this does not detract from the fact that sexual difference is fundamental in a way that none of the other forms of difference are—humans share with other living forms some form of sexual differentiation, and sexual differentiation is vital for the reproduction of the human race.

It is also important to note that the category of 'inter-sectionality'[49] that has widely taken hold in the feminist movement may itself downplay the biological domain. There was significant political motivation for the introduction of the term. Feminists were setting out to counter the 'heteronormativity' of the claim that 'all' women experience oppression in similar, if not identical, ways. One difficulty with the expression 'inter-sectionality', however, is that if it is read as suggesting that women are not simply women, but are also black, white, rich, poor, heterosexual, or homosexual, it is clearly true, and each dimension is significant in its own way. But it may be difficult to ascertain which of these differences is to count as an 'inter-sectional' value. How do we determine which are to count? It is also important not to deny that there are biological categories as well as social ones. The biological and the social may indeed interconnect and the social may shape and influence the biological. However, it is important, I have been arguing in this book, not to lose sight altogether of the natural and the biological and, indeed, to note the foundational character of the biological.

None of the claims I have been making in this book can be conclusively proven in the sense that, for example, the verificationists or indeed some Kantians would want. I have been suggesting that what counts as nature, in particular, can itself be understood by means of a metaphor, but one that does not entail that biological and natural entities and powers are not really existent.

In this chapter, I have, through a couple of readings of the text of *Fear and Trembling*, continued the argument of the previous chapter, that it is possible to read at least some of Kierkegaard's texts in terms of a model of a body that can birth. Of course none of this represents conclusive evidence that Kierkegaard believes in the view I am attempting to ascribe to him, any more than it represents conclusive evidence that the view is right. Yet the above suggests (i) that Kierkegaard believes in a process system; (ii) that he does not think it appropriate to describe this process in 'logical' terms but rather in terms that make reference to 'actuality'; (iii) that there is evidence that 'woman' is, in some way, superior to 'man'; and (iv) that there are many references to the power of procreation and to birth. This in no way amounts to conclusive proof, but it does at least offer food for thought, and it suggests that the hypothesis I am proposing makes sense of many of Kierkegaard's remarks, across a range of his texts.

NOTES

1. Søren Kierkegaard, *Practice in Christianity*, ed. and trans. Howard V. Hong and Edna H. Hong (Princeton: Princeton University Press, 1985).
2. Kierkegaard, *Practice in Christianity*, 224.
3. FT, 123.
4. Ibid.
5. Ibid., 87.
6. Ibid., 137.
7. There are a number of different interpretations of the meaning of this. For example, Anthony Quinn ('Kierkegaard's Christian Ethics', in *The Cambridge Companion to Kierkegaard*, ed. Alistair Hannay and Gordon C. Marino [Cambridge: Cambridge University Press, 1998], 349–375) argues that the absurdity refers to the contrast between religious duty and ethical obligation. Quinn argues for a divine command interpretation of Abraham's position, where God's command is placed higher than Abraham's paternal obligation. However, this interpretation is contested by others, including Evans (C. Evans, *Kierkegaard's Ethic of Love* [Oxford: Oxford University Press, 2004]), who argues that it is not Abraham's willingness to draw the knife that is absurd, but rather his belief both that he will be required to kill Isaac and that he will get him back.
8. The epitome of this is, again, Hannah Arendt's description of Eichmann, who substitutes faith in the Fuhrer for belief in the Categorical Imperative (see Hannah Arendt, *Eichmann in Jerusalem: A Report on the Banality of Evil* [Harmondsworth: Penguin, 2006]). Indeed, Kierkegaard is seen to be prescient here in that he noted that the one who has sold his soul to the devil is condemned to

silence, just as those who witnessed some of the horrors of Auschwitz became incapable of speech. See, for example, the words of Susan Sontag (Sontag, *On Photography* [Harmondsworth: Penguin, 2008]).

9. FT, 63.

10. John Lippitt, *The Routledge Philosophy Guidebook to Kierkegaard's Fear and Trembling* (London: Routledge, 2003).

11. Ibid., 74.

12. Ibid., 70.

13. FT, 70.

14. Kant, CJ, 112.

15. CJ §25, 106.

16. Robert Wicks, *Kant on Judgment* (London: Routledge, 2007), 103.

17. Kant, CJ, paragraph 28.

18. Kant, CJ §29, 124.

19. Kant, CJ §86; Wicks, 246.

20. Kant, CJ §87, 338–339; Wicks, 224.

21. Kant, CJ §88, 348.

22. David Hume, *Dialogues concerning Natural Religion and Other Writings* (1779), ed. D. Coleman (Cambridge: Cambridge University Press, 2007).

23. CUP, 312.

24. David Kangas, *Kierkegaard's Instant: On Beginnings* (Bloomington: Indiana University Press, 2007), 159.

25. FT, 57.

26. Kangas, *Kierkegaard's Instant*, 151.

27. See Lippitt, *The Routledge Philosophy Guidebook*, 22.

28. FT, 45.

29. Ibid., 45–46.

30. Ibid., 45.

31. Ibid., 46.

32. Edward Mooney and Dana Barnea, *Birth and Love in Fear and Trembling and the Symposium* (website, dated Sunday, 1 December 2013, accessed 21 May 2014), 6.

33. FT, 46.

34. Ibid.

35. Ibid., 48.

36. Regine Olsen was the young woman with whom the young Kierkegaard was initially infatuated. They became engaged. After a period of engagement, Kierkegaard broke it off. Regine was devastated. Kierkegaard set about trying to make her hate him.

37. Mooney and Barnea, *Birth and Love*, 2.

38. FT, 134.

39. FT, 77.

40. Victor Frankl, *Man's Search for Meaning* (Boston: Beacon Press, 2006), 38–39.

41. Maurice Merleau-Ponty, *The Visible and the Invisible*, trans. Alphonso Lingis (London: Routledge, 1962).

42. Irigaray Luce, *An Ethics of Sexual Difference*, trans. Carolyn Burke and Gillian C. Gill (London: Athlone Press, 1993).

43. Judith Butler, 'Gender as Performance: An Interview with Judith Butler', interviewed by Peter Osborne and Lynne Segal, *Radical Philosophy* (1994), 32–39.

44. As I argued in my book *Enlightened Women* (Alison Assiter, *Enlightened Women* [London: Routledge, 1996]).

45. Lena Gunnarsson, *The Contradictions of Love: Towards a Feminist Ontology of Sociosexuality* (London: Routledge, 2014).

46. Carrie Hull, *The Ontology of Sex* (London: Routledge, 2006).

47. Judith Butler, *Gender Trouble* (London: Routledge, 1990), 137.

48. See Elisabeth Grosz, *Becoming Undone: Darwinian Reflections on Life, Politics and Art* (Durham and London: Duke University Press, 2011).

49. See, for example, Nira Yuval-Davis, *The Politics of Belonging* (London: Sage, 2012).

9

NATURE AS A BODY THAT CAN BIRTH

In this chapter, I will suggest that the metaphor of birth for the whole of nature, in particular, not only can be applied to Søren Kierkegaard's thought but also has much to recommend it in its own right. In order to make this point, I will draw on contemporary biology.[1]

I would like to begin by responding to the claim that any such view anthropomorphizes nature or the whole in a way that is impossible, following and extending the arguments of Martin Heidegger and Emmanuel Levinas, among others. This latter kind of argument takes the following form: Limited finite beings experience the whole as in some sense undetermined. For Levinas, all we can say about Being is that it is an 'il y a' or a 'there is'. To conceive of the whole in an anthropomorphic manner may indeed be to remain trapped in what G. W. F. Hegel calls a 'bad infinity'—an infinity that is conceptualized as the negation of finitude. Hegel writes about this notion in *The Science of Logic*:

> The infinite, however, is held to be absolute without qualification for it is determined expressly as the negation of the absolute. . . . But even so, the infinite is not yet really free from limitation and finitude; the main point is to distinguish the genuine Notion of infinity from the bad infinite, the infinity of reason from the infinity of the understanding.[2]

The model of a series of birthing bodies, if it could be imagined as extending to infinity, would constitute a 'bad' infinity because genuine infinity could only be conceptual, a complete idea of reason. The concept, for example, of a perfect circle would be an example of a 'good infinity'.[3]

Moreover, if the ultimate 'being' or process is to give rise to beings that are themselves in process, if it is to give rise to beings that are incomplete, then, so the argument runs, the whole must contain, within itself, this possibility. Levinas[4] reasoned along these lines, with his *il y a* that grounds beings. According to one critic of Levinas' notion of the whole, Michael Lewis, however, even Levinas' conception is incapable of making sense of a self that is capable of freedom—a being that can never be 'complete', one that is never whole and unified. As Lewis puts it, 'the fact that the ego has a limit compels it to doubt the limitlessness of its understanding'.[5] This is not only a point, it is claimed, about our understanding of Being, but also about Being itself. Death constitutes, in Heideggerian terms, 'my own otherness'. Describing the 'grounding' of free beings who have limited understanding presupposes a whole that is somehow 'lacking'. There is no complete whole. Being in the ultimate sense contains a void. According to this reasoning, then, the whole must contain a void within itself. Levinas' *il y a*, in spite of his apparent move away from this, according to his critics, is a generalized expression of anonymous Being. This, as Stella Sandford has argued, 'sees the return . . . to a certain Platonism'.[6]

Another way of expressing the claim that the whole is imperfect is to argue that thinking of a perfect whole presupposes an absolute non-situated intelligence and, since God is dead, there is no such intelligence. There is nothing outside the whole. Whatever it is upon which beings are grounded must be situated within beings and not outside them.[7] Lewis[8] argues that, at least for the early Heidegger, this 'otherness' that is both within beings and outside them is nature. Humans are unable to conceptualize such a domain, however, as they cannot step outside their own frameworks and view them from the outside; they cannot conceptualize this natural ground other than as a 'lack', a 'void' in their own being. This can only be revealed through, in Derrida's language, the 'trace' or the 'non presence of the other inscribed within the sense of the present'.[9] Being as a whole, then, is not whole but incomplete and thus capable of radical transformation.

In a differently conceived critique of the notion I am proposing, Slavoj Žižek argues, as we saw in the first couple of chapters, that Kierkegaard rejects Friedrich Wilhelm Joseph Schelling's descriptions of a God that has 'moods and states' for one of 'absolute transcendence of whom no anthropomorphic predicates can be applied'.[10] Žižek claims that Kierkegaard rejects and indeed ironically satirizes such a notion. [11] On the other hand, however, in a wonderfully ironic piece, Kierkegaard writes, 'Julius Muller said it very well. "By creating man, God theomorphizes—precisely therefore man does not anthropomorphize when he supposes God as a being resembling man."' [12]

In a significant recent addition to this kind of view, Michael Burns has argued that Kierkegaard prefigures dialectical materialism, in his emphasis upon the ontological openness of reality. [13]

AN ALTERNATIVE

It seems to me, however, extending the arguments of the first chapter, that to conceive of the whole as containing a void, a 'lack', or a paradoxical 'nothing' may be to remain within a 'conceptual' form of thought that excludes embodiment. It may be, despite claims to the contrary, in some way still to focus on mental characteristics. Beings are no longer minds 'looking out' at a static world, and yet the perspective may assume rather mobile embodied thought that 'sees' or 'experiences' the world from multiply moving perspectives. In some complex fashion, however, it remains a mind. The finitude of being, in the above model of the whole or Being, is conceptualized in terms of incompleteness. A metaphysic of 'becoming' is contrasted with one of substantiality. The metaphysic of becoming, in this view, can only be conceptualized in terms of 'lack'— the lack of a completely formed whole. Being as a whole must either be complete—a whole self-sufficient substance—or the negation of this—a lack, an incomplete whole.

Is it not possible, moreover, to regard the approach that sees the whole as a lack or as chaos as the inverse of Kantianism? Unless it is organized by the categories and by the forms of space and time, Immanuel Kant's matter is chaotic, fearful, and unlimited in its power. So fearful, indeed, is Kant of the power of this matter that he dreams up ever more layers of ordering—there must be the imagination which schematizes the categories, and then, in turn, there are judgements of beauty, which unify and harmonize the powers of imagination and understanding. [14]

But what if the metaphysic of becoming challenges this dualism? What if there is a different way of conceiving the whole that presupposes neither a whole self-sufficient 'thing' nor a void or an inchoate 'something'? What if it presupposes 'something' that is neither 'some thing' nor 'no thing'? Perhaps, by contrast, the 'whole' can be genuinely conceptualized in terms of a living, organic process. Perhaps this whole has a 'beginning' that is neither Being, conceived as Substance, nor Nothing, nor is it chaos.

Moreover, we can find, in Kierkegaard's writings, or at least in the work of Victor Eremita, in *Either-Or*,[15] a specific criticism of the Hegelian notion of infinity described in the opening paragraph of this chapter. In his work *A Few Words about the Infinite*, which appeared in 1828, Johan Ludvig Heiberg defended a Hegelian notion of infinity against what he, following Hegel, called a 'bad infinity'. Heiberg refers to the first stage of being—positive being. This is the notion articulated in common sense when it conceptualizes determinate things considered to be self-sufficient substances. But, Heiberg argues, a thing needs a restriction if it is to be determinate. Absolute Being and Absolute non-Being are equivalent. A limit of this takes any two things to be indifferent to one another. This goes on ad infinitum and is equivalent to a bad infinity.

Good infinity, by contrast, sees each thing as interrelated with every other. And ultimately each is united with every other in a deep speculative unity of the concept.

In EO, however, Eremita suggests that there are aspects of this that confuse ethics and logic. He appears to be suggesting that those who read Hegel as suggesting a movement of spirit towards a speculative unity of the concept negate a crucial aspect of lived experience. There is, in fact, always a remainder, in everything that is experienced. We can neither know nor be united with God nor with the infinite. The life of the aesthete is in some fashion determined, just as the movement of spirit in some versions of Hegelian mediation is determined. Judge William argues that the aesthete 'bears a strange resemblance to the pet theory of the newer philosophy, that the principle of contradiction is annulled. You mediate contradictions in a higher madness, philosophy mediates them in a higher unity. At this point you are united with the philosophers. What unites you is that life comes to a stop'.[16] Kierkegaard, or at least some of his pseudonyms, challenges both the Fichtean 'absolute I' and the Hegelian infinity. In CI[17] Kierkegaard, in the section on Johann Gottlieb Fichte, argues that Fichte's 'infinite I' is always an absolute negative infinity, lacking both finitude and content. The Fichtean 'I', according to Kierkegaard in CI, remains in the Cartesian framework insofar as it attempts to posit the world from its perspective, whereas in fact there is always something prior to the process of self-reflection.

BODY THAT CAN BIRTH AND BIRTHING METAPHORS

The model of processes of birthing as well as a body that can birth challenges this dualism of Being/Chaos. A body that is capable of birthing is one that can produce another from within itself. The other that is produced can, in some cases, itself be capable of conscious thought. The process of giving birth is a natural one that takes place without conscious thought. The capacity, in its turn, is a force or a power. The metaphor for this process, I have been suggesting, in Kierkegaard's work is the body of the woman and the capacity or the power possessed by this body. This process suggests neither a whole self-sufficient substance à la Aristotle nor the inverse of such a substance—a paradoxical, chaotic 'core'. The model that conceptualizes the whole either in terms of a 'whole thing', as a thing containing a void, or as itself a void is one of a pair of oppositions, albeit an opposing pair that incorporates paradoxicality. So infinity is conceived either as in opposition to finitude—the bad infinity—or as an infinity that, paradoxically, incorporates finitude within itself. But suppose there is another possibility—that these ways of thinking fail properly to register corporeality and the capacity of certain bodies to give birth. This alternative way of thinking would not solely register birth as an indicator of the perspectival nature of a person's thinking and as an indicator of finitude, but would offer an alternative model of process, the process of one being emerging out of another. Moreover, it can be used as a metaphor for the whole of nature. The way I have been deploying the notion in this book, it does not only incorporate human beings—either *homo sapiens* or the Neanderthal kind. The birth of one human from another is a process of the emergence of another human from a self. The metaphorical 'birth' of a parasite or a bacterium from another or, in the case of some, from itself is an analogous process. It is, in other words, a process that occurs throughout nature, and it is one that Kant himself described, as noted, in his third *Critique*. The seed gives rise to the tree. In its turn the tree is capable of producing seeds that begin the process all over again. The tree, in its turn, is cause and effect of itself. Its various parts sustain it—the bark, the leaves and so on—and enable it to continue in existence. The body that has birthed, then, sustains and reproduces itself. The model can also incorporate the notion of 'unprethinkable being'—the ground of the whole that may be un-conceptualizable, indeed paradoxical, when viewed from the standpoint of a particular finite self, which seems to me to be so important in the work of Kierkegaard.

On this model, it is not necessary to think in terms of good or bad models of infinity or in terms of completeness or incompleteness. The model of infinity outlined above, while it purports to be thinking in temporal or process terms, may remain, in fact, trapped in a model of the whole in substantial terms. Instead of rethinking this substantiality, however, it negates it, and is then left in a position of paradox. Kierkegaard's paradoxes, then, the examples of the Christ figure or of Abraham, may be paradoxical only when viewed from the vantage point of Kantian or perhaps Adlerian speculative reason. But seen from the perspective of a genuine process system, such 'contradictions' would not be contradictions at all, but merely aspects of the emergence of the body from its ground. This process, to reiterate, cannot be made comprehensible from the perspective of a purely rational, apparently whole and self-sufficient self.

The model of birthing may also allow us to reintroduce into the foundation of being the ethical dimension. It is important to note that among the processes of birth in nature is the birth of one *homo sapiens* from another. In this case, one body that is capable of conscious thought, and of reflection on the whole, produces another independent being that has the same qualities. Such beings are capable of ethical engagement with one another and with the rest of nature. It is vitally important, as noted throughout this book, that the ethical dimension is reintroduced into ontology in the fashion of the ancient Greeks, although understood radically differently from the way in which Plato, for example, conceptualized it. Kierkegaard himself is exemplary in this respect. Plato, as noted, was interested in Being partly because he wanted to understand, like his mentor Socrates, in what the good really consists.

In our present age, where, as Bernard Stiegler has put it, 'it is the future of terrestrial life that is at stake with unprecedented urgency',[18] the question is all the more pressing. Edmund Husserl, of course, although he put it very differently, spoke, after the First World War, of a crisis of science: the exclusiveness with which the total world view of modern man, in the second half of the nineteenth century, let itself be determined by the positive sciences and blinded by the 'prosperity' they produced meant an indifferent turning away from the questions which are decisive for a genuine humanity'.[19]

Traditionally, there have been two very broad interpretations of the nature of Being, and these are expressed in the following words of Alain Badiou: 'In Bergson we find a philosophy of vital interiority, a thesis on the identity of being and becoming; a philosophy of life and change'.[20] Badiou counters this with a philosophy of the concept, the possibility of philosophical formalism of thought and of the symbolic. But, he writes, 'at stake in any such question is the human subject for it is here that the two orientations coincide'.[21] The self is at once a living organism and a creator of concepts. If we are, therefore, to 'ground' this living organism, that is also a creator of concepts, in a theory of the nature of Being, then this grounding must make these two aspects of the subject possible.

The body that can birth is a helpful metaphor for a process system and it can ground the self as creator of concepts. Being a creator of concepts would be among its capacities or its powers. The model of a birthing body is one that has been mentioned by male 'process philosophers', and yet it has rarely been discussed or taken seriously as a metaphor or, indeed, as a real process. It is a speculative hypothesis that can make sense (i) of a reality that is made up of force flows and capacities; and (ii) it is a model that can be made to serve an important ethical purpose, and this purpose, as I shall argue, is not confined to making sense of women's bodies, or serving the ends of women.

NATURE AS A LIVING BODY

There are contemporary biologists who take the idea of nature as a living system seriously. Not being, myself, a biologist, I cannot properly evaluate these theories. However, I would like simply to mention one such theory to illustrate that a close analogue of the picture I am offering here is taken seriously by some contemporary biologists. My proposal is not, therefore, merely a wild speculative hypothesis.

These biologists take nature—mother nature, as she is often called—as a living system. As the contemporary biologists H. R. Maturana and F. J. Varela[22] have argued, life extends all the way down to the bacterium. Life as a whole, in its turn, can be conceptualized along the lines articulated by Kant in the third *Critique*, as a 'system' that is cause and effect of itself. Life is described by biologists Maturana and Varela as an 'auto-poietic system'.[23] Such systems are self-organizing and self-controlling, and they do not require the inputs and outputs that are presupposed by heteronomous systems. They offer 'a naturalised, biological account of Kant's notion of a natural purpose'.[24] Every part of a natural purpose exists for the sake of the other parts, but also reciprocally produces them.

A thing, as noted above, appears to be a natural purpose, for Kant, if 'it is both cause and effect of itself'.[25] A tree reproduces itself over successive generations. Each generation of trees plays a role in the causal chain—being an effect of the previous one and the cause of future genera-tions. Each individual tree, in its turn, produces and reproduces itself through its own growth and generation. Moreover, each part of the tree is dependent on every other part. Thus, this Kantian notion could be viewed as an autopoietic system.

A minimal notion of an autopoietic system, for the above contempo-rary biologists, is a living cell. In the view of these contemporary biolo-gists, furthermore, cognition is a dynamic phenomenon that ought, in its turn, to be understood as an instance of autopoiesis. So the brain is such a system, with 'behaviour that is neither random nor ordered and predict-able; rather, it is in- between, exhibiting changing and unstable pat-terns'.[26] Cognition, then, is constituted by a relationship between the agent and its environment.[27] The theory, furthermore, allows for emer-gent processes: processes that arise out of the organization of the ele-ments of the whole. Part and whole work together.

Extending this conception of system to the whole of nature, the latter can be viewed as a Gaia. James Lovelock[28] hypothesizes that the totality of living organisms, the atmosphere, the oceans, the rocks and the soil, makes up a single planetary entity that is self-regulating and self-sustain-ing. Organisms interact with their environment to form a self-regulating system. According to the theory, the 'biota'—for example, the compo-nents listed above—evolve together with their environment. So organ-isms don't merely 'adapt' to a 'dead' world, but rather they 'live with a world that is the breath and bones of their ancestors and that they are now sustaining'.[29] The whole earth is a self-regulating system, made up 'from all of life, including the air, the oceans and the surface rocks, not just organisms alone'.[30] '*Gaia* is best thought of as a super-organism'.[31]

Lovelock argues that the world evolved from early simple bacterial forms towards the oxygen-enriched atmosphere that supports more complex life forms. Geo-physiology, which is the discipline of Gaia theory, in Lovelock's words 'sees the organisms of the Earth evolving by Darwinian natural selection in an environment that is the product of their ancestors and not simply a consequence of the earth's geological history. Thus the oxygen of the atmosphere is almost wholly the product of photosynthetic organisms and without it there would be no animals or invertebrates, nor would we burn fuels'.[32] Lovelock, as noted, sees Gaia as a superorganism. Lynn Margolis, by contrast, describes it as an autopoietic system like a cell: 'The simplest, smallest known autopoietic entity is the single cell. The largest is probably *Gaia*'.[33]

Critics of this notion argue that the Gaia is not a reproducing individual and it should not therefore be accorded the status of a living entity. Evan Thompson's suggestion, however, in response to this, is that the criticism assumes an evolutionary, reproductive process. If the Gaia is construed, rather, 'as a self-producing but non-reproducing individual' then the objection does not apply. Gaia would be a superorganism just like a cell. The latter would be among the smallest such systems and the former among the largest. Both are self-sustaining and self-regulating systems. In a response to his critics who have made this point, Lovelock writes, 'But something that lives a quarter of the age of the universe surely does not need to reproduce, and perhaps *Gaia*'s natural selection takes place internally as organisms and their environment evolve in a tightly coupled union'.[34] Indeed, the earth does not produce (or not as far as we know) further earths that are autonomous from this one. But it does make sense to suggest that the earth is self-reproducing or that it constantly gives birth to itself.

Living systems, moreover, must be understood partially in terms of norms. A living cell modifies its behaviour according to internal norms of its activity.[35] A bacterium, according to this conception, partially operates in accordance with the norms that its autonomy brings about. In an interpretation of this process, Hans Jonas[36] has argued that we must attribute a rudimentary notion of freedom to the bacterium. The bacterium has an internal identity and 'needful freedom'. Thompson characterizes this by offering an account of the 'motile bacterium' that swims about in a gradient of sugar. The cells make a 'choice' to swim in the direction of increased exposure to sugar.[37] As the reader may expect, following Kierkegaard, I have distinguished the kind of freedom experienced by human and rational beings from this notion. Nonetheless, the picture I have been painting, derived from Kierkegaard and Schelling, is one of a living and active nature, that exemplifies, if you like, degrees of freedom, with humans possessing the most developed form of it.

Varela's system is a living and dynamic one, that is dependent not only on inert and external causal relations, but upon norms that govern each autopoietic system as well as relations among systems and between them and the whole. In turn, if biologists were to ask the question about the ground of the whole, then they might be led to something like Schelling and Kierkegaard's conception of the ground. Overall, the metaphor of ground and consequent, deriving from Schelling, encapsulates this process.

It is interesting, moreover, to note the origin of the word 'Gaia'. The Gaia theory is named after the Greek goddess of that name, who, in Greek mythology, was the personification of the earth. Gaia was the mother of all—she was the goddess who gave birth to the universe.

Kierkegaard, to reiterate material from an earlier chapter, discussing the origin of the universe, referred to a different Greek goddess—Persephone. In Kierkegaard's words, quoted in chapter 7: 'Yet Persephone is only a reflection of the beginning of the beginning of this condition. The beginning itself is a surprise; only in the conclusion does consciousness become clear'.[38] Persephone is, in Greek mythology, queen of the underworld, but she is also the personification of vegetation. She is a power or a force that appears in the spring. She can give birth to generative natural powers and capacities, but she also plays some role in the generation of capacities for wrongdoing.

In chapter 7, I referred to Hilarius Bookbinder's *Stages on Life's Way.* Kierkegaard there makes the claim that the female sex is more perfect than the male in the context of the formation of the earth. Originally, according to Kierkegaard, as noted in that chapter, there was only one sex. Earth was formed in the likeness of another figure from Greek mythology—Pandora.

There are analogies, then, between the work of contemporary biologists and the hypothesis I have been attributing, throughout the book, to Kierkegaard. The metaphor of a body that can birth encapsulates the ideas of these biologists. Such a body is cause and effect of itself in Kant's sense. In contrast to Kant's view, however, it is a hylozoist system.[39] The foetus gives rise to the baby. If that body, in its turn, is a female body, then it can give rise to further foetuses and it can contribute to reproducing the species. But the body that can birth itself is not the evolutionary process; it is, rather, the individual system with these various capacities and powers. In other words, it need not always be conceptualized in terms of a reproducing system that produces autonomous entities, but can sometimes be viewed, instead, as a productive system that has reproduction among its emergent properties or powers.

If the 'birthing' notion is construed, also, and separately, as an evolutionary process that occurs through time, then it can also serve as a metaphor for a process system. The capacity to give birth, then, is an account of the capacity or the power to produce a whole being (and the whole, in turn, is dependent upon its ground). The process of birthing outlines the generative nature of the ground, which, using Schelling's terminology, becomes a ground at the point at which it brings into being its consequent. The mother, in other words, becomes a mother at the point at which she produces her child.

In other words, there are at least two separate conceptions of the birthing body and birthing processes. One is the Gaia notion—the whole planetary system as a living and self-sustaining one. My own argument, though, derived from Schelling and Kierkegaard, extends the Gaia conception. The suggestion is that the earth is itself grounded in a capacity or a power that gave rise to it.

The second notion of birth, however, is a particular conception of a process within this whole, a process of generation of beings from their grounds. This process, it is important to add, requires appropriate conditions in order to maintain its self-sustaining character. It is possible, indeed, for such a system, unless it is maintained, to destroy itself. A system of living entities, characterized in terms of bodies that birth, needs to be cared for if those entities are to be sustained. Schelling, as noted, described the yearning of the one to give birth to itself also as the power of love.

Each element of this overall organic system needs to be maintained and sustained through love. A mother, according to the psychoanalyst Donald Winnicott,[40] by taking care of her infant, teaches it that life is worth living. The mother, here, does not have to be a female human. It simply needs to be some caring figure who enables the child to develop the feeling that life is worth living. Thus, the metaphor I have been

developing throughout the book is a metaphor that contains ethical power. It suggests that the natural world is an organic and living system but
also a system that requires care and love. Its various component parts—
the various aspects of organic matter that it comprises—need to be cared
for and loved if they are to be sustained. Love, as I and others[41] have
written elsewhere, is an important component of Kierkegaard's substantial ethic. He writes in *Works of Love* about the importance of loving our
neighbour, which I have argued includes those close to us as well as
strangers. But he also writes about the need to love ourselves before we
can love others. 'Whoever has any knowledge of people will certainly
admit that just as he has often wished to be able to will them to relinquish
self-love, he has also had to wish that it were possible to teach them to
love themselves'.[42]

THE ETHICAL DIMENSION

When we think ethically as humans about other humans we think in terms
of our responsibilities or obligations to others. If nature as a whole is a
living entity, then this responsibility is extended so as to incorporate its
various constituent parts and processes. The metaphysical model of nature gives rise, as Plato's did for him, to an ethic. It is an ethic that is vital
for the contemporary world.

Being, in this view, conceptualized as a body that can birth, will be
equivalent to nature. The ethical concern includes a need to care for the
nature that, in Quentin Meillassoux's words, 'preexists' the human, and, I
would like to add, makes the human possible. While humans frequently
depend upon machines and have, indeed, been argued by many today to
constitute a hybrid of human/machine, or a cyborg,[43] machines are not, or
not yet, by themselves living things, nor are they autopoietic systems.[44]
Even the robots that appear to function on their own, without a human
operating them, have been consciously produced by a human and pro-
grammed by a human.[45] If they do become able to sustain themselves,
perhaps to reproduce themselves and to maintain and care for their kind,
then my view will be different. However, at the present time, machines,
indeed, have the potential to destroy the very nature on which humans
rely.

Indeed, it was the very mechanization of human processes that partially enabled the most extreme horror of the twentieth century, although the logic that gave rise to this extreme horror was, as several have argued, present in earlier epochs.[46] Those who proclaim a continuity in consciousness between humans and machines may inadvertently be colluding in the logic that allows for the reduction of all living forms, including all human life, to 'bare life', or *zoe*, that can be killed but not sacrificed. Lovelock indeed has argued that 'our' emissions of carbon dioxide perturbs the self-regulating system that is the earth.[47]

This is not at all to say, on the other hand, that the human being, as a tool user, is not intrinsically connected to technical objects. Ranging from simple agricultural objects to complex *techné*, the human being evolves as, in the words of Andy Clark, an 'extended mind'.[48] The human mind, in other words, is interconnected with body, world, and action. In important works, to summarize the details of a complex argument, Stiegler has claimed that the present phase of capitalist development, deploying the extraordinary power of digital networks, that suggest the infinite recoverability of human memory, in fact leads to greater and greater degrees of powerlessness. This encompasses not only a loss of knowledge, but also a loss of the very essence of humanity—the notion of being in the world, or of existing.[49] In his book *What Makes Life Worth Living*, Stiegler presents his view of the original *pharmakon*. The first *pharmakon*, he writes, is Winnicott's 'transitional object'. The transitional object, for the very young child, 'instils in the child the feeling that life is worth living'.[50] This notion is both positive and also potentially poisonous. The significance of the *pharmakon*, according to Stiegler, was first brought to our attention in contemporary philosophy 'with Jacques Derrida's commentary on the Phaedrus'.[51] Writing, as *hypomnesis, hypomnematon*—artificial memory—is opposed to *anamnesis*, or thinking for oneself. While for Plato, Stiegler argues, these two notions were separated, in fact they combine together. But in the present era of capitalist development, the potentially poisonous side of the *pharmakon* is able to take precedence over its positive aspect, and the mnemo-technologies that are being developed on a massive scale are potentially able to affect desire itself. Not only producers, but also consumers, find themselves dis-individuated. Modern capitalism is capable of destroying desire itself. 'The destruction of desire (which is also to say, of attention and care) which leads to a drive based economy, that is an essentially destructive economy, is a new limit encountered by capitalism, this time not only as mode of production, but also as mode of consumption defined as a way of life, that is *bio-power become psychopower*.[52] Stiegler maintains that the negative aspects of the economy must be turned into positives. The negative aspects of the notion of the *pharmakon* must be turned right-side up into positives. Libidinal energy must be transformed. While consumption destroys its object, 'libido is on the contrary what takes care of its object'.[53] Addressing the problems of contemporary capitalism, therefore, according to Stiegler, involves not simply abandoning fossil energy but rather abandoning a drive-based economy and 'reconstituting libidinal energy'.[54] Energy that is focused on industrial and technological production, he suggests, must be refocused on 'a new social rationality, producing motivation, motives for living together, that is for taking care of the world and those who live within it—producing a new *savoir-vivre*'.[55]

The metaphor of the body that can birth can act as a ground for this kind of an ethic and a politics. While the metaphor of the whole as chaos might itself ground a chaotic or nihilistic ethic, the metaphor of the body that can birth can sustain a caring ethic. This caring ethic is necessary for the maintenance of the whole.

KANT AS THE ORIGINATOR OF THE VIEW

Partial inspiration for the view that reality is, at its core, a body that can birth comes from, as I have noted, Kant, who refers, in the third *Critique*, to the earth as a 'common original mother'.[56] He writes, to quote again, 'He can make mother earth (like a large animal as it were) emerge from her state of chaos, and make her lap promptly give birth initially to creatures of a less purposive form, with these then giving birth to others that became better adapted to their place of origin and to their relations to one another, until in the end this womb itself rigidified, ossified, and confined itself to bearing definite species that would no longer degenerate, so that the diversity remained as it had turned out when that fertile formative force ceased to operate'.[57] But Kant, as we have seen, ultimately rejects this model. One reason that he does not give, however, for this rejection may be that, at the time he was writing, the active role of the female in procreation was not known.[58]

The idea of nature as a body that can birth (i) makes some significant sense in the contemporary world and (ii) is compatible with a number of remarks in Kierkegaard's work. It also contributes to the response to the well-known difficulty, alluded to in previous chapters, that appears in Kant's work, the problem of explaining how it is possible freely to do wrong. This difficulty, I have suggested and will continue to argue, arises, for Kant, significantly because of his metaphysic. Kierkegaard, as I have argued throughout this book, challenges this metaphysic.

In this chapter I have set out to argue that the metaphor of Being, or the whole, as a body that can birth, as well as the ultimate 'non-ground'— the yearning of the whole to give birth to itself—is not only to be found in Kierkegaard's corpus, but is also a plausible model in its own right. Not only, I have suggested, is it plausible as a metaphor for the whole, but it is also a model that is compatible with the kind of ethic that is vital in our contemporary world, if humanity is not to destroy both itself and the conditions that allow the human race to survive.

NOTES

1. I do not wish to claim that the science on which I will draw constitutes the 'best' science of the day since I am not competent to make such a judgement. Moreover, since I am not claiming, in this book, that the perspective I have been outlining constitutes the 'best' perspective there can be, at this moment in time, I do not think it is necessary to engage in the topic of what constitutes the 'best' science of the day. In this sense my drawing on contemporary science is a different exercise from that of some contemporary metaphysicians. James Ladyman and Don Ross are examples of philosophers who do set out to draw on what they call the 'best' science of the day; see, for example, James Ladyman and Don Ross, *Everything Must Go: Metaphysics Naturalised* (Oxford: Oxford University Press, 2010).

2. George W. F. Hegel, *The Science of Logic*, trans. Arnold Miller (New York: Humanity Books, 1969), 137. One of the main commentators on this subject is Stephen Houlgate, *The Opening of Hegel's Logic: From Being to Infinity* (West Lafayette: Purdue University Press, 2006), especially chapter 22, 'True Infinity'.

3. Hegel, *The Science of Logic*, trans. George di Giovanni (Cambridge: Cambridge University Press, 2010).

4. E. Levinas, *Totality and Infinity: An Essay on Exteriority*, trans. Alphonso Lingis (The Hague: Martinus Nijhoff, 1979).

5. Mike Lewis, *Heidegger beyond Deconstruction* (London: Continuum, 2007), 88.

6. Stella Sandford, *The Metaphysics of Love* (London: Athlone Press, 2000), 13. I am not sure that I wholly concur with this reading, since it suggests a transcendent notion that may not be quite what is meant here. But it is certainly a whole that is conceived without any gaps.

7. Once again this is not only an epistemic point. Kant expressed the connection between epistemic and ontological points in this domain in his mathematical Antinomies. He argued there that the difficulty of providing consistent arguments about the whole world demonstrates not only a limit of our knowledge but also that it does not make sense to regard the 'world as a whole' as an entity. Kant himself would not have drawn the conclusion that the whole therefore becomes an imperfect entity. However, since he argued that contradictory claims can be proven about it, then it would not seem an implausible conclusion to draw, even on his premises, that it itself becomes a paradoxical entity.

8. Lewis, *Heidegger beyond Deconstruction*.

9. Jacques Derrida, *Of Grammatology* (1974, 1971), trans. Gayatri Chakravorty Spivak (Indianapolis: Hackett Publishing; Baltimore: Johns Hopkins University Press, 1997).

10. Žižek, PV, 89.

11. Ibid.

12. JP, vol. 1, p. 29, note 76.

13. Michael Burns, *A Fractured Dialectic: Soren Kierkegaard between Idealism and Materialism* (London: Rowman & Littlefield International, 2014).

14. Kant, CJ.

15. Søren Kierkegaard, *Either-Or* (2 vols.), trans. David F. Swenson and Lilian Marvin Swenson (New York: Doubleday, Anchor Books, 1959).

16. EO II, 174.

17. CI, 273.

18. Bernard Stiegler, *What Makes Life Worth Living: On Pharmacology*, trans. Daniel Ross (Cambridge: Polity Press, 2013), 5.

19. Edmund Husserl, *The Crisis of European Sciences and Transcendental Phenomenology*, trans. David Carr (Evanston, IL: Northwestern University Press, 1969), 24.

20. Alain Badiou, *The Adventure of French Philosophy*, trans. Bruno Bosteels (London: Verso, 2012), liii.

21. Ibid.

22. See H. R. Maturana and F. J. Varela, *Autopoiesis and Cognition: The Realization of the Living*, ed. Robert S. Cohen and Marx W. Wartofsky, (Boston: D. Reidel, 1980); and H. R. Maturana and F. J. Varela, *The Tree of Knowledge:*

The Biological Roots of Human Understanding (Boston: Shambhala Publications, 1987).

23. Ibid.

24. Evan Thompson, *Mind in Life: Biology, Phenomenology, and the Sciences of Mind* (Cambridge: Belknap Press, 2007), 140. It is important to note that, in their early work, Maturana and Varela did not see autopoietic systems as teleological. They saw them rather as purposeless and analogous to 'autopoietic machines' (see Maturana and Varela, *Autopoiesis and Cognition*). Yet later, partly in response to the criticisms of, for example, Robert Rosen (Robert Rosen, *Life Itself: A Comprehensive Inquiry into the Nature, Origin and Fabrication of Life* [New York: Columbia University Press, 1991]), Varela came to revise his view. (See F. J. Varela, 'Organism: A Meshwork of Selfless Selves', in *Organism and the Origin of Self*, ed. A. Tauber [Dortrecht: Kluwer Academic Publishers, 1990], 79–107; and Thompson, *Mind in Life*, chapter 6).

25. Kant, CJ, 249.

26. Thompson, *Mind in Life*, 40.

27. See Ibid., 119.

28. James Lovelock, *Gaia: A New Look at Life on Earth* (Oxford: Oxford University Press, 1979).

29. Thompson, *Mind in Life*, 120.

30. James Lovelock, *A Final Warning: The Vanishing Face of Gaia* (London: Penguin, 2009), 112.

31. James Lovelock, *The Ages of Gaia* (New York: W.W. Norton, 1998), 15.

32. Lovelock, *A Final Warning*, 31.

33. L. Margulis, 'Biologists Can't Define Life', in *From Gaia to Selfish Genes: Selected Writings in the Life Sciences*, ed. C. Barlow (Cambridge: MIT Press, 1991), 237.

34. Lovelock, *A Final Warning*, 127.

35. Thompson, *Mind in Life*, 74.

36. Hans Jonas, *The Phenomenon of Life: Towards a Philosophical Biology* (Chicago: Chicago University Press, 1966).

37. Thompson, *Mind in Life*, 157.

38. Kierkegaard, quoted in chapter 7 of this book.

39. In other words, it is a system where these processes really exist in nature as opposed to Kant's view, which has them being merely regulative ideas on the part of beings like us. For Kant we view nature as though it is purposive. It is not really purposive.

40. See Donald Winnicott, *Playing and Reality* (London: Routledge, 1971).

41. See Alison Assiter, *Kierkegaard, Metaphysics and Political Theory: Unfinished Selves* (London: Continuum, 2009); and Alison Assiter and Margherita

Tonon (eds.), *Kierkegaard and the Political* (Cambridge: Cambridge Scholars Press, 2012).

42. WL, 23.

43. See, for one of the earliest and most influential statements of this position, Donna Haraway, 'A Cyborg Manifesto: Science, Technology and Socialist-Feminism in the Late Twentieth Century', in *Simians, Cyborgs and Women: The Reinvention of Nature* (New York: Routledge, 1991), 149–181; see also the work of Margrit Shildrick, for example, *Embodying the Monster: Encounters with the Vulnerable Self* (London: Sage, 2011), in this area.

44. There is a body of work that has attempted to argue not only that it is possible to produce a reproducing machine but also that this has already been done. See, for example, V. Zykov, E. Mytilinaios, B. Adams, and H. Lipson, 'Robotics: Self-Reproducing Machines', *Nature* 435 (12 May 2005), 163–164. However, as Robert Rosen has argued, it is very difficult to remove the fact that there has been a creator of the machine. However capable a complex machine might be of self-replicating, through, for example, the creation of cubes that can be attached, detached, and reattached to one another in a large number of shapes and orders, such a machine requires a creator. See Robert Rosen, *Life Itself: A Comprehensive Inquiry into the Nature, Origin and Fabrication of Life* (New York: Columbia University Press, 1991).

45. See, for example, those who defend the thesis of 'pan-psychism', among them Galen Strawson et al., *Consciousness and Its Place in Nature: Does Physicalism Entail Pan-psychism?*, ed. Anthony Freeman (Exeter: Imprint Academic, 2006).

46. See Giorgio Agamben, *Homo Sacer: Sovereign Power and Bare Life*, trans. Daniel Heller-Roazen (Stanford: Stanford University Press, 1998), for arguments to this effect.

47. Lovelock, *A Final Warning*.

48. See Andy Clark and David Chalmers, 'The Extended Mind', *Analysis* 58, no. 1 (1998), 7–19.

49. See Bernard Stiegler, *The Decadence of Industrial Democracies, vol. 1, Disbelief and Discredit*, trans. Daniel Ross and Suzanne Arnold (Cambridge: Polity Press, 2011).

50. Bernard Stiegler, *What Makes Life Worth Living: On Pharmacology* (Cambridge: Polity Press, 2010), 1.

51. Ibid., 2.

52. Ibid., 88.

53. Ibid., 92.

54. Ibid.

55. Ibid., 93–94.

56. Kant, CJ, 304.

57. Ibid.

58. See, for example, Catherine Gallagher and Thomas Laqueur, edited with introduction, *The Making of the Modern Body* (Berkeley and Los Angeles: University of California Press, 1987). It is important to note that this argument has been disputed, however.

10

THE AGE OF REVOLUTION AND THE PRESENT AGE

I would like, in this final chapter, to demonstrate the application of some of the foregoing in a particular area—that of the political domain. There are many who argue that Søren Kierkegaard's writing and the political are oxymoronic. Kierkegaard is, in their view, essentially a religious thinker and, at best, he was indifferent to the political. At worst, indeed, he was actively against it. He was, it is said, against the French and the Danish revolutions. David Wood, for example, writes that Kierkegaard's political insights are, perhaps, 'something like a reactionary residue we should walk past on our way to his original thoughts'.[1] At the very best, his political insights are unhelpful for anyone who wishes to attempt, by this means, to make the world a better place—he was, to quote Wood once more, 'a royalist, a misogynist and fought a rearguard action against the more communitarian Christianity gaining ascendency in Denmark at the time'.[2] It seems clear, indeed, that Kierkegaard did not develop a relational sense of self by reference to human others, but rather saw the self as relating to itself through the medium of God. For Anti-Climacus, the self is itself only when it is related, in Sylvia Walsh's words, 'in total dependency to the power that established it'.[3] One can, then, become a self 'only through the relationship to God'.[4]

For some who have found political and indeed feminist inspiration in Kierkegaard's writings, it has been in the earlier pseudonymous works. So Christine Battersby, for example, whose work inspired me and led to my fascination with Kierkegaard's rich and rewarding texts, sees the later works as more misogynistic and less useful for her project of difference feminism than the earlier writing. Indeed, she writes that *Two Ages* is not simply 'apolitical, it is anti political'.[5]

Moreover, for those who seek religious inspiration in his works, particularly his later writings, it is a desecration of his legacy to suggest that his work can shape the political domain. If one commentates on Kierkegaard's works and disregards the religious, as it is assumed one must if one focuses on the political, then one misses the crucial and deeply original aspects of Kierkegaard's writings. I myself, indeed, stand accused of this.[6]

I will argue, in this chapter, by contrast, that Kierkegaard's work *Two Ages: A Literary Review* suggests that a certain notion of the political actually prefigures the religious and, indeed, that this political notion has much in common for him with the relation between a finite limited self and God. I will argue, furthermore, that the conception of revolution outlined by Kierkegaard in this text may be modelled on the account of process I have been describing throughout the book.

One exception[7] to the lack of interest in Kierkegaard and the political domain is Merold Westphal in his *Kierkegaard's Critique of Reason and Society*. His account of the political in Kierkegaard has some commonality with the view I would like to offer here. According to Westphal, Kierkegaard offers a critique of the conception of reason that he believed was expressed in his own epoch. The 'spectre' he suggests Kierkegaard sees haunting humanity is the 'amoral herd'.[8] In a claim that echoes something of this book, Westphal views Camus as developing Kierkegaard's thought, in the latter's focus on the 'terror that self-deified humanity unleashes upon itself'.[9] Properly religious discourse, which is not normally a majority outlook, for him offers a critique of this 'ideology' of his period. The language of faith subverts the established order and offers an alternative: a radically new form of discourse.

TWO AGES

Two Ages was written after CUP[10]—indeed, Kierkegaard interrupted his writing of it to complete the latter—and by Kierkegaard in his own name. Strictly, he wrote the text as a literary review[11] and produced it after he had decided to discontinue writing. The text is a review of a novel by

Thomasine Gyllembourg. Some argue, indeed, that Kierkegaard saw it as acceptable, after he had vowed to discontinue writing, to pen a review, which has a different character from a prose book or article.

Far from critiquing the 'age of revolution' in *Two Ages*, Kierkegaard is much more critical, in the text, of the 'present age', which had succeeded the period of revolution (although not yet the 1848 revolutions).[12] Although Kierkegaard writes that he is simply describing the two ages and offering no commentary on them, the chapter is full of critical invective on the 'present age' and somewhat positive commentary on the revolutionary period. I would like, in the next section of the chapter, to outline some of this positive commentary and compare it with his description of the religious.

Similarities between the Religious and the Age of Revolution

While, of course, the view Kierkegaard really extols is that which follows the 'inspired leap of religiousness', the 'age of revolution' 'takes action'[13] with passion, whereas the 'present age' is a 'reflective age devoid of passion'.[14] He writes, 'The age of revolution is essentially passionate therefore it has not nullified the principle of contradiction and can become either good or evil'.[15] So there is an opening in the revolutionary age, for selves to become genuine selves and for them to act as moral agents. They have a choice whether or not to follow a moral ideal from an infinite source. This is precisely the dilemma Haufniensis is preoccupied with in CA.

The revolutionary age is also, and interestingly, an 'age of revelation'. This does not, of course, mean revelation by an infinitely compassionate God, but it is interesting that Kierkegaard uses this word. It is an age of revelation 'by a manifestation of energy that unquestionably is a definite something and does not deceptively change under the influence of conjectural criticism concerning what the age really wants'.[16] In other words, the age of revolution is clear and decisive about its ideals; it is active and engaged and is not liable to alter its projects when facing hypothetical and indeed 'conjectural' criticism about its aims. This contrasts dramatically with the present age, where the fickle 'public' engages in incessant 'chatter' and disables anyone from becoming any kind of self.

One similarity between the religious self and the 'age of revolution', then, is that both feature 'revelation' in some form. I suggest this might be read as implying that, just as the self as it becomes free effectively receives revelation from the *ungrund*, so too does the revolutionary, in the moment of revolution. The moment of revolution, at its inception, then, functions as a possible rebirth, as a new beginning.

'The age of revolution', Kierkegaard writes, 'is essentially passionate, and therefore it essentially has form'.[17] Insofar as it is passionate and has form, it also 'has culture'. The tension and the resilience of the inner being are the 'measure of essential culture'.[18] Kierkegaard compares the age of revolution to a 'maidservant genuinely I love'. She is 'genuinely cultured'. Being cultured, perhaps, is distinct from merely mindlessly following the herd, doing as others do, which characterizes the 'present age'. I'd like, now, to expand on how this notion illustrates a further commonality between the religious and the age of revolution.

In his book *Kierkegaard, Religion and the 19th Century Crisis of Culture*,[19] George Pattison refers to *Two Ages* alongside his discussion of the sublime, culture,[20] and time. Pattison sees something positive in Kierkegaard's description of the revolutionary age. He writes that although, for Kierkegaard, a person only finds 'definitive rest' in the highest idea, 'which is the religious', the age of revolution nonetheless contrasts with a 'fossilised formalism' 'which has lost the originality of the ethical'.[21] Yet Pattison's reading of Kierkegaard's age of revolution has Kierkegaard remain sceptical about such an age.

I pointed out earlier that the Danish word *tiden*, as Pattison notes, which is translated appropriately as 'the age', can also mean 'time'. One could read Kierkegaard, here, then, as suggesting 'what a life lived in time without any perspective on eternity might give itself over to. In fact such a life gives itself over to "the momentary"'. For Pattison, 'this may (in the form least respected by Kierkegaard) express itself as jumping on political bandwagons, or it may appear as the dedicated following of fashion in music, clothes, art, the whole merry-go-round of seeing and being-seen, the world of the eye, the gaze, in which people "keep a careful eye on each other (*passé paa hinanden med Oinene*)"'.[22]

The culture of modernity, then, is, for Pattison, the culture of those whose horizons are filled by the 'time that now is', the momentary, the shock of the new. This is a culture therefore that excludes the fearful fascination of anxiety and sublimity. But there may be a way other than Pattison's of viewing the texts both of CA and TA, that would allow us to see the age of revolution, and Kierkegaard's reference to culture, differently. Typically we see time, as I have claimed in this book, in terms of spatializing metaphors. Haufniensis, by contrast, emphasizes an ontology of process, where each spatialized moment contains elements of past and future.

As noted earlier as well, Kierkegaard is also expressing reservations about a teleological conception of time. For David Kangas, a teleological reading presupposes a continuous temporality defined by the movement of self-consciousness in coming to itself. The 'highest' stage would be the one that best expressed its principle. But Kierkegaard, as we have seen, does not accept this kind of Hegelian system. Kierkegaard's self holds itself open not to absolute being but to non-being. The final chapter of CA articulates the relation between faith and anxiety, 'anxiety being a relation to the nothing of possibility. Faith is sinking into what absolves itself from being, a relation to what cannot be gathered into presence'.[23]

Using Kangas and noting the argument of the rest of the book, we can read the description of the 'age of revolution' differently. The age of revolution is notable in several respects. First, it expresses, as Slavoj Žižek has put it, in the moment of revolution 'an act of freedom which momentarily suspends the nexus of historical causality, that is, in revolt, the noumenal dimension transpires'.[24] It expresses this because, insofar as this is possible, in the finite limited temporal world of beings like us, it represents some kind of radical break with previous causal patterns. In this respect, it can express a dimension Pattison evokes in his discussion, which is the Kantian sublime. The latter comes into play, as noted before, and now in Pattison's words, 'at the precise point where appearances resist or escape being formed into a single, beautiful representation'.[25] Revolution, in the moment, resists categorization in 'normal' spatiotemporal form. It represents a break with these normal conventional categories.

Thus, a second sense in which the 'age of revolution' is notable is that it offers an immediate and tangible realization of a process ontology. It speaks, in its immediacy (as Kierkegaard refers to it), to such an ontology; it brings one up short, and gives the lie to those who spatialize temporality; it gives the lie to those who see the world of their vision in terms of a continuous present. If only in metaphorical form, therefore, it offers an immediate illustration of the significance of an active process ontology, as contrasted with one that has the subject look out, as Kant does, on a world that it has constructed for itself, a world of static substances related in terms of Newtonian causation.

Thirdly, then, the 'age of revolution' can prefigure the eternal—it is passionate and engaged in a manner that is akin to the subject when she is consumed with anxiety and facing her relation to God.

But, and fourthly, the 'age of revolution' also suggests a way of viewing the eternal itself, to which Kierkegaard subscribes, and that is that the eternal is not a Hegelian absolute that represents a knowable reality. Rather, as Kangas has noted in relation to *The Concept of Irony*, Kierkegaard 'reverses this archeo-teleological structure'.[26] The possibility of possibility is possibility beyond a horizon of being. The model for this, once more, is Schelling's *ungrund* or the 'unprethinkable'. There is no such thing as absolute presence in the manner of, for example, Descartes. Presence always contains something that 'thought cannot think'.

Friedrich Wilhelm Joseph Schelling, as noted throughout the book, introduces this notion[27] in order to account for the possibility of evil. As Kangas puts it, 'to grasp evil in its positivity, according to Schelling, requires allowing ontological space in relation to the absolute for an act that is both singular and radically self-determining. An irremediable gap in being, or presence, is necessary that extends all the way into the absolute—hence the notion of the indeterminate *Grund* as what lies "beyond absolute identity"'.[28] In this reading, God exists as an eternal resolution to subordinate the will of the ground to the will of existence. God indefinitely 'ejects love'.[29] The unity that is indivisible in God must be divisible in the human being—expressed as the possibility of both good and evil. To put this differently, process philosophy extends all the way up and all the way down. There is no 'substance' that is God who possesses the properties of omniscience and omnipresence. There is no Being at the beginning or the end of the process that is a simple, Absolute substance. There ought to be, in this system, therefore, something that precedes the actuality of God and that is the possibility of God: just as the fact of a child must presuppose the process of giving birth to the child. However, given that God initiates the whole process, the logic that is applicable to the rest of the system may be subverted here. Unlike any other ground and consequent, God's ground and consequent may be both simultaneous and infinitely operative.

All of this is glimpsed in the moment of revolution. Revolution upsets the taken-for-granted world. Revolution offers up an image of a 'break' in the causal chain that we frequently (unless we are living in the Middle East today) experience as normal and invincible. It offers up an image of the way reality, experienced for Kierkegaard in SUD and CUP, appears to the anxious and despairing subject. It is therefore to be applauded, although, of course, this applause cannot be unequivocal.

I would like to offer one further piece of evidence of a commonality between the age of revolution and the relation between the individual self and God. Sylvia Walsh, in her important book *Living Christianity*,[30] offers a deep analysis of the inward suffering of the true Christian as described mainly in Kierkegaard's late works. She writes of the distinction drawn by Kierkegaard in the *Upbuilding Discourses* and in the late religious writings between the 'merely human' or temporal viewpoint and the 'eternal perspective'.

In adopting the eternal viewpoint, it is important to 'perceive the spiritual usefulness of suffering. The merely human or temporal attitude regards suffering as useful only when it can be shown to serve some (temporal) good cause and to be a benefit to others. The eternal sees things *inversely*: the usefulness of suffering is determined by whether sufferers are willing to let it help them to the highest, and instead of their suffering being a benefit to others it is a burden to others and to themselves'.[31]

She continues to argue that one can find freedom in this suffering. The suffering remains but it becomes positive through the freedom received from it. One may recall (although this is written in the early pseudonymous period of Kierkegaard's works) the description of the knight of faith in *Fear and Trembling*, or the knight of the infinite. He 'takes pleasure' in taking part in everything. He delights 'in everything he senses—the new omnibuses, the Sound'.[32] 'Abraham had faith and he did not doubt. He believed the absurd'.[33] 'Humanly' speaking—or rather, speaking from the perspective of Kantian reason—to believe both that Abraham will be required to kill Isaac and that he will get Isaac back is absurd. Humanly speaking, at least from the perspective of Aristotelian logic and the law of the excluded middle, holding both beliefs simultaneously would be absurd. But given that Abraham had faith, it is not absurd. Seen in the way I described earlier, in terms of the process system, the two beliefs are not necessarily incompatible.[34]

While there is no doubt a difference between this description and the later evocation of suffering and martyrdom as conditions and prerequisites of faith, there is nonetheless a similarity between them. The knight of faith from *Fear and Trembling* does not wish to show off that he is different from the rest; his outward appearance is of utter normality and this belies the inner despair, anxiety, and then calm acceptance of the requirement from God. Again, as Walsh writes, 'suffering becomes a joy in following Christ first of all because it signifies that one has chosen rightly, that one is advancing on the right way, and that the way of hardship is the way of perfection'.[35]

These are precisely the characteristics required of the true revolutionary. The one quality described in Walsh's reading of the singular self, who finds him or herself through God in Kierkegaard's later religious works, that differentiates him or her from the revolutionary, who has a fervent and absolute desire to change the world, is that the latter is 'merely human'.

In other respects, the characteristics of the true revolutionary fit admirably those of the individual suffering before God. The revolutionary experiences suffering, which may be inward—the loss of taken-for-granted everyday realities—or outward—the loss of family and friends. All of this takes place because of a belief, which may or may not be religiously informed, in some ideal that the person is aware he or she may never directly experience. Thus, 'humanly speaking', they lose taken-for-granted everyday realities. They may lose home, family, jobs, and normal life, but they gain a passion for action and for a cause with which they strongly identify. This contrasts, as Kierkegaard puts it, with a 'fossilised formalism' which is a characteristic of the 'present age'.[36] The revolutionaries may indeed believe (in their cause) as Abraham believed in God 'by virtue of the absurd'. No doubt, in the midst of revolution, it is absurd to believe that some real and significantly better form of life is possible. Perhaps many revolutionaries both do and do not believe that a better world is possible and carry on being prepared for both eventualities, but in the supreme belief that their ideal will triumph, if not in eternity then at least in some far distant future.

Indeed, the sorts of thing real revolutionaries lose—one may recall, for example, the 1789 Revolution, the Russian Revolution of 1917, the Iranian Revolution of 1979, or the twenty-first-century revolutions in the Middle East—are precisely those Kierkegaard denigrates in his description of the 'present age'—the age of 'levelling', an age of 'publicity'. They lose the form of conventionality represented by Mrs. Waller (a character from the text), the normality of the 'ethical' life—marriage, convention.

The revolutionary age, moreover, might be described, using the metaphors outlined earlier, as a kind of rebirth. A philosopher who was influenced by Kierkegaard and who described him as one who offers 'the deepest interpretation of Cartesian doubt in that for him doubt is at the heart of human existence'[37] is Hannah Arendt. She is one later philosopher who also uses metaphors of birth in her work. Freedom, for her, is beginning anew; it is a form of rebirth. By acting in certain ways individuals reenact their births. Every time we really act as a free person we perform something new; we engage with the world in radically different ways, as if we were being reborn. As Arendt puts it, 'the new beginning inherent in birth can make itself felt in the world only because the newcomer possesses the capacity of beginning something anew, that is, of acting. . . . [R]evolutions are the only political events which confront us directly and inevitably with the problem of beginning'.[38] The French Revolution, the Paris Commune of 1871, the creation of Soviets during the Russian Revolution, the French Resistance to Hitler in the Second World War, each in its turn confronted us with the problem of beginning. In doing so, according to Arendt, the revolutionaries rediscovered the truth known to the ancient Greeks that action is the supreme blessing of human life, that which bestows significance on the lives of individuals. To act effectively means to introduce the new. This is frequently done collectively, with others.[39]

Likewise for Kierkegaard, revolution enacts freedom. Freedom, as I have been arguing in this text, originally 'comes into being' in Eve and is then reenacted as a form of rebirth each time a person or a group acts in a genuinely free manner.

Kierkegaard's 'present age', by contrast with these revolutionary periods, is an age 'where nothing happens but still there is instant publicity'.[40] It is an age 'where great and good actions are past'.[41] It is an age devoid of passion where actions and decisions are scarce. In the 'present age' 'not even a suicide does away with himself with passion'.[42] The revolutionary age is a period where action is important, while the latter is an age of 'inertia and reflection'.

Kierkegaard critiques the revolutionary age: he describes it as 'essentially crude' by contrast with the person 'turned inward [to God]', who 'is never crude'. It may also be 'riotous, wild, ruthless towards everything but its idea'.[43] The revolution may turn violent and crude if it is given over to 'talkativeness', and if there is no uniting idea then people may end up 'shoving and pressing and rubbing against one another in pointless externality'.[44]

There is no doubt that it is the inward relation of the 'single individual' to God that, for Kierkegaard, is the highest idea. 'From the standpoint of the idea, a person finds definitive rest only in the highest idea which is the religious',[45] whereas the 'age of revolution' is only provisional. Yet the 'age of revolution' is 'essentially passionate and therefore it has "propriety"'. It has, I am suggesting, many features in common with the religious.

The Aesthetic, the Age of Revolution, and the Religious

In an earlier chapter, I wrote about 'Silhouettes'[46] in *Either-Or*. There, 'A' discusses the difficulty, also expressed in this present chapter, of gaining awareness via sight. Sight tends to privilege the form of knowing that imagines the self as a seeing eye, looking out on static substances, and for whom time is represented as a series of static moments, a series of 'nows'. When a person is in sorrow, vision is in shadow; we do not have full sight, and it seems that what is hidden from view offers a more accurate depiction of reality than what is presented fully to the seeing eye.

A similar story is presented, now by Kierkegaard writing in his own name, in TA. Kierkegaard clearly likes Gyllembourg's writings. He 'gladly'[47] picks up her work to read. In TA, he recounts a tale of two lovers, who in the early stages of their relationship are passionate; later, this is lost and they become much closer to simple reflections of their age. They come to reflect the domestic side of their age and are akin to other characters outlined in the 'present age'. When they initially meet, by contrast, we are given 'an authentic portrayal of great passions'.[48] Kierkegaard extols passionate activity in a range of contexts. One of the most passionate activities of which any human is capable is the process of giving birth, the production of another from within a self. Like the process of revolution as well as the relationship between the individual and God, the process of birthing involves suffering. Like the individual who discovers religious belief, for whom suffering becomes a joy, so too, for the individuals involved in the process of birth, suffering becomes a joy, a joy in the production of new life.

In this chapter, I have offered an account of one way in which the 'birthing' metaphor may be applied to a radically different area of Kierkegaard's writings: in this case, the political domain. I have suggested that the period Kierkegaard, writing in his own name, describes as the revolutionary age has resonances with the religious. I have argued that it is, at least, provisional for the latter, in that they have many features in common. I have further suggested that the metaphor of birth may usefully be applied to the notion of revolution—the bringing into being, or at least the hope of bringing about, a new political order. This chapter concludes the main part of the book. It remains only to attempt to draw the threads together, in a conclusion.

NOTES

1. David Wood, 'The Singular Universal One More Time', in *Kierkegaard and the Political*, ed. Alison Assiter and Margherita Tonon (Cambridge: Cambridge Scholars Press, 2012), 7–25.

2. Ibid., 90.

3. Sylvia Walsh, *Living Christianity: Kierkegaard's Dialectic of Christian Existence* (University Park: Pennsylvania State University Press, 2005), 29.

4. SUD, 30.

5. Christine Battersby, 'Kierkegaard: The Phantom of the Public and the Sexual Politics of Crowds', in *Kierkegaard and the Political*, eds. Alison Assiter and Margherita Tonon (Cambridge, Cambridge Scholars Press), 41.

6. When I wrote my book *Kierkegaard, Metaphysics and Political Theory*, I was not, as I now am to a much greater extent, deeply engaged with Kierkegaard's work.

7. A further significant and recent exception is Michael Burns, *Kierkegaard and the Matter of Philosophy: A Fractured Dialectic* (London: Rowman and Littlefield, 2015), in a series edited by myself and Evert van der Zweerde.

8. Merold Westphal, *Kierkegaard's Critique of Reason and Society* (University Park: Pennsylvania University Press, 1991), 40.

9. Ibid., 40.

10. Kierkegaard delivered the manuscript of *Concluding Unscientific Postscript* to the printer in December 1845; he set aside work on *Two Ages* to work on the former, only returning to it after he had delivered CUP (see Hong's introduction to *Two Ages*, x).

11. See JP, vol. 2, 5877 (paper VII, A19), supplement p. 119.

12. The age of revolution, in Kierkegaard's text, following a similar structure in Gyllembourg's novel, was the period of the French Revolution, while the 'present age' was the 1840s but prior to the 1848 revolutions.

13. TA, 70.

14. Ibid., 72.

15. Ibid., 66.

16. Ibid.

17. Ibid., 61.

18. Ibid.

19. George Pattison, *Kierkegaard, Religion and the 19th Century Crisis of Culture* (Cambridge: Cambridge University Press, 2002).

20. See also W. Hartog, 'The Physician as a Physician of Culture: Kierkegaard, Nietzsche and the Diagnosis of Modern Culture', *Kierkegaard Studies Yearbook* 1 (2012), 267–300.

21. Pattison, *Kierkegaard, Religion and the 19th Century Crisis of Culture*, 65.

22. TA, 78, quoted in Pattison, *Kierkegaard, Religion and the 19th Century Crisis of Culture*, 20.

23. David Kangas, *Kierkegaard's Instant: On Beginnings* (Bloomington: Indiana University Press, 2007), 8.

24. Slavoj Žižek, *The Sublime Object of Ideology* (London: Verso, 1989), 109.

25. Pattison, *Kierkegaard, Religion and the 19th Century Crisis of Culture*, 6.

26. Kangas, *Kierkegaard's Instant*, 167.

27. I discussed this in my article 'Kant, Kierkegaard and Freedom and Evil', *Royal Institute of Philosophy Supplement* 72 (2013), 275–296.

28. Kangas, *Kierkegaard's Instant*, 168.

29. Ibid.

30. Walsh, *Living Christianity*.

31. Ibid., 117 (italics in original).

32. FT, 68–69.

33. Ibid., 54.

34. See the earlier discussion of this in chapter 8.

35. Walsh, *Living Christianity*, 121.

36. TA, 65.

37. Hannah Arendt, *The Human Condition* (Chicago: Chicago University Press, 1989), 275.

38. Hannah Arendt, *The Origins of Totalitarianism*, 3rd ed. (New York: Harcourt Brace, 1951), 21.

39. See Arendt, *The Human Condition*, 9.

40. TA, 70.

41. Ibid., 68.

42. Ibid.

43. Ibid., 62.

44. Ibid., 63.

45. Ibid., 65.

46. Alison Assiter, 'Kierkegaard, Battersby and Feminism', *Women: A Cultural Review* 22, nos. 2–3 (Summer/Autumn 2011).

47. TA, 16.

48. Ibid., 39.

CONCLUSION

I have set out, in this book, as noted in the introduction, to place some of Søren Kierkegaard's thinking firmly in the context of the German Idealist tradition. In this respect, this work shares something important in common with those whose work I considered in the first two chapters—Slavoj Žižek and Michael Burns,[1] among others—who have gone against the grain in reading Kierkegaard. In other respects, however, I have moved away from Žižek, or Burns, or from those who have been labelled speculative realists. In particular, I have taken issue with the focus of the latter group on reality as being thoroughly contingent at its core, or, more strongly, on reality as inherently chaotic. I have two reservations about these kinds of views, both as applied to the thought of Kierkegaard and in their own right. The first is that I am not entirely convinced by the arguments for reality being chaotic—at least those considered in the first couple of chapters of this book. But the second, which seems to me to be at least as significant, is that the claim that reality is chaotic may lend itself to a nihilistic ethic that seems to me to be counterproductive in the contemporary world. By contrast, we need, in the present epoch, a metaphysic that can ground the possibility of a different kind of ethic.

In suggesting my alternative to the above view, I have been specifically concerned with Kierkegaard's response to a problem in Immanuel Kant's thought—the problem of explaining how it is possible freely to do wrong. I have sought to demonstrate how Friedrich Wilhelm Joseph Schelling, in his *Freiheitsschrift*, noted and responded to this difficulty faced by Kant. In his turn, again, Kierkegaard, writing in *The Concept of Anxiety*, offered his own solution to Kant's problem.

I have suggested, furthermore, that the difficulty faced by Kant is connected to his Newtonianism and to his being compelled, partially because of this commitment, to develop a dual notion of the self. It is also, I have suggested, linked to his desire, a desire that again stems from his Newtonianism, not to allow 'purposes' really to exist in the natural world.

Schelling, by contrast, sees the natural world as inherently full of life and dynamism. This dynamic natural world, in his picture, is grounded ultimately in something—his *ungrund*—that is incomprehensible from the perspective of finite reasoning beings, but that can be described in metaphorical terms. One of the significant metaphors he deploys, I have suggested, is that of the 'yearning' or the 'longing' of the 'one' to give birth to itself.

Kierkegaard, then, picks up these concerns of both Kant and Schelling. In the course of his response to both thinkers he also, I have argued in this book, develops a process ontology that can be read through various metaphors of birth. I have suggested that these metaphors are deployed in Kierkegaard's works in several different ways: to describe the whole of nature and the 'grounding of this nature', and also to outline the process of the emergence of freedom and consciousness in the natural world.

While many of the commentators who have noted Kierkegaard's views on women have seen them in negative terms, I have suggested, to the contrary, that he intends to valourize the perspective outlined on women. He sometimes symbolically occupies the role of a woman. He is sceptical of the model of the self defended by Kant—the self as an autonomous self-sufficient thing governed by its own reasoning powers. Rather, I have suggested, Kierkegaard valourizes the capacity of women to give birth and values the significance, associated with women, but actually applicable to all, of dependence—on other finite beings but also, ultimately, on a 'power' that is transcendent to all finite beings. He further uses 'woman' as a metaphor for his conception of time.

I have suggested, then, that there is evidence, from a range of Kierkegaard's writings, to suggest that he views the birthing body as highly significant for his ontology and therefore that the role of the body of woman is important for him. He draws on Schelling for this model.

In chapter 9 I suggested that the metaphor of a body that can birth and of some sort of 'longing' to give birth, on the part of the whole of nature, is not merely a wild fanciful outpouring of my imagination, but is rather one that is taken seriously by some contemporary biologists. Such a model lends itself to an ethic—an ethic of care that incorporates care for the environment. If nature is itself living and active, and humans are part of that living and active world, then humans have a responsibility to care not only for one another, but also for that world, rather than, as we may be doing at the moment, gradually destroying the natural world.

The metaphysical model I have been describing, then, incorporates an ethic. Plato attempts to make sense, in metaphorical form, of the 'Good beyond Being'. Schelling's *ungrund*, his metaphor of the 'yearning of the one to give birth to itself', lies beyond what can be expressed in the terms of a certain conception of rational thought. Much of Kierkegaard's work stretches the imagination and, through metaphor, expresses the limits of a particular conception of reason. I have suggested that his metaphors of birth allow us to make sense both of the natural world and of the need for ethical concern for this world. Through this reading of Kierkegaard, then, we can perhaps come to see that the notion of reason that derives partly from an implicit substance ontology and a certain conception of epistemology may hamper both science and ethics, in the broadest senses.

NOTE

1. I would also like to mention the interesting work of two further recent scholars of Kierkegaard who are moving in this direction—Maria J. Binetti and Elisabete de Sousa.

BIBLIOGRAPHY

WORKS BY KIERKEGAARD, WITH THEIR STANDARD ABBREVIATIONS

Kierkegaard, Søren. *The Book on Adler*. Edited and translated by Howard V. Hong and Edna H. Hong. Princeton: Princeton University Press, 1998.

Kierkegaard, Søren. *The Concept of Anxiety*. Edited and translated by Reidar Thomte, in collaboration with Albert B. Anderson. Princeton: Princeton University Press, 1980. CA.

Kierkegaard, Søren. *The Concept of Irony*. Translated by Howard V. Hong and Edna H. Hong. Princeton: Princeton University Press, 1989. CI.

Kierkegaard, Søren. *Concluding Unscientific Postscript to Philosophical Fragments*, vol. 1. Edited and translated by Howard V. Hong and Edna H. Hong. Princeton: Princeton University Press, 1992. CUP.

Kierkegaard, Søren. *Eighteen Upbuilding Discourses*. Edited and translated by Howard V. Hong and Edna H. Hong. Princeton: Princeton University Press, 1990. EUD.

Kierkegaard, Søren. *Either-Or*. Parts I and II. Edited and translated by Howard V. Hong and Edna H. Hong. Bloomington: Indiana University Press, 1987. EO.

Kierkegaard, Søren. *Fear and Trembling*. Translated by Alistair Hannay. London: Penguin, 2003. FT.

Kierkegaard, Søren. *Journals and Papers*, 7 volumes. Translated by Howard V. Hong and Edna H. Hong. Bloomington: Indiana University Press, 1967–1978. JP.

Kierkegaard, Søren. *Notes on Schelling's Berlin Lectures*. In *The Concept of Irony with Continual Reference to Socrates and the Notes*. Edited and translated by Howard V. Hong and Edna H. Hong. Princeton: Princeton University Press, 1989.

Kierkegaard, Søren. *Papers and Journals: A Selection*. Harmondsworth: Penguin, 1996. PJ.

Kierkegaard, Søren. *Philosophical Fragments: Johannes Climacus*. Translated by Howard V. Hong and Edna H. Hong. Princeton: Princeton University Press, 1985. PF.

Kierkegaard, Søren. *Practice in Christianity*. Edited and translated by Howard V. Hong and Edna H. Hong. Princeton: Princeton University Press, 1985.

Kierkegaard, Søren. *Repetition*. Translated by Walter Lowrie. New York: Harper and Row, 1964.

Kierkegaard, Søren. *Repetition and Philosophical Crumbs*. Translated by M. G. Piety, with an introduction and notes by Edward Mooney and M. G. Piety. Oxford: Oxford University Press, 2009. R.

Kierkegaard, Søren. *The Sickness unto Death*. Translated by Howard V. Hong and Edna H. Hong. Princeton: Princeton University Press, 1980. SUD.

Kierkegaard, Søren. *Stages on Life's Way*. Edited and translated by Howard V. Hong and Edna H. Hong. Princeton: Princeton University Press, 1980. SLW.

Kierkegaard, Søren. *Two Ages: The Age of Revolution and the Present Age, a Literary Review*. Edited and translated by Howard V. Hong and Edna H. Hong. Princeton: Princeton University Press, 1978. TA.

Kierkegaard, Søren. *Works of Love*. Translated by Howard V. Hong and Edna H. Hong. Princeton: Princeton University Press, 1995. WL.

OTHER WORKS

Agamben, Giorgio. *Homo Sacer: Sovereign Power and Bare Life*. Translated by Daniel Heller-Roazen. Stanford: Stanford University Press, 1998.

Allison, Henry. *Kant's Theory of Freedom*. Cambridge: Cambridge University Press, 1990.

Allison, Henry. *Kant's Transcendental Idealism: An Interpretation and Defence*. New Haven, CT: Yale University Press, 1983.

Arendt, Hannah. *Eichmann in Jerusalem: A Report on the Banality of Evil*. Harmondsworth: Penguin, 2006.

Arendt, Hannah. *The Human Condition*. Chicago: Chicago University Press, 1989.

Arendt, Hannah. *The Origins of Totalitarianism*, 3rd ed. New York: Harcourt Brace, 1951.

Aristotle. *Metaphysics*. Translated by W. D. Ross. London: Penguin, 2004.

Assiter, Alison. *Enlightened Women*. London: Routledge, 1996.

Assiter, Alison. 'Kierkegaard and the Ground of Morality'. *Acta Kierkegaardiana* (2012).

Assiter, Alison. 'Kierkegaard, Battersby and Feminism'. *Women: A Cultural Review* 22, nos. 2–3 (Summer/Autumn 2011).

Assiter, Alison. *Kierkegaard, Metaphysics and Political Theory*. London: Continuum, 2009.

Badiou, Alain. *The Adventure of French Philosophy*. Translated by Bruno Bosteels. London: Continuum, 2012.

Banham, Gary. *Kant's Practical Philosophy: From Critique to Doctrine*. Basingstoke: Palgrave Macmillan, 2006.

Battersby, Christine. 'Kierkegaard: The Phantom of the Public and the Sexual Politics of Crowds'. In *Kierkegaard and the Political*, edited by Alison Assiter and Margherita Tonon. Cambridge: Cambridge Scholars Press, 2012.

Battersby, Christine. *The Phenomenal Woman: Feminist Metaphysics and the Patterns of Identity*. London: Routledge, 1998.

Bayne, Steven M. *Kant on Causation: On the Fivefold Routes to the Principle of Causation*. New York: State University of New York Press, 2004.

Beck, Lewis White. *Commentary on Kant's Critique of Practical Reason*. Chicago: University of Chicago Press, 1960 (1984).

Beck, Lewis White. 'Five Concepts of Freedom in Kant'. In *Philosophical Analysis and Reconstruction*, edited by Stephan Korner and J. T. J. Scredznick. Dortrecht: Nijhoff, 1987.

Beiser, Frederick. *The Fate of Reason: German Philosophy from Kant to Fichte*. Cambridge: Harvard University Press, 1987.

Bhaskar, Roy. *A Realist Theory of Science*. London: Verso, 1997.

Binetti, Maria J. 'Kierkegaard's Ethical Stage in Hegel's Logical Categories: Actual Possibility, Reality, Necessity, Cosmos and History'. *Journal of Natural and Social Philosophy* 3, nos. 2–3 (2007).

Bowie, Andrew. *Schelling and Modern European Philosophy*. London: Routledge, 1993.

Brassier, Ray. 'The Enigma of Reason'. *Collapse II*. Edited by R. McKay. Oxford: Urbanomie, 2007.

Burns, Michael. 'A Fractured Dialectic: Kierkegaard and Political Ontology after Zizek'. In *Kierkegaard and the Political*, edited by Alison Assiter and Margherita Tonon. Cambridge: Cambridge Scholars Press, 2012.

Burns, Michael. *Kierkegaard and the Matter of Philosophy: A Fractured Dialectic*. London: Rowman & Littlefield International, 2015.

Butler, Judith. 'Gender as Performance: An Interview with Judith Butler'. Interviewed by Peter Osborne and Lynne Segal. *Radical Philosophy* (1994), 32–39.

Butler, Judith. *Gender Trouble*. London: Routledge, 1990.

Camus, Albert. *The Myth of Sisyphus*. Translated by Justin O'Brian. London: Penguin, 2005.

Carlisle, Claire. *Kierkegaard: A Guide for the Perplexed*. London: Continuum, 2009.

Carlisle, Claire. *Kierkegaard's Philosophy of Becoming, Movements and Positions*. New York: State University of New York Press, 2005.

Chanter, Tina. *Whose Antigone? The Tragic Marginalisation of Slavery*. New York: State University of New York Press, 2011.

Clark, Andy, and David Chalmers. 'The Extended Mind'. *Analysis* 58, no. 1 (1998), 7–19.

Connell, George. 'Knights and Knaves of the Living Dead: Kierkegaard's Use of Living Death as a Metaphor for Despair'. In *Kierkegaard and Death*, edited by Patrick Stokes and Adam Buben. Bloomington: Indiana University Press, 2011.

Dainton, Barry. *Stream of Consciousness: Unity and Continuity in Conscious Experience*. London: Routledge, 2000.

Deleuze, Gilles, and Felix Guattari. *A Thousand Plateaus: Capitalism and Schizophrenia*. London: Continuum, 1987.

Deleuze, Gilles, and Felix Guattari. *What Is Philosophy?* Translated by Hugh Tomlinson and Graham Burchell. New York: Columbia University Press, 1994.

Derrida, Jacques. *Of Grammatology* (1974, 1971). Translated by Gayatri Chakravorty Spivak. Indianapolis: Hackett Publishing; Baltimore: Johns Hopkins University Press, 1997.

Dunham, Jeremy, Iain Hamilton Grant, and Sean Watson. *Idealism: The History of a Philosophy*. London: Acumen, 2011.

Evans, C. Stephen. *Kierkegaard's Ethic of Love*. Oxford: Oxford University Press, 2004.

Evans, C. Stephen. *Kierkegaard's 'Fragments' and 'Postscript'*. Amherst, MA: Humanity Books, 1999.

Fox Keller, Evelyn. *Making Sense of Life, Explaining Biological Development with Models, Metaphors, and Machines*. Cambridge: Harvard University Press, 2003.

Frankfurt, Harry. 'Freedom of the Will and the Concept of a Person'. *Journal of Philosophy* 68 (1971), 5–20.

Frankl, Victor. *Man's Search for Meaning*. Boston: Beacon Press, 2006, 197–225.

Freydberg, Bernard. *Schelling's Dialogical Freedom Essay*. Albany: State University of New York Press, 2008.

Gallagher, Catherine, and Thomas Laqueur, edited with introduction. *The Making of the Modern Body*. Berkeley and Los Angeles: University of California Press, 1987.

Gardner, Patrick. *Kierkegaard*. Oxford: Oxford University Press, 1998.

Garf, Joakim. *Soren Kierkegaard, a Biography*. Translated by Bruce H. Kimmse. Princeton: Princeton University Press, 2005.

Gironi, Fabio. 'Between Naturalism and Rationalism: A New Realist Landscape'. *Journal of Critical Realism* 11, no. 3 (2012).

Grant, Iain Hamilton. *Philosophies of Nature after Schelling*. London: Continuum, 2006.

Green, Ronald. *Kierkegaard and Kant: The Hidden Debt*. Albany: State University of New York Press, 1992.

Grosz, Elisabeth. *Time Travels*. Durham: Duke University Press, 2005.

Gunnarsson, Lena. *The Contradictions of Love: Towards a Feminist Ontology of Sociosexuality*. London: Routledge, 2014.

Guyer, Paul. *Kant*. Oxford: Routledge, 2006.

Haar, Michael. *The Uses and Abuses of History*. London: Bobbs Merrill, 1957.

Hallward, Peter. *The Speculative Turn: Continental Materialism and Realism*. Edited by Levi Bryant, Nick Srnicek, and Graham Harman. Melbourne: re.press, 2011.

Hamann, Johan Georg. *Sämtliche Werke Historisch-Kritische Ausgabe*. Edited by J. Nadler. Vienna: Herder, 1949.

Hampson, Daphne. *Kierkegaard: Exposition and Critique*. Oxford: Oxford University Press, 2013.

Hannay, Alistair. *Kierkegaard: A Biography*. Cambridge: Cambridge University Press, 2001.

Haraway, Donna. 'A Cyborg Manifesto: Science, Technology and Socialist-Feminism in the Late Twentieth Century'. In *Simians, Cyborgs and Women: The Reinvention of Nature*. New York: Routledge, 1991.

Hartog, W. 'The Physician as a Physician of Culture: Kierkegaard, Nietzsche and the Diagnosis of Modern Culture'. *Kierkegaard Studies Yearbook* 1 (2012), 267–300.

Hegel, Georg W. F. *The Science of Logic*. Translated by A. V. Miller. New York: Humanity Books, 1969.

Heidegger, Martin. *Being and Time*. Translated by John Maquarrie and Edward Robinson. Oxford: Blackwell, 1993.

Heidegger, Martin. 'The Origin of a Work of Art'. In *Poetry, Language, Thought*. Translated by Albert Hofstadter. New York: Harper and Row, 1971.

Heidegger, Martin. *What Is Called Thinking*. Translated by Glenn Gray. New York: Harper, 1968.

Hesse, M. 'Tropical Talk: The Myth of the Literal'. *Aristotelian Society* 61 (1987, supplement), 297–310.

Heuser, Marie-Louise. 'Schelling's Concept of Self-Organization'. In *Evolution of Dynamical Structures in Complex Systems*, edited by R. Friedrich and A. Wunderlin. Springer Proceedings in Physics. Berlin/Heidelberg/New York: Springer, 1992.

Houlgate, Stephen. *The Opening of Hegel's Logic: From Being to Infinity*. West Lafayette, IN: Purdue University Press, 2006.

Hull, Carrie. *The Ontology of Sex*. London: Routledge, 2006.

Hume, David. *Dialogues concerning Natural Religion and Other Writings* (1779). Edited by D. Coleman. Cambridge: Cambridge University Press, 2007.

Husserl, Edmund. *The Crisis of European Sciences and Transcendental Phenomenology*. Translated by David Carr. Evanston, IL: Northwestern University Press, 1969.

Irigaray, Luce. *An Ethics of Sexual Difference*. Translated by G. Gill and C. Burke. London: Continuum, 2004.

Irigaray, Luce. *Speculum of the Other Woman*. Translated by Gillian C. Gill. Ithaca: Cornell University Press, 1985.

Johnson, Mark. *The Body in the Mind, the Bodily Basis of Meaning, Imagination and Reason*. Chicago: University of Chicago Press, 1987.

Jonas, Hans. *The Imperative of Responsibility: In Search of an Ethics for the Technological Age*. Chicago: Chicago University Press, 1984.

Jones, Rachel. *Irigaray*. Cambridge: Polity, 2011.

Kangas, David. *Kierkegaard's Instant: On Beginnings*. Bloomington: Indiana University Press, 2007.

Kant, Immanuel. *Critique of Judgment*. Translated by Werner S. Pluhar. Indianapolis: Hackett Publishing, 1987. CJ.

Kant, Immanuel. *Critique of Practical Reason*. Edited and translated by Mary Gregor. Cambridge: Cambridge University Press, 1997. CPrR.

Kant, Immanuel. *Critique of Pure Reason*. Translated by Norman Kemp Smith. London: Macmillan, 1970. CPR.

Kant, Immanuel. *Gesammelte Schriften* (Akademieausgabe). Berlin: Königlich Preußische Akademie der Wissenschaften, 1900.

Kant, Immanuel. *Groundwork of the Metaphysics of Morals*. Introduction by Christine Korsgaard. Translated by Mary Gregor and Jens Timmerman. Cambridge: Cambridge University Press, 2012. GM.

Kant, Immanuel. *Metaphysical Foundations of Natural Science*. Edited and translated by Michael Friedman. Cambridge: Cambridge University Press, 2004.

Kant, Immanuel. *Religion within the Limits of Reason Alone*. Translated by Theodore M. Green and Hoyd Hudson. New York: Harper and Row, 1960. RA.

Korsgaard, Christine. *The Sources of Normativity*. Cambridge: Cambridge University Press, 1996.

Kosch, Michelle. *Freedom and Reason in Kant, Schelling and Kierkegaard*. Oxford: Oxford University Press, 2006.

Ladyman, James, and Don Ross. *Everything Must Go: Metaphysics Naturalised.* Oxford: Oxford University Press, 2010.

Ladyman, James, and Don Ross. 'The World in the Data'. In *Scientific Metaphysics.* Oxford: Oxford University Press, 2013.

Laqueur, Thomas. *Making Sex: Body and Gender from the Greeks to Freud.* Boston: Harvard University Press, 1992.

Lawrence, J. P. 'Schelling's Metaphysics of Evil'. In *The New Schelling*, edited by Judith Norman and Alistair Welchman. London: Continuum, 2004.

Lawson-Tancred, Hugh. *De Anima.* London: Penguin Classics, 1986.

Leibniz, Gottfried. *Theodicy: Essays on the Goodness of God, the Freedom of Man and the Origin of Evil.* In *The Philosophical Works of Leibniz.* Translated by George M. Duncan. New Haven, CT: Tuttle, Morehouse & Taylor, 1890.

Leon, Celine. *Neither/Nor of the Second Sex: Kierkegaard on Women, Sexual Difference and Sexual Relations.* Macon, GA: Mercer University Press, 2008.

Leon, Celine, and Sylvia Walsh (eds.). *Feminist Interpretations of Soren Kierkegaard.* University Park: Pennsylvania University Press, 1997.

Levinas, E. *Totality and Infinity: An Essay on Exteriority.* Translated by Alphonso Lingis. The Hague: Martinus Nijhoff, 1979.

Lewis, Michael. *Heidegger beyond Deconstruction.* London: Continuum, 2007.

Lippitt, John. *The Routledge Philosophy Guidebook to Kierkegaard's Fear and Trembling.* London: Routledge, 2003.

Lovelock, James. *The Ages of Gaia.* New York: W.W. Norton, 1998.

Lovelock, James. *A Final Warning: The Vanishing Face of Gaia.* London: Penguin, 2009.

Lovelock, James. *Gaia: A New Look at Life on Earth.* Oxford: Oxford University Press, 1979.

Malabou, Catherine. *The Future of Hegel: Plasticity, Temporality and Dialectic.* Translated by Lisabeth During. London: Routledge, 2005.

Malik, Habib C. *Receiving Soren Kierkegaard: The Early Impact and Transmission of His Thought.* Washington, DC: The Catholic University of America Press, 1997.

Margulis, L. 'Biologists Can't Define Life'. In *From Gaia to Selfish Genes: Selected Writings in the Life Sciences*, edited by C. Barlow. Cambridge: MIT Press, 1991.

Marino, Gordon. 'Anxiety in the Concept of Anxiety'. In *The Cambridge Companion to Kierkegaard*, edited by Alistair Hannay and Gordon C. Marino. Cambridge: Cambridge University Press, 1998.

Maturana, H. R., and F. J. Varela. *Autopoiesis and Cognition: The Realization of the Living.* Edited by Robert S. Cohen, Marx W. Wartofsky, and H. R. Maturana. Boston: D. Reidel, 1980.

Maturana, H. R., and F. J. Varela. *The Tree of Knowledge: The Biological Roots of Human Understanding.* Boston: Shambhala Publications, 1987.

McCarthy, V. 'Schelling and Kierkegaard on Freedom and Fall'. In *International Kierkegaard Commentary: The Concept of Anxiety*, edited by Robert Perkins. Macon: Mercer University Press, 1985.

McDonald, William. Entry on Soren Kierkegaard. In *Stanford Encyclopedia of Philosophy.* Section 4. First published 3 December 1996; substantive revision 27 July 2012. Available online at Plato.Stanford.edu. Accessed 25 January 2015.

McDowell, John. *Having the World in View.* Cambridge: Harvard University Press, 2009.

McGrath, Alister E. *The Blackwell Encyclopedia of Modern Christian Thought.* Oxford: Blackwell Publishing, 1993.

Meillassoux, Quentin. *After Finitude.* London: Verso, 2009.

Merleau-Ponty, Maurice. *The Visible and the Invisible.* Translated by Alphonso Lingis. London: Routledge, 1962.

Michalson, Gordon. *Fallen Freedom: Kant on Radical Evil and Moral Regeneration.* Cambridge: Cambridge University Press, 1990.

Mooney, Edward. 'Postscript Ethics: Putting Personality on Stage'. In *Ethics, Love and Faith in Kierkegaard*, edited by Edward Mooney. Bloomington: Indiana University Press, 2008.

Mooney, Edward. *Selves in Discord and Resolve.* Basingstoke: Routledge, 1996.

Mooney, Edward, and Dana Barnea. *Birth and Love in Fear and Trembling and the Symposium*. Website, dated Sunday, 1 December 2013. Accessed 21 May 2014.

Morgan, Seiriol. 'The Missing Formal Proof of Humanity's Radical Evil in Kant's Religion'. *Philosophical Review* 114, no. 1 (January 2005).

Nagel, Tom. *Mind and Cosmos*. Oxford: Oxford University Press, 2012.

Newton, Isaac. *Philosophical Writings*. Edited by A. Janiak. Cambridge: Cambridge University Press, 2004.

Nietzsche, Friedrich. *The Birth of Tragedy*. Cambridge: Cambridge University Press, 2010.

O'Neill, Onora. *Constructions of Reason: Explorations of Kant's Practical Philosophy*. Cambridge: Cambridge University Press, 1989.

Pattison, George. *Kierkegaard, Religion and the 19th Century Crisis of Culture*. Cambridge: Cambridge University Press, 2002.

Pattison, George. *Kierkegaard's Upbuilding Discourses: Philosophy, Literature and Theology*. London: Routledge, 2002.

Pattison, George. *The Philosophy of Kierkegaard*. Chesham: Acumen, 2003.

Perkins, Robert. *Woman-Bashing in Kierkegaard's 'In Vino Veritas': A Reinscription of Plato's Symposium*. In *Feminist Interpretations of Soren Kierkegaard*, edited by Celine Leon and Sylvia Walsh. University Park: Pennsylvania University Press, 1997.

Plato. *Symposium*. Translated by A. Nehamas and P. Woodruff. In *Complete Writings*, edited by J. M. Cooper and T. S. Hutchinson. Indianapolis: Hackett Publishing, 1997.

Plato. *Timaeus*. Translated by D. Lee. Harmondsworth: Penguin, 1977.

Pyper, Hugh. *The Joy of Kierkegaard: Essays on Kierkegaard as a Biblical Reader*. Oakville: Equinox, 2011.

Quinn, Anthony. 'Kierkegaard's Christian Ethics'. In *The Cambridge Companion to Kierkegaard*, edited by Alistair Hannay and Gordon C. Marino. Cambridge: Cambridge University Press, 1998.

Ricoeur, Paul. 'Philosophy after Kierkegaard'. In *Kierkegaard: A Critical Reader*, edited by Jonathan Ree and Jane Chamberlain. Oxford: Blackwell, 1998.

Rorty, Richard. *Philosophy and the Myth of Nature*. Oxford: Blackwell, 1983.

Rosen, Robert. *Life Itself: A Comprehensive Inquiry into the Nature, Origin and Fabrication of Life*. New York: Columbia University Press, 1991.

Rudd, Anthony. *Kierkegaard and the Limits of the Ethical*. Oxford: Clarendon Press, 1997.

Sandford, Stella. *The Metaphysics of Love*. London: Athlone Press, 2000.

Sartre, Jean-Paul. 'Existentialism Is a Humanism'. In *Existentialism from Dostoevsky to Sartre*, edited by Walter Kaufmann. Ohio: Meridian Books, 1964, 287–311.

Schelling, F. W. J. *Ages of the World*. Translated by Frederick de Wolfe Bolman. New York: Columbia University Press, 1942.

Schelling, F. W. J. 'I'. In *Schelling Werke*, edited by Manfred Schroder. Munchen: E.H. Back, 1959.

Schelling, F. W. J. 'On the World Soul'. Translated and with an introduction by I. H. Grant. *Collapse VI: Geo/Philosophy* (6), Urbanomic (2010), edited by R. Mackay, 58–95.

Schelling, Friedrich W. J. *Philosophical Investigations into the Essence of Human Freedom*. Translated by Jeff Love and Johannes Schmidt. New York: State University of New York Press, 2006.

Schelling, F. W. J. *The Philosophy of Art*. Minneapolis: University of Minnesota Press, 1989.

Schmid, C. C. E. *Versuch Einer Moralphilosophie*. Jena: Cröcker, 1790.

Sedley, David. *The Cambridge Companion to Greek and Roman Philosophy*, 1st ed. Cambridge: Cambridge University Press, 2003.

Shakespeare, Steven. *Kierkegaard, Language and the Reality of God*. Basingstoke: Ashgate, 2001.

Sontag, Susan. *On Photography*. Harmondsworth: Penguin, 2008.

Spinoza, Benedict de. *Ethics*. Edited and translated by Edwin Curley, with an introduction by Stuart Hampshire. Harmondsworth: Penguin Classics, 1994.

Stack, George. *Kierkegaard's Existential Ethics*. Tuscaloosa: The University of Alabama Press, 1977.

Stern, Robert. *Understanding Moral Obligation: Kant, Hegel, Kierkegaard.* Cambridge: Cambridge University Press, 2012.

Stewart, Jon. *Kierkegaard's Relations to Hegel Reconsidered.* Cambridge: Cambridge University Press, 2003.

Stewart, Jon. 'The Notion of Actuality in Kierkegaard and Schelling's Influence'. *Ars B revis: A nuari o de la Càtedra Ramon Llull Blanquerna* 17 (2011), 237–253.

Stiegler, Bernard. *The Decadence of Industrial Democracies, vol.1, Disbelief and Discredit.* Translated by Daniel Ross and Suzanne Arnold. Cambridge: Polity Press, 2011.

Stiegler, Bernard. *What Makes Life Worth Living: On Pharmacology.* Cambridge: Polity Press, 2010.

Strawson, Galen, et al. *Consciousness and Its Place in Nature: Does Physicalism Entail Panpsychism?* Edited by Anthony Freeman. Exeter: Imprint Academic, 2006.

Strawson, Peter. *The Bounds of Sense.* London: Methuen, 1966.

Stronge, Will. 'An Inquiry into the Concept of Chaos and Matters Connected Therewith: A Reading of Nietzsche and Schelling'. MA thesis, Kingston University, 2013.

Thompson, Evan. *Mind in Life: Biology, Phenomenology, and the Sciences of Mind.* Cambridge: Belknap Press, 2007.

Thulstrup, Neils. *Kierkegaard's Relation to Hegel.* Translated by George L. Stengren. Princeton, NJ: Princeton University Press, 1980.

Tonon, Margherita. 'Suffering from Modernity'. In *Kierkegaard and the Political*, edited by Alison Assiter and Margherita Tonon. Cambridge: Cambridge Scholars Press, 2012.

Walsh, Sylvia. *Living Christianity: Kierkegaard's Dialectic of Christian Existence.* University Park: Pennsylvania State University Press, 2005.

Westphal, Merold. *Becoming a Self.* West Lafayette: Purdue University Press, 1996.

Westphal, Merold. *Kierkegaard's Critique of Reason and Society.* University Park: Pennsylvania University Press, 1991.

White, Alan. *Schelling: An Introduction to the System of Freedom.* New Haven, CT: Yale University Press, 1983.

Wicks, Robert. *Kant on Judgment.* London: Routledge, 2007.

Winnicott, Donald. *Playing and Reality.* London: Routledge, 1971.

Wood, A. *Kant's Ethical Thought.* Cambridge: Cambridge University Press, 1999.

Wood, D. 'Thinking God in the Wake of Kierkegaard'. In *Kierkegaard: A Critical Reader*, edited by Jonathan Ree and Jane Chamberlain. Oxford: Blackwell, 1998.

Young, Iris Marion. *On Female Body Experience: 'Throwing Like a Girl' and Other Essays.* New York: Oxford University Press, 2005.

Žižek, Slavoj. *The Parallax View.* Cambridge: MIT Press, 2009. PV.

Žižek, Slavoj. *The Sublime Object of Ideology.* London: Verso, 1989.

Zupancic, Alenca. *Ethics of the Real: Kant and Lacan.* London: Verso, 2000.

Zykov, V., E. Mytilinaios, B. Adams, and H. Lipson. 'Robotics: Self-Reproducing Machines'. *Nature* 435 (12 May 2005), 163–164.

INDEX